"New Testament professors might remind us that if Paul were to take our seminary exegesis classes, he'd fail because he doesn't use the historical-critical method, which shows that there's something not quite right about what we teach. Graves joins a new wave of scholarship that challenges the adequacy of the historical-critical method, takes comprehensive theological exegesis seriously, and finds in the Scriptures themselves nothing less than Scripture interpreting Scripture in an unfolding drama that leads us into the wisdom of God. Knowing what an author meant in context may be the place to begin, but once we hear the text, we realize the Word of God is alive and at times takes us to unanticipated and wholly glorious places."

—**Scot McKnight**, Northern Seminary

"Graves's excellent work gives us a fresh appreciation of inner-biblical exegesis, showing how we can—and should!—continue to interpret Scripture for our times. He sets out clearly the principles and methods he uses, and he illustrates these through a study of well-selected themes. This is a careful and insightful contribution to biblical interpretation."

—**Havilah Dharamraj**, South Asia Institute of Advanced Christian Studies

"Through five interesting themes, Graves splendidly reveals how inner-biblical interpretation takes shape in the Old and New Testaments and its importance for Christian interpretation and application. He is a wise and discerning biblical exegete and evaluator of both ancient Near Eastern and early Christian sources. Readers can learn so much from this book about the spectrum of wisdom that the Bible offers for Christians today."

—**Michael D. Matlock**, Asbury Theological Seminary

"In this book, 'emphasis is placed on how the interpreting text applies or qualifies its inherited biblical tradition.' In other words, Scripture interpreting Scripture is part of what shapes scriptural meaning long before we start to talk of the history of interpretation. This inspires and guides us in our own interpretation today. The book wears its learning lightly, yet the occasional turn to the biblical languages reveals the scholarly substructure. For example, corporate responsibility is clearly a key notion that has become unfashionable but is here well articulated. The Bible's concern for boundaries as real and necessary but also as starting points for relationship is also appreciated. An informed and rewarding operation in biblical theology is within these pages. It is wide ranging across the canon, judicious, and wise, a book from which the whole church (lay and expert) can learn much."

—**Mark** ⸏⸏⸏⸏ ⸏⸏⸏⸏⸏⸏⸏⸏⸏ ⸏⸏ ⸏⸏ Wycliffe College, Toronto

"The Reformation principle 'Scripture interprets Scripture' receives a fresh treatment by Graves. While affirming the coherence of Scripture in Christ, the book carefully engages with the unique contribution of individual authors in their ancient cultural contexts, and in so doing provides thoughtful insights on the web of connections that link Old and New Testaments. By examining inner-biblical interpretation, both how one Old Testament text interprets another and how the New Testament authors interpret the Old Testament, Graves unveils principles of interpretation at work within Scripture, which modern interpreters can use to interpret and apply Scripture's teachings today. Interpretation is shown to be a process—one whose goal is the clear communication of the Word of God to the modern hearer."

—**Jason Soenksen,** Concordia University Wisconsin

How Scripture
Interprets
Scripture

What Biblical Writers Can Teach Us
about Reading the Bible

MICHAEL GRAVES

B
Baker Academic
a division of Baker Publishing Group
Grand Rapids, Michigan

© 2021 by Michael Graves

Published by Baker Academic
a division of Baker Publishing Group
PO Box 6287, Grand Rapids, MI 49516-6287
www.bakeracademic.com

Printed in the United States of America

Library of Congress Cataloging-in-Publication Data
Names: Graves, Michael, 1973– author.
Title: How scripture interprets scripture : what biblical writers can teach us about reading the Bible / Michael Graves.
Description: Grand Rapids, Michigan : Baker Academic, a division of Baker Publishing Group, [2021] | Includes bibliographical references and indexes.
Identifiers: LCCN 2021018961 | ISBN 9781540964540 (casebound) | ISBN 9781540962003 (paperback) | ISBN 9781493432332 (ebook)
Subjects: LCSH: Bible—Criticism, interpretation, etc.
Classification: LCC BS511.3 .G73 2021 | DDC 220.6—dc23
LC record available at https://lccn.loc.gov/2021018961

Unless otherwise indicated, Scripture translations are the author's own.

Baker Publishing Group publications use paper produced from sustainable forestry practices and post-consumer waste whenever possible.

21 22 23 24 25 26 27   7 6 5 4 3 2 1

To Gary United Methodist Church in Wheaton

Contents

Acknowledgments

I would like to express my sincere gratitude to Wheaton College for granting me a research sabbatical in the spring term of 2020 to work on this book. For all the students who have taken my courses at Wheaton College over the past seventeen years, and for the many faithful students of the Bible whom I have had the pleasure to teach in local churches, I am truly thankful.

My experience working with Baker Academic has been very positive. I have benefited from encouragement and sound advice from Jim Kinney. Jennifer Hale has done an excellent job managing the production of the book. I am grateful to my graduate assistant at Wheaton College, Amy Allan, for her valuable assistance in proofreading and preparing the indexes.

This year has been special for our family. While I was writing this book, my son, Ben, married a wonderful person, Caroline. We could not be more thankful.

This book is dedicated to the people of Gary United Methodist Church in Wheaton, Illinois, who have been an abundant source of encouragement to our family. Gary Church is filled with the love of Jesus. This is an ideal setting for good biblical interpretation.

1

Introduction

Interpreting Scripture and Inner-Biblical Interpretation

M any people today doubt that the Bible has anything meaningful to say in our contemporary context. Even within the church, the usefulness of Scripture for helping Christians to navigate today's complex world is often not fully recognized. It is my belief and the testimony of Christians throughout the centuries that the Bible remains relevant and teaches what is essential for human well-being. Christians have traditionally accepted the truthfulness and usefulness of Scripture as necessary corollaries of believing in Jesus. Our confidence in Scripture is grounded in the testimony of Jesus and the early church. Jesus accepted Israel's Scriptures (that is, the Old Testament) as sacred and authoritative. Christians who lived after the apostles commended these same sacred books as Scripture, together with other books pertaining to Jesus that eventually became the New Testament. Moreover, the Bible has continued to "work" in the lives of Christians to instruct, encourage, warn, and comfort. The purpose of this book is to illustrate and explain what we can learn about biblical interpretation by paying attention to how Scripture interprets Scripture. This kind of interpretation aims to help us grow closer to God, cultivate Christian virtues, and make wise decisions that demonstrate love for God and for our neighbors.

Within Scripture, we find examples of "inner-biblical interpretation"—that is, passages in which a biblical author appropriates and reapplies an older biblical tradition. Such passages often handle their biblical sources with striking sensitivity to context and theological imagination. In certain cases, only one facet of the older meaning is brought into the new setting. Sometimes an early biblical tradition is applied in different ways by later biblical writers. Core theological ideas typically stand behind both the earliest form of a scriptural tradition and its reapplications in later biblical texts. The phenomenon of inner-biblical interpretation provides insight into how we should interpret Scripture generally and also contributes to our understanding of Scripture's teaching on specific topics.

The first chapter of this book will present four key concepts that provide an entryway into the process of biblical interpretation. These concepts are as follows: (1) Scripture was meant to be interpreted with an attitude of reverence and with the expectation that we will learn divine wisdom; (2) we understand Scripture best when we pay attention to the ancient contexts of biblical statements as the starting point for our process of interpretation; (3) we need to read widely in the Bible to hear the whole counsel of Scripture, because the Bible contains a variety of perspectives on complex topics and each of these biblical perspectives conveys important insights; and (4) we should seek not just the contribution of each individual text but also a coherent picture of what Scripture as a whole has to say in addressing any given topic. These concepts suggest a process of interpretation that leads from the study of individual texts to a coherent statement of biblical teaching. As we will see, this process represents an application of principles learned from how Scripture interprets Scripture. It also allows insights gained from inner-biblical interpretation on specific passages to inform our present-day application.

After this first chapter on the key concepts of interpretation, five chapters follow that apply these concepts to specific topics in Scripture. The purpose of these chapters is to show how the phenomenon of inner-biblical interpretation illuminates both the topic in question and the nature of reading the Bible. The chapter topics are as follows: corporate and individual responsibility; insiders and outsiders; marriage, polygamy, and divorce; sacrificial offerings; and the afterlife. Although none of these can be addressed comprehensively, and other topics could be discussed, these chapters will be sufficient to illustrate the approach suggested by this book and show the need and value of this kind of interpretation.

In the final chapter, I will sum up key insights from each of the chapters. I will also make general observations about how Scripture interprets Scripture and suggest specific principles that can guide contemporary biblical interpretation. I hope to make clear why it is so important that we read both deeply and widely in Scripture. Furthermore, I will attempt to show that the historical tradition of inner-biblical interpretation that grows out of the Old Testament and blossoms in the New Testament finds an authentic continuation in the early church. Finally, I will argue that the Bible, even though it contains ancient texts from cultures very different from our own, equips us with the insights we need to apply biblical teaching wisely today. By interpreting Scripture well and putting it into practice, we can grow in our knowledge of God, live out our Christian calling, and help shape our world to be better, in many ways, than the one in which the biblical writers lived.

Scripture Was Meant to Be Interpreted with Reverence and Expectation

The term "interpretation" can be used in different senses. For example, if an ancient Greek letter written in an obscure style with a number of rare words was found, scholars trying to reconstruct the letter's original meaning as intended by the author could be said to be "interpreting" its meaning. In other words, they are interpreting the linguistic and cultural evidence in order to reconstruct the historical sense of the document. In this book, I typically mean something more than this by "interpretation." What I have in mind is closer to the interpretation offered by judges when they are interpreting a law to settle a contemporary dispute. The historical sense can (some would say "should") serve as the foundation for how the law is applied, but what the judge must decide is how the primary idea of the law bears on a present circumstance. To take another example, professional historians must interpret the past in order to write history; that is, they must look at the evidence and decide what was important, which events caused others, and how this should be told to present-day readers. Two good historians might offer different narrative accounts of the same period because many important things could be selected to recount, different themes could be emphasized, and audiences change. When I talk about interpreting the Bible, I have in mind the whole process, from studying biblical texts in their historical contexts, to ascertaining what ideas and values are present in the text, to discerning what is important for a certain audience to know, and perhaps to stating how the audience should respond. It is in this broad sense of "interpretation" that the Bible was meant to be interpreted. This has been the belief of Christians from the beginning as part of believing in biblical inspiration.

A challenge for contemporary readers of the Bible, and perhaps a reason why the Bible is not more widely read, is that biblical texts do not speak directly to our specific circumstances. For example, the Bible does not give us direct, context-specific instructions, such as "Go to this store and buy that shirt," or "Take this job, not that one." If God sent messages of this sort through the Bible, there would be little need for interpretation. The original context of each message would be our context, and the directions would be perfectly clear. We could simply do as we were told and know that we were following God's will. But as it is, the Bible does not contain messages written directly to us. Instead, the Bible is filled with various kinds of prose and poetry that address situations from the past. Some comments here and there feel directly relevant, but much of the Bible concerns ancient peoples, unfamiliar rituals, and cultural practices that are foreign to our present experience. In fact, it is common even for Christians who hold the Bible in high regard to turn primarily to other sources for guidance on how to live.

It should be stated, of course, that good advice that derives from or appropriately supports biblical teaching is valuable. Nevertheless, there is no substitute for directly encountering the Bible for ourselves. The very process of reading the Bible cultivates wisdom, orients our love in the proper direction, and inspires us to act rightly. We cannot obtain these benefits at the same level simply by listening to someone else report to us what Scripture teaches. Christians who are blessed with the opportunity to study the Bible should exercise responsible stewardship of this blessing. Still, how can reading ancient biblical texts, which do not speak directly into our present circumstances, help us to grow closer to God and other people? The answer is that we are meant to interpret them. Through interpretation the Bible is translated into wisdom that can shape us as people and guide our specific choices. The very idea that God inspired biblical texts for our instruction requires that we are meant to interpret them and apply them to our lives.

By way of example, we can contrast the ancient Code of Hammurabi with the US Constitution. Although the Code of Hammurabi sets forth ideals and values, no community still looks to it for binding law, and consequently no tradition of contemporizing interpretation surrounds it. The US Constitution, on the other hand, remains authoritative for citizens of the United States, and consequently it has been and continues to be interpreted for its contemporary relevance. Another example from US history is the phrase "All men are created equal" from the Declaration of Independence. It contains a core idea that is central to US civic thought (that is, the fundamental equality of all people) but has continued to be interpreted and applied more broadly (for example, to include women and people of all races) in light of later insights. The key point is that when a text from the past remains meaningful, people mediate its meaning to their present circumstances through interpretation.

A few moments of reflection on the Bible's content make clear that it was meant to be interpreted for later times. This is evident, for example, where the Bible relates stories and codes that assume cultural elements that no longer exist for most of us, such as polygamy and slavery. Biblical passages that involve these topics presumably have something to teach us without requiring that we revive these practices. Again, the need for interpretation is obvious when we consider issues in today's world, such as "How should I vote?" or "Is genetic science good or bad?"—which the Bible does not speak about directly but which can be addressed using biblical teaching. At a deeper level, the important role of interpretation becomes apparent when we see biblical texts that seem to lean in opposite directions. For example, on the basis of what the men of Judah did in Ezra 10:3–5, one might suppose that it is biblical teaching to divorce a spouse who is outside the faith. However, because of Paul's words in 1 Corinthians 7:12–14, one would think that it is not biblical teaching to do this. Both Ezra 10 and 1 Corinthians 7 have specific contexts, and we need to interpret these texts in light of their contexts, in light of each other, and within the framework of the Bible as a whole. The best Christian response to complexity in the Bible is to interpret it with reverence and faithful expectation.

As this book will illustrate in detail, that the Bible is meant for interpretation is made perfectly clear from how biblical writers interact with prior biblical traditions. Many examples will be given in the following chapters. For the present, I can mention the interpretation of Deuteronomy 23:3 ("No Ammonite or Moabite may enter the assembly of the Lord, even to the tenth generation") reflected in Nehemiah 13:1–3, and Paul's application of Deuteronomy 25:4 ("Do not muzzle an ox while it is threshing") to his own situation of laboring as an apostle (1 Cor. 9:7–12). While biblical texts have specific contexts that should be understood as part of responsible interpretation, biblical writers themselves testify to the fact that divinely ordained values, principles, and practices can be faithfully applied to new settings.[1]

An important dimension of interpreting Scripture for contemporary application is exploring all the facets of meaning that a text contains. Abraham's binding and near sacrifice of Isaac serves as a good example (Gen. 22). In this passage, God commands Abraham to take his son Isaac and sacrifice him as a burnt offering on a mountain, but at the last minute, God tells Abraham not to sacrifice Isaac. A literal account of the narrative would describe the events

---

1. For examples where New Testament writers derive lessons from Old Testament narratives, see 1 Cor. 5:6–8; 10:1–13; Rom. 4:16–25; Heb. 11; James 2:25; 5:10–11, 17–18; 2 Pet. 2:4–10, 13–16; 1 John 3:11–12; Jude 7, 11. On God's intent that Old Testament texts should teach later generations, see Rom. 15:3–4; 2 Tim. 3:14–17. Biblical references are given in the order of their importance wherever this is helpful for a given point. Otherwise, they are given in canonical order.

that take place. But at a deeper level, what is this narrative about? Because it begins by saying that God was testing Abraham (v. 1), we might surmise that we are to learn something from how Abraham responds. Abraham's willingness to obey (vv. 16–17: "Because you have done this, . . . I will bless you") suggests that the patriarch's obedience is being commended to the reader. Abraham also demonstrates trust in God, and Hebrews 11:17–19 uses this passage to commend the virtue of faith. James 2:21–24 interprets this passage to show that faith is brought to maturity in our actions. Within its broader literary context, this narrative confirms God's promises to Abraham (Gen. 22:17–18), serves as a model for sacrifice as substitution (v. 13), and provides a vivid pictorial rejection of human sacrifice. Even these facets of meaning do not exhaust what could be said about this remarkable passage.

At the same time, we cannot validly claim that a text is about anything we wish. There are limits to what a text might mean. For example, the story of Abraham binding Isaac in Genesis 22 is not in any recognizable sense about socialism or capitalism. Even if numerous facets of meaning interlock in the unfolding of a narrative, only those facets with solid basis in the wording and ideas of the text are valid. Moreover, even some interpretations that could conceivably be derived from a text should be rejected because of the broader contexts that surround the passage. For example, someone might claim that Genesis encourages child sacrifice. Such an interpretation might suggest itself to a reader who encounters this text in isolation, but in the context of the Pentateuch it does not hold up. The process of interpretation helps us to see the abundant richness of the text's meaning, but it does not allow for any and every meaning imaginable.

Biblical interpretation can be challenging. On difficult topics, serious disagreements sometimes arise between Christians. Nevertheless, the process of biblical interpretation is too important not to discuss. If we are to benefit from the teaching of Scripture, we need to articulate an interpretive approach that is faithful to the text and equitable to one another. To this end, the principles of biblical interpretation must go beyond advice on what not to do with the Bible. We do not want an environment in Christian education where the more we know about the Bible, the less it applies to our lives. This does not make for useful sermons or healthy Christians, and it does not reflect historical Christianity. The goal of this book is to suggest a positive approach to biblical interpretation that takes its cues from how biblical authors interpreted prior biblical traditions. In order to put this approach into practice, we need to come to the Bible ready to participate actively in the interpretive process, with a humble spirit of obedience to God and a trusting expectation that God has something to teach us from every biblical text.

The Starting Points for Interpretation Are the Ancient Contexts of the Bible

Christian biblical interpretation can be thought of as a process. The best starting point for this process is careful study of each biblical book against the backdrop of whatever we can surmise about its original context. Modern biblical scholarship has brought sharper focus to this aspect of biblical interpretation, but the intentions of the Bible's human authors as envisioned in their historical contexts was likewise a concern for the best interpreters in the early church.[2] Words have meaning in specific linguistic-cultural contexts. For example, when a nineteenth-century English Christmas carol refers to birds that "sing loud their carol gay,"[3] the sense of the word "gay" in this historical setting is different from the sense it normally carries in the twenty-first century. If we want to give an accurate account of why the text before us uses the specific words that it does, we need to conceptualize a human author who lived in a certain time and place and who wrote with a specific audience in mind.

It is true that different kinds of literature express the writer's aims in different ways. In an expository text, such as the book of Amos or the book of Romans, the writer presents a certain persona and sets forth an argument in a relatively straightforward manner. In other types of literature, such as the narratives in 1–2 Samuel or the poetry of the Psalms, the writer's aims are often suggested rather than stated outright. Moreover, literature can convey more than just ideas. The Psalms, for example, can stir up feelings, invoke memories, and rouse the reader to action. We should not be simplistic about what authors intend when they write or how much access we have to their inner thoughts. Nevertheless, meaningful literature exists because writers employ linguistic conventions at their disposal to create compositions that resonate with an audience. We should seek to interpret texts in light of the writer's conventions as best we can.

The study of biblical books in their ancient contexts is important for several reasons. First, attention to the historical settings of biblical books allows us to see the distinct contribution that each passage makes. This opens up the rich variety of the Bible and is preferable to seeing the entire sacred text as a series of figurative articulations of the same three or four points over and over again. Second, making the historical sense the basis for interpretation keeps us in contact with the text's ideas. When interpreters become untethered from the Bible in its historical contexts, they often miss out on important lessons because the only ideas they hear are the ones they brought with them. Third,

2. See Graves, *Inspiration and Interpretation*, 73–75, 162–63.
3. See "The Sun of Righteousness," in *Christmas Carols*, 60.

by grounding ourselves in the concrete world of biblical texts, we can learn to reapply Scripture's core ideas to our own context in ways that are equally concrete. For example, when we take the time to understand what Paul meant when he admonished Christians to greet one another with a holy kiss,[4] we are reminded that our greetings to one another should not only flow from deep affection but also manifest themselves in tangible ways that are suited to our context.

The method of biblical interpretation that I explain in this book takes as foundational the meanings of biblical texts in their historical contexts. By the word "context," I have in mind (1) the cultural contexts of the biblical writers, (2) their specific historical circumstances, (3) the types of literature they composed, and (4) their location within the Bible's narrative of creation and redemption. I will say something brief about each of these.

1. The various books of the Bible were written in specific cultural contexts. These contexts become evident to us when we read about aspects of these cultures that are different from our own. The writers of most biblical books lived in cultures that, in one way or another, assumed that temples should be built for deities and animal sacrifices should be made to those deities, that some form of slavery was acceptable, and that women did not have the same status as men. In the Old Testament, individuals are told to "gird up their loins." This presumes a certain type of clothing and communicates something specific in its context (often, "Make yourself ready"). In the New Testament, Jesus washes his disciples' feet (John 13:5). This presumes certain customs related to footwear, hygiene, and status, and what Jesus did expresses a special kind of service in that context. Sometimes the words we use in our English translations fail to make clear the cultural difference between the world of the text and our world. For example, the ancient Greek word *gynē*, "woman," could be used for the female participant in the institution of *gamos* (or in Latin, *matrimonium*), akin to our "marriage," and the word *anēr*, "man," could be used for the male participant. When we translate *gynē* as "wife" and *anēr* as "husband" in the New Testament, we may forget that the institution addressed in these passages is not the same as marriage in contemporary Western countries. But to equate the ancient institution of *matrimonium* with today's practice of marriage is no more valid than to equate the master of a slave with an employer, or the ancient emperor of Rome with a modern president. Comparisons can be made, but the cultural situations differ and matter for interpretation.

Most readers perceive instinctively that acknowledging the Bible's authority does not require that we bring the entire cultural world of the Bible into

4. Rom. 16:16; 1 Cor. 16:20; 2 Cor. 13:12; 1 Thess. 5:26.

our own. This perception is confirmed by the fact that there is not just one culture represented in the Bible, but many. The cultural setting of Abraham is not the same as that of David and Solomon, which differs from the world of King Josiah, which differs from Daniel's context in Babylon, which differs from the Persian setting of Esther. The Greco-Roman world of the New Testament is different too, and one can distinguish between the Roman Judea of the Gospels and the Greco-Roman environment presupposed in 1 Corinthians. All of this shows that we who believe in the inspiration of the Bible should not try to reproduce biblical culture in our world, because there is no single "biblical culture" to imitate. Instead, we need to discern what Scripture teaches as interpreted against the backdrop of the biblical writers' cultures and then apply this teaching to our context.

2. The specific historical circumstances of the writer constitute another dimension of a biblical text's context. In today's world, if the mayor of a town gave a public address in the aftermath of a forest fire, the content of the mayor's speech would make better sense to us if we knew about this event. In the Bible, the book of Haggai illustrates how the message of a biblical book is illuminated by the understanding of its specific historical setting, which for Haggai is the postexilic period as described in the book of Ezra, when the temple was rebuilt.[5] It is evident that if we know something about the specific occasion that prompted an author to compose a text, we will gain some insight into the text's meaning.

One complicating factor for much of the Old Testament is that we have little evidence to use in identifying when the books were written and under what circumstances. Because Samuel dies in 1 Samuel 25, it is safe to assume that he did not write 2 Samuel. The book of Judges, which narrates events that took place before the reigns of Saul and David, refers to something that held true "until the day of the exile of the land" (Judg. 18:30), which shows that this text reached its final form later and through some sort of editorial process. The book of Psalms is another biblical book that contains early material, including Davidic psalms and a "prayer of Moses" (Ps. 90), and also material written in response to the Babylonian exile (e.g., Ps. 137). The book of Psalms was evidently put together out of a variety of sources from different periods, as shown also by the editorial seams that have been added at the end of the book units.[6] With these and most Old Testament books, we cannot know for sure when exactly they reached their final form or what circumstances led

5. See Hag. 1:1, 14–15; 2:1–2, 10, 20; Ezra 5:1; 6:14.

6. See Pss. 41:13; 72:19–20; 89:52; 106:48; 150:1–6 (and all of Pss. 147–50). Although not a tightly edited book, the book of Psalms seems to have received some editorial attention as part of its composition. See Tucker and Grant, *Psalms*, 2:19–29.

to their promulgation and acceptance as finished books. Moreover, the fact that Old Testament books were composed in stages means that any given text might have engaged more than one historical circumstance. In the case of a psalm, for example, the text might have initially addressed a situation in the life of David, and later the editor of the Psalms made intentional use of it in giving shape to the whole book. Although the value of knowing the specific circumstances of the writer is undeniable, with the Old Testament we typically do not have enough information to be precise.

Even for the Old Testament, however, we occasionally get clues as to when a certain unit of text might have been written. Such clues include passages in which the writer comments on a previous condition that no longer holds (e.g., Gen. 12:6) or mentions something that remains "until this day" (e.g., Josh. 16:10). Moreover, earlier language is sometimes distinct from later language (e.g., Joshua is older than Esther), and the rhetorical aims of the writer give us some sense of what circumstances are being addressed. With the New Testament, the time frames within which books were written are better known. In terms of the circumstances of composition, we have a clearer understanding for the New Testament letters and are less clear about the Gospels and Acts. For the New Testament to some extent, and especially for the Old Testament, we will often have to be content with a general sense of the times and circumstances in which the authors or editors wrote. I will return to this topic of composition and chronology below when I explain how biblical writers interpret older biblical traditions.

3. In a given cultural context, writers may compose different types of literature that serve distinct purposes and follow specific conventions. More importantly, the types of literature employed in one culture may not correspond to those used in another. A type or category of literature is referred to as a "genre." The idea that biblical writers composed their books according to the conventions of ancient literary genres is another aspect of exploring the Bible's ancient context.

We can understand the concept of genre by reflecting on the different sets of expectations we bring to different kinds of writing, such as a piece of serious journalism, a comic book, historical fiction, a fable, a repair manual, or an autobiography. The key idea is that when an author chooses to write in a defined genre, the conventions of the genre create a set of expectations that are shared between the author and the readers. Readers then know what to expect and can evaluate the work according to the genre's conventions. For serious journalism, a competent reader will know to ask, Is it factual? Does it lead off with major ideas? Is the writing clear and appropriately concise? This same reader will bring different sets of expectations to a comic book or fable (both highly inventive, but distinct), or to a repair manual or auto-biography (both purportedly factual, but quite different). As for the Bible, to the extent we can understand the conventions assumed by the writer and intended readers, we will better grasp what the biblical writers communicated in their historical contexts.

Much profit is to be gained by thinking about literary genres in the Bible. But the types of literature we find in the Bible do not necessarily correspond to the literary genres with which we are most familiar today. We should pay careful attention to clues within each biblical book to determine as much as possible how the author expected the text to be read. Parallels with ancient literature inside and outside the Bible provide examples of possible literary types. Some of the genre categories applied to biblical books and units within books include law, historical narrative, vision report, short story, lament, proverb, parable, letter, and apocalyptic.[7]

At the same time, we should not overestimate how much we know about the genres of biblical literature. First, most biblical books do not bear enough resemblance to other ancient sources to suggest that they belong to the same genre or follow the same conventions. For example, there is nothing in ancient Near Eastern literature that appears to be the same genre as the Pentateuch or Isaiah or 1–2 Samuel. Some sections of a biblical book may resemble other literature (e.g., parts of Gen. 1–11 resemble certain ancient hymns, epics, and myths),[8] and this can offer help in identifying the type of source material used. But it does not necessarily tell us how the material is employed in its new context. Second, even where substantial literary connections exist at the book level (such as between Egyptian proverbs and the biblical book of Proverbs), we cannot conclude from the points of similarity that the texts are similar at every point, especially because the texts in question come from different cultures. Third, the conventions that governed how ancient texts outside the Bible were interpreted are often no clearer to us than the conventions that guided biblical writers. All of these ancient texts, biblical and nonbiblical alike, are difficult to interpret. In raising these concerns, I do not wish to minimize the contributions that the study of ancient history, languages, and cultures makes to our understanding of the Bible. We should be cautious, however, in what we claim to know about ancient genres and the rules that supposedly governed them.

The need for caution may be illustrated with reference to biblical law and ancient Near Eastern law. Much of the concrete legal material in the

---

7. E.g., see Gorman, *Elements of Biblical Exegesis*, 92–94; Chapman and Sweeney, *Cambridge Companion*.

8. For these terms, see Hallo and Younger, *Context of Scripture*, 1:v–x.

Pentateuch (e.g., the ox that gores, theft, murder, etc.) belongs to a tradition of ancient Near Eastern law that goes back to the third millennium BC.[9] Around a dozen legal texts from this tradition have come to light, the most famous being the "Code" of Hammurabi from the Old Babylonian period (eighteenth century BC). In all probability, this document did not function as a law code in the modern sense. It leaves many essential topics untreated and is not cited in the numerous legal decisions preserved from the Old Babylonian period.[10] Different theories have been proposed to explain its purpose—for example, that Hammurabi's law collection served as royal propaganda to show that the king had ruled justly or that it was compiled for the purpose of training scribes. Raymond Westbrook suggests that Hammurabi's law collection served as a reference work for royal courts in deciding difficult cases.[11] It is noteworthy that this text was copied for a thousand years with very little change in the substance of its laws. Perhaps this shows that Hammurabi's collection was more like a work of literature or philosophy, intended not to settle individual cases (since it was not updated, even though practical laws must have changed) but rather to inspire right thinking in the judicial sphere.[12] Interestingly, Westbrook also points out that, for certain Hittite law collections, scribes did update the legal content, as if these Hittite codes played some role in the practical judicial process.[13] To sum up, the purpose and usage of the Code of Hammurabi is not entirely clear, and in any case, there is reason to think that Hittite law collections were used differently. Ancient Near Eastern law collections provide excellent paradigms for thinking about how legal material might have functioned in ancient Israel, but there is no obvious genre with fixed conventions or rules that the biblical texts must follow. The best way to discover how this material was employed in the Bible is to look at the biblical passages themselves.

The legal material in the Bible shares much in common with the substance of ancient Near Eastern law, but it also has its own unique framework and reception history. Key collections of biblical law that parallel ancient

9. See Westbrook, *Law from the Tigris to the Tiber*, 300, 306; Levinson, *Legal Revision and Religious Renewal*, 23–24.

10. See Westbrook, *Law from the Tigris to the Tiber*, 320–22; Westbrook, "Biblical and Cuneiform Law Codes," 247–64; Levinson, *Legal Revision and Religious Renewal*, 23–25; Bottéro, *Mesopotamia*, 156–69. Westbrook, "Biblical and Cuneiform Law Codes," 249, cites two cases that may represent some kind of practical application for Hammurabi's collection.

11. Westbrook, "Biblical Law and Cuneiform Law Codes," 254.

12. On Hammurabi's collection as literature or philosophy, see Levinson, *Legal Revision and Religious Renewal*, 24. On the Code of Hammurabi as a model intended to inspire, see Bottéro, *Mesopotamia*, 167. As Bottéro states, "It was instructive and educative in the judicial order."

13. Westbrook, "Biblical Law and Cuneiform Law Codes," 255–56.

Near Eastern law are found in Exodus 21–23 and Deuteronomy 15–25. As with other ancient law collections, biblical law is far from comprehensive; therefore, it probably did not function as a law code in the modern sense. We may assume that judges in early Israel looked to these laws as models of justice to help them adjudicate in a wide variety of cases. In this way, the use of Mosaic law in ancient Israel may have been similar to the use of law in one or another surrounding culture. The setting for Israel's laws, however, is unique. Biblical law is located within a framework that emphasizes God's covenant with Israel, and the laws in Exodus are presented as coming from God (Exod. 21:1), not from a human king. In the context of the Sinai revelation, the legal "ordinances" (*mišpāṭîm*, Exod. 24:3) in Exodus 21–23 are given by God through Moses to the people of Israel, who say, "All the words that the LORD has spoken, we will do" (24:3). The Pentateuch therefore portrays Israel at Sinai as a community that has entered into covenant with God to observe these legal rulings in some sense. At first, Moses and his immediate assistants (18:25–26) may have implemented the specific rules given at Sinai, using judicial discretion informed by core values (e.g., 22:21). Beyond this, they probably made rulings on other cases based on principles derived from revealed laws and fresh Mosaic revelations (see Num. 15:34–35; 36:5–9). After the death of Moses, the legal traditions found in Deuteronomy may have served as authoritative elaboration on the earlier legal material in order to provide further values and principles to help judges make rulings (see Deut. 26:16–17). Biblical laws came to be included in the books that ultimately formed the Pentateuch, where they could serve not only as inspiration for good legal decisions but also as records of God's justice and as witnesses to Israel's covenant obligations.

As for the reception of Mosaic legal material in other biblical texts, much remains uncertain, but a few significant points are worthy of mention. Although the narratives of Judges (e.g., Judg. 4:4–5) and 1–2 Samuel (e.g., 1 Sam. 7:15–17) refer to figures who served as judges in a judicial sense, they do not indicate how Mosaic law functioned in this process. The basic orientation and tone of what these biblical texts commend is in line with Mosaic law, but there is no indication that specific laws were being cited to justify particular rulings.[14] This lack of verbatim reference to Mosaic law also holds true for

14. The book of Ruth shows how Israel's legal traditions could function as moral guidance or legal precedent, even when not explicitly cited. Not only does Ruth 2 illustrate principles of gleaning and generosity (Lev. 19:9–10; Deut. 24:19–22), but Ruth 4 presupposes the laws of levirate marriage (Deut. 25:5–10) and land redemption (Lev. 25:25–28; cf. Num. 27:8–11), albeit practiced in a way that appears idiosyncratic from the perspective of preserved biblical law. According to Berman, *Inconsistency in the Torah*, 137–47, the structure of the book of Ruth was

most prophetic literature. Nevertheless, we see in the prophets clear indications that legal traditions were known and recognized as authoritative; for
example, Amos 2:8 condemns those who lie down on garments taken in pledge
(Exod. 22:26–27), Hosea 4:2 presupposes the Ten Commandments (Exod.
20:1–17), Jeremiah 2:34 assumes a specific Mosaic law about theft (Exod.
22:2–3), and Ezekiel 18:5–18 alludes to a number of legal principles (e.g.,
Lev. 18:19, 20; Exod. 22:21, 25–27; 23:2–3).[15] According to 2 Kings 22–23,
King Josiah ordered the people of Judah to follow the "commandments,
decrees, and statutes" contained in a "scroll of the Torah" that was found in
the temple (2 Kings 22:8, 11; 23:3).[16] During the Persian period, Nehemiah
the governor (Neh. 8:9) and Ezra the priest and expert in the Torah (Ezra 7:6,
10, 12, 21) received Persian imperial authorization to institute Mosaic law as
part of their management of the province. Ezra was directed by the Persians
to appoint judges and magistrates to teach and enforce "the law of your God"
along with "the law of the king" on penalty of death, banishment, confisca-
tion of property, or imprisonment, as appropriate to the offense (Ezra 7:6,
12, 25–26). The books of Ezra and Nehemiah record the implementation of
Mosaic laws related to sacrifice (Ezra 3:2), putting away foreign wives (Ezra
10:1–17; Neh. 13:1–3), and Sabbath observance (Neh. 13:15–22).[17] In the New
Testament, the exact status of Old Testament law is not always clear, but
Jesus sometimes invokes a specific Mosaic commandment as authoritative
(e.g., Matt. 15:3–4), as does the apostle Paul (1 Cor. 9:8–9).[18] As the reception
history shows, biblical laws were interpreted as applicable and authoritative
in a variety of ways in different contexts.

In considering the historical context of the Bible, it is important to remember that the types of literature represented in Scripture are not precisely
the same as those we use today. As we study the Bible, we should pay careful

---

shaped by laws in Deut. 24:16–25:10. But the author of Ruth felt free to modify how the legal
ideas were applied, because these laws were seen not as sources of fixed rulings, but as resources
for the legal reasoning of later jurists. Berman invokes as a parallel case the relationship between
the Neo-Babylonian work "Nebuchadnezzar King of Justice" and the Code of Hammurabi.

15. Other examples where the book of Jeremiah presupposes legal material known from
the Pentateuch include Jer. 3:1, on divorce (Deut. 24:1–4), and Jer. 34:8–9, on slave release (Lev.
25:10; Deut. 15:12–18). Ezekiel shows special interest in traditions related to the temple, ritual
purity, and sacrifice.

16. The scroll of the Torah that inspired Josiah's reforms probably corresponded in substance
to the book of Deuteronomy. On the relationship between Josiah's reforms and the book of
Deuteronomy, see McConville, *Deuteronomy*, 21–33.

17. For historical studies of the Persian context, see Fried, *Priest and the Great King*, 217–27;
and Cataldo, *Theocratic Yehud?*, 101–17.

18. For a brief survey of how Christians have understood the relevance of Old Testament
laws, see Sprinkle, *Biblical Law and Its Relevance*, 1–27.

attention to textual clues that signal how the text might have functioned in its original context. Ancient literature related to the Bible can be valuable for our understanding. Two important points, however, should be emphasized: (1) What we know about the genres and conventions of ancient literature is limited. Therefore, whether we are trying to label a text as history, myth, epic, or something else, our conclusions should be measured to fit the evidence. (2) As shown by the reception history of biblical law across the canon of Scripture, biblical texts contain principles, values, and images that can be reapplied in new contexts beyond what might be expected from their original usage.

4. The Christian Bible presents a story of creation and redemption. Major events in this story include the rebellion of Adam and Eve, the giving of the Torah at Sinai, the exile in Babylon, and the birth, death, and resurrection of Jesus. When we study the Bible, we should pay attention to how each biblical text fits into this story, especially in relation to the ministry of Jesus.

Within the story of the Old Testament from creation to the return from exile, it is often useful to remember where a specific narrative is located vis-à-vis other revelatory events. For example, given biblical prohibitions against child sacrifice (Deut. 12:30–31; 18:10; Lev. 18:21; 20:2–5), it may be surprising that Abraham does not question the command to sacrifice Isaac (Gen. 22:1–14) in the same way that he questions the destruction of Sodom (Gen. 18:22–33). It must be remembered, however, that Abraham's binding of Isaac takes place before the revelation at Sinai. Within the narrative of the Pentateuch, Abraham did not yet know what to think about this practice.

The most important factor in properly recognizing the redemptive-historical context of a biblical text is its location before, during, or after the ministry of Jesus. According to the Bible's story of redemption, the coming of Jesus both fulfilled the ideals of the Old Testament and also transformed the significance of its rules. For example, Old Testament regulations pertaining to animal sacrifice and food taboos no longer apply to Christians as they did to Israel prior to the coming of Jesus, even though the texts that discuss these topics remain sacred Scripture for the church. The period of Jesus's earthly ministry constitutes a unique theological-historical context. For example, Jesus can still direct someone to make an offering according to Mosaic law (Matt. 8:4), although his death and resurrection will render these offerings unnecessary. As another example, Jesus's disciples do not fast while he is present with them, but they will fast again when he is taken away (Matt. 9:14–15). I will return to the subject of Jesus and biblical interpretation below. For the present, it suffices to say that when interpreting the Old Testament, we must take into consideration the fact that these texts were written before and in preparation for the life, death, and resurrection of Jesus.

The Bible Addresses Complex Topics by Giving
a Variety of Perspectives

As the following chapters will show, the Bible sometimes offers a variety of perspectives on particular topics. This does not mean that various biblical texts stand in irreconcilable contradiction to one another. One could imagine a collection of texts that are so diverse in their underlying values and trajectories that no coherent way of life could emerge from them. The Bible is not such a collection. Part of the reason for the Bible's diversity is that scriptural revelation is contextual; that is, the message of Scripture was contextually appropriate at the time when it was written. Biblical books addressed specific audiences, dealt with particular circumstances, and were suited to the recipients' capacity to comprehend and act. The variety of contexts partly explains the variety we see in the Bible. At the same time, the presence of diverse perspectives in the Bible should not be seen as an unfortunate by-product of its historical rootedness. On the contrary, the fact that Scripture offers different angles on certain topics contributes significantly to its didactic usefulness. The variety of perspectives contained in the Bible helps us to understand complex realities so that we can respond to these realities with wisdom.

The constructive value of diversity is evident in passages where a biblical writer affirms two different perspectives in proximity, as if to challenge the reader to sort out the precise nuance of each statement and discover their harmonization or appropriate applications. For example, in the narrative of Saul's rejection God "regrets" making Saul king as the just response to Saul's disobedience (1 Sam. 15:11), and yet God does not "regret" in human fashion (1 Sam. 15:29) when Saul pleads for another chance as if God has acted rashly. Similarly, Proverbs 26:4–5 offers contrasting advice on how to respond to a fool, so as to challenge us to consider the potential outcome when deciding whether to answer, and the Gospel of John presents the paradox of Jesus's earthly identity, that "the Father is greater than I" (John 14:28) and also "I and the Father are one" (John 10:30).

It should be recognized, of course, that there are different kinds and degrees of diversity.[19] In some cases, discrepancies in detail between biblical passages probably reflect nothing more than different sources that variously achieved the conventional level of detail needed for accuracy and vividness. Examples include simple discrepancies in calculating numbers (e.g., 1 Kings 9:28; 2 Chron. 8:18) and the question of one or two angels at Jesus's empty tomb

19. This subject is dealt with in a slightly different and useful way by Goldingay, *Theological Diversity*.

(Matt. 28:1–7; Luke 24:1–8). In other cases, the diversity between passages is substantive and reflects the specific aims or context of the author. Thus, the Gospel of Matthew recounts the story of Jesus cursing the fig tree, with the tree withering immediately to emphasize the power of faithful prayer (Matt. 21:18–22), whereas Mark adds to this story the account of Jesus cleansing the temple, with the tree withering the following day so as to emphasize the theme of judgment (Mark 11:12–26). The diversity here stems from the aim of each Gospel writer. As for context, a famous example is the contrast between (1) the LORD inciting David to take a census, as narrated in an earlier period when the call to monotheism was the dominant concern (2 Sam. 24:1), over against (2) Satan inciting David to take the census as narrated at a later time, when the dominant concern was David's enigmatic disobedience (1 Chron. 21:1). Both perspectives have something to contribute (cf. the roles of God and Satan in Job 1–2), but each writer explained the account in a way that best suited the needs of the specific context. In some situations, biblical writers may have advocated for positions that were seen at the time as opposing sides of a dispute (e.g., Ruth vs. Ezra-Nehemiah on foreign wives). Even in these cases, regardless of how much coherence the human writers might have recognized, the reception of all these books as Scripture means that each passage contributes in its own way to the coherent message of the Bible that we are responsible to discern.

Belief in the unity of Scripture does not require that all biblical texts say the same thing; rather, the expectation is that the various things Scripture says can be put together into a meaningful whole. One should not think of the Bible as a painting that is "unified," in the sense of a canvas covered with solid green or solid red. Instead, the Bible is like a painting made up of many colors: blues, greens, reds, browns, and so forth—all of which come together to make a coherent and meaningful picture. We learn to perceive this picture as we become more practiced in the art of biblical interpretation.

We Should Seek a Coherent Picture of What Scripture Teaches

Christian belief in biblical inspiration leads us to expect that all biblical texts fit together into a coherent theology. Therefore, if the Bible exhibits some measure of diversity in its content, how do we organize all biblical texts into a unified theological whole? The answer is that we need to identify the core values that stand at the center of biblical teaching. As we identify these values stated explicitly in Scripture, we will be able to recognize them throughout the Bible as the values that underlie other passages, until we see a network of values that unite all biblical texts and fit together harmoniously. We can have confidence that we are on the right track with our theological interpretation when (1) we ground our core values in the life and teaching of Jesus and (2) the unity of the Bible manifests itself in the network of core values more clearly than it does when we merely line up every statement in the Bible side by side without interpretation.

The place to start in identifying Scripture's core values is the life and teachings of Jesus. As for his life, Jesus the divine Word willingly humbled himself to take on the form of a servant and chose to suffer death on a cross for the sake of the world, even though the world did not recognize him. Rather than striking out in vengeance, Jesus asked for forgiveness on our behalf. Jesus was raised by the Father and given all authority in heaven and on earth, and he will return as the righteous judge of all. The narrative of Jesus's miraculous birth, life, death, and resurrection establishes a paradigm for Scripture's core values.

Moreover, Jesus made several statements about Scripture that bring the core of biblical teaching to light. According to Jesus, the principle "Whatever you want people to do for you, so also you should do for them" is equivalent to the Law and the Prophets (Matt. 7:12). Elsewhere, Jesus states that all the Law and the Prophets depend on two commandments: "Love the Lord your God with all your heart and with all your soul and with all your mind" (cf. Deut. 6:5), which is the greatest and first commandment, and "love your neighbor as yourself" (cf. Lev. 19:18; Gal. 5:14), which is the second. Jesus says this with some variation in all three Synoptic Gospels (Matt. 22:34–40; Mark 12:28–31; Luke 10:25–27), with the concept "love your neighbor" explained in Luke through the parable of the good Samaritan, so as to include anyone who may need neighborly care. When the rich young ruler asks Jesus, "What must I do to inherit eternal life?" Jesus lists several of the Ten Commandments and then tells the young man to sell everything, give to the poor, and follow him (Luke 18:18–22; Matt. 19:16–21; Mark 10:17–21). When challenged about his work on the Sabbath, Jesus justifies himself by appealing to David (1 Sam. 21) and citing Hosea 6:6, "I desire mercy, not sacrifice" (Matt. 12:1–8). In discussing ritual purity, Jesus lists the sins that come from the heart that make us unclean, such as sexual immorality, theft, murder, greed, malice, deceit, and envy (Mark 7:17–23). While rebuking the Pharisees for hypocrisy, Jesus refers to justice, mercy, and faith as the "weightier matters of the law" (Matt. 23:23–24).

The above passages show how Jesus summed up the core values of the Old Testament. In terms of content, Jesus focused on dispositions and actions that flow from proper reverence for God and right moral behavior, showing clear ethical standards and abundant mercy. As for interpretive methodology, according to Jesus not all commandments function in the same way. Some commandments sum up others. Certain commandments depend on others. Specific commandments are weightier than others. The weightier commands on which others depend express Scripture's core values. All biblical passages, of course, are inspired and meant for instruction (2 Tim. 3:16–17). But some passages articulate the Bible's core more clearly.[20] Core biblical values should guide our interpretation of Scripture, especially of "less weighty" passages that show how the Bible's core teaching manifests itself in specific circumstances. Although not all biblical passages play the same role, as part of inspired Scripture they complement one another.

In biblical interpretation, a careful balance must be struck between reading each passage through the lens of core biblical teaching and allowing each text to make its own unique contribution. On the one hand, every biblical text offers special insight. This is why we start with the specific wording of the text in its historical context. The fact that different passages come at topics from different angles is part of what makes the Bible useful. On the other hand, what we interpret any biblical text to be teaching must reflect the fact that all Scripture was inspired by the one true God. We should expect certain points of tension, and of course there will be issues we do not fully understand. But in the end, the purpose of Scripture is to lead us to God and guide our steps. Therefore, as we ask what key ideas, values, and principles contained in this passage represent the divinely intended teaching, we should be searching for an interpretation that can serve as part of one coherent theological message.

For Christian readers of Scripture, interpretation involves certain goals and guardrails that keep them on track. The goals of biblical interpretation are expressed by Jesus in his statements on Scripture—for example, that we are to love God and our neighbor.[21] This can be articulated in other ways, as when Paul speaks in light of Christ's resurrection about his own aim in life: "That I may know him and the power of his resurrection and the fellowship of his sufferings, being conformed to his death so that in some way I might attain to the resurrection from the dead" (Phil. 3:10–11). As for guardrails, church families and reason are especially important.

---

20. This is why Bible readers have always been especially drawn to favorite passages, such as Exod. 20:1–17 (the Ten Commandments); 1 Pet. 1:16 ("Be holy, because I am holy"); Jer. 9:23–24; Mic. 6:8; Rom. 14:17; Gal. 5:22–25; James 3:17–18; 1 John 4:10; and many others. Generally speaking, these texts are presented as summative or foundational principles in their literary contexts, but what marks them as core teaching is their content—that is, the clarity with which they express Jesus's embodiment of Scripture and the underlying values that hold all Scripture together.

21. See Augustine's comments on the goal of biblical interpretation in *On Christian Teaching* 1.36.40.

In ways understood differently by different groups of Christians, but that are essential in some way for all, church tradition and our church families function as guardrails for biblical interpretation.[22] It has never been seen as the task of Christians to invent a new religion out of the Bible, but rather to believe and practice the gospel as taught by the apostles and preached in the churches in accordance with biblical teaching. Churches and traditions should be reformed on the basis of Scripture, but our interpretations of Scripture should also be guided by the guardrails of the whole Christian family, past and present. Within the context of church life, we also gain wisdom from our Christian experience. In a host of ways pertaining to the practical application of Scripture, how we experience God can help us discern between competing possibilities. This experience, however, should itself be interpreted and weighed in the context of our church families.

Another guardrail for biblical interpretation is reason. The idea of scriptural revelation presupposes that human beings collectively (although not every person) are equipped with sufficient reasoning powers to transmit, read, translate, and interpret texts. Our capacity to think clearly and with moral rectitude enables us to examine the Scriptures and deal justly with one another. Due to our human limitations and sinful proclivities, the concept of reason as a tool for biblical interpretation should not be construed in an exclusively individual way. Because other people are endowed with reason, and the scope of every individual's understanding is limited, each interpreter should be eager to learn from others, and humility is always in order. Furthermore, although reason serves as the "operating system" for interpretation, it does not generate the "data" out of which theology is constructed. Our role as thoughtful interpreters is to organize the authoritative materials that are given to us, which are found primarily in the canon of Scripture but also include truths known from nature (natural revelation) and Christian witness (tradition). Among these sources of theology, Scripture functions as the unique standard for the others.

To sum up this section, if we are to apply biblical texts in a responsible manner, we should interpret them in a way that is informed by the coherent theological message of Scripture. The network of core values that unify the Bible will reflect God's values as revealed in Jesus. Theological interpretation is not simply reading all biblical texts in the light of a single formulation of

---

22. For example, Christian sources in the second and third centuries mention a "rule of faith" that succinctly summarizes core Christian teaching as transmitted in churches founded by the apostles. These "rule of faith" statements probably served as baptismal confessions (e.g., Irenaeus, *Against Heresies* 1.10.1; 3.4.2), although they could also function as brief outlines of scriptural teaching on Jesus. See Ferguson, *Rule of Faith*.

doctrine; it requires that we pay attention to how each biblical text fits with the rest of the Bible. The discovery of this theological interconnectedness is an important dimension of interpreting Scripture. Special insight into the Bible's interconnections can be gained by paying careful attention to how one biblical text interprets another.

How Scripture Interprets Scripture

In certain places in Scripture, a biblical writer may show that he is aware of an older biblical tradition and reapply it to his own context.[23] Such instances provide instructive case studies for how a theme embedded in one setting can be redeployed in a different setting. Each biblical text gives a proper application of the theme, but we also learn something enlightening about the interpretive process by seeing what the later writer does with the earlier tradition. In a general way, the phenomenon of inner-biblical interpretation serves as a paradigm for our entire approach to interpreting Scripture theologically with an eye toward fresh application. More specifically, the insights gained from how Scripture interprets Scripture can offer valuable assistance as we seek to find the theological unity underlying all biblical passages on a given theme.[24]

Although the benefits of studying inner-biblical interpretation seem obvious, it is not always a simple task to identify where in Scripture one biblical text interprets another. Of course, where New Testament texts quote the Old Testament, we clearly see inner-biblical interpretation at work.[25] It would be unfortunate, however, to overlook the many ways that Scripture interprets Scripture even within the Old Testament. To ignore this aspect of inner-biblical interpretation is not only to miss out on numerous insights that individual Old Testament passages convey but also to leave unappreciated how

23. Given the customs related to gender in the ancient cultures of the Bible, and especially the lack of opportunities for women to engage in literary activity, I am assuming that biblical writers were male. In the end, however, we do not know that all biblical writers were male. My translations of Scripture in this book are meant to reflect the culturally embedded dimension of biblical texts so as to highlight the gap between the biblical world and our world, and thus one key aspect of interpretation. Therefore, I do not employ gender-neutral language for biblical translations in this book, as I would do in other contexts.

24. An important historical study of "inner-biblical exegesis" is Fishbane, *Biblical Interpretation in Ancient Israel*. See also the bibliographical essay on inner-biblical exegesis in Levinson, *Legal Revision and Religious Renewal*, 95–181. For a recent book on Deuteronomy's "amendments" to the Covenant Code (Exod. 20:22–23:19), which include new formulations that supplement and sometimes replace earlier statutes, see Mattison, *Rewriting and Revision as Amendment*.

25. This subject has benefited from many insightful studies, including Hays, *Echoes of Scripture*; Beale, *Handbook on the New Testament*; Moyise, *Paul and Scripture*.

interpretive trends already evident in the Old Testament find their consumma-
tion in the New Testament. The major challenge in studying this phenomenon
in the Old Testament, however, is that we do not have as clear a picture as
we would like of when each Old Testament text was written. This makes it
hard in many cases to be sure which text is interpreting the other. Still, as
noted above (point 2, under "The Starting Points for Interpretation"), there
are sometimes clues in biblical texts that allow us to identify a general time
frame for composition, and often the nature of how a given tradition is used
in two texts allows us to determine with some certainty the relative chronology of the texts. Thus, even if we cannot state with absolute certainty the
date of final composition for Exodus or Amos, it is reasonable to conclude
that the law about taking a garment in pledge in Exodus 22:26–27 predates
the allusion to this law in Amos 2:8. Through cautious historical judgments
based on biblical scholarship assessed through the eyes of faith, I will attempt
to identify general chronological relationships between texts where possible
and try to learn what lessons I can from inner-biblical interpretation in both
the Old Testament and the New Testament.

In order to manage these historical challenges responsibly, I will discuss
examples of inner-biblical interpretation at two levels. First, I will highlight
any passages where I think that one biblical text is aware of a prior biblical
tradition and makes interpretive use of it. In some cases, the later writer
may be familiar with an earlier biblical book very much as we have it, and
in other cases the later writer might know the earlier tradition even though
the completed version of the biblical book that transmits this tradition to us
was not available. Second, in certain cases I will suggest that different biblical texts that come from roughly the same time period and take up the same
topic from different angles are in dialogue with each other. It is likely, in many
cases, that one text or the other knows a specific tradition from the other
stream of thought, but at the very least, such instances point to a dialogue
on the topic where each text is responding to the position of the other. These
parallel biblical texts that appear to be in dialogue with one another represent
another form of Scripture interpreting Scripture.

In treating specific cases of inner-biblical interpretation, I will not interpret these texts in such a way that later texts are seen as simply rejecting or
subverting earlier biblical traditions. There is always some kind of "commentary" on the inherited tradition that is expressed through the new usage,
which can include reapplying, supplementing, answering, and countering the
earlier tradition. But I will be looking for the didactic value of *each* text, not
just the later one. Moreover, in the end I will ask how these texts fit together
theologically in the context of the Bible's core values.

As mentioned above, it should be kept in mind that both earlier texts (inherited traditions) and later texts that offer comment (interpreting texts) are located in specific cultural and historical contexts. This means that all the texts require interpretation for application. I will not argue that we can always find a single theological trajectory that is moving in a specific direction. Because ideas develop over time, even within the Bible (for example, regarding the afterlife), it is often possible on a given topic to observe development of thought toward a certain end.[26] Such developments will naturally manifest themselves in how later biblical texts interpret received biblical traditions. Still, in principle there is no reason why a later biblical writer cannot apply an earlier biblical tradition in a way that fails to adhere to a specific trajectory—if, for example, the needs of the later writer require an application that does not exhibit development. I will point out movements of thought where I think they exist, but I see this kind of movement as a product of developments in the historical contexts of the writers, not necessarily as divinely ordained trajectories that lead to an ideal goal.

One of the primary reasons for studying inner-biblical interpretation is to set the stage for our own contemporary application. The following chapters will draw on insights gathered from specific examples of inner-biblical interpretation in order to help guide this process.

How Each Chapter Below Is Organized

In the following chapters, I provide overview discussions of themes that are addressed in Scripture from a variety of angles where inner-biblical interpretation plays an important role. These chapters show how the phenomenon of inner-biblical interpretation can inform our general approach to interpretation. They also illustrate how specific instances of inner-biblical interpretation can help us to perceive the Bible's coherent message on complex topics. Two of the chapters deal with broad conceptual categories that represent opposite poles on a spectrum and can be emphasized in different ways: "Corporate and Individual Responsibility" (chap. 2), and "Insiders and Outsiders" (chap. 3). The next two chapters address concrete practices that were basic to the ancient societies of the Bible and yet could be understood and lived out variously: "Marriage, Polygamy, and Divorce" (chap. 4), and "Sacrificial Offerings" (chap. 5). The final thematic chapter discusses a topic of central interest in Christian theology: "The Afterlife" (chap. 6).

26. A useful book in this regard is Webb, *Slaves, Women, and Homosexuals.*

Each chapter presents three sections: (1) Biblical Perspectives: This is an overview of important biblical treatments of the theme, organized in such a way as to highlight diversity of perspectives where they exist. Biblical texts are discussed with reference to their cultural, historical, and literary contexts. At this stage, I do not attempt to resolve any tensions that may exist among the various texts. (2) Inner-Biblical Insights: In this section, specific passages are discussed that exhibit inner-biblical interpretation. Emphasis is placed on how the interpreting text applies or qualifies its inherited biblical tradition. To sum up, I identify key theological insights about the theme that emerges from these passages. (3) Putting the Pieces Together: I conclude each chapter by proposing an interpretive framework for the chapter's theme that is informed both by the inner-biblical insights and by Scripture's core values as exemplified in Jesus. Based on this framework, I suggest ways to interpret the various biblical perspectives so that (a) each makes its own distinctive contribution and (b) the different passages fit together into a coherent theological whole.

My goal in these chapters is to explain what biblical writers can teach us about how to read the Bible with faithfulness to its inspired message and with wisdom in applying that message today. Clearly, the idea that Scripture interprets Scripture cannot be taken to mean that the Bible comes already interpreted, with no role for human interpreters. On the contrary, the manner in which biblical writers make use of prior biblical traditions suggests a process of interpretation that involves contemporary readers who receive the message of Scripture and mediate it to the present world.

2

Corporate and Individual Responsibility

Individual Responsibility within Community Obligations

That we belong to a group that bears corporate responsibility for certain outcomes and that we are individually responsible for our actions are perspectives that stand in tension with each other, and yet they are not incompatible. Both aspects of this dichotomy play some role in every society. Yet cultures differ in balancing or even defining these categories. Plus, the way corporate and individual responsibility interact in real human experience is always complex. All of this generates some diversity in how the Bible handles this topic.

The theme of corporate and individual responsibility serves as a useful starting point for our exploration of inner-biblical interpretation. First, issues of cultural difference come into play, both between biblical texts and between the cultures of the Bible and today's Western societies. Second, although the transition from Old Testament to New Testament involves a shift in focus, aspects of corporate and individual responsibility figure prominently in both testaments. Third, a significant Old Testament statement on transgenerational punishment (Exod. 20:5–6) receives clear inner-biblical treatment within the Old Testament itself. Finally, the limited scope of this topic makes it relatively simple to identify inner-biblical insights, but putting the various perspectives together into a coherent theological whole presents special challenges.

Biblical Perspectives

I will begin this section by summarizing biblical perspectives on corporate punishment in the Old Testament and also corporate responsibility to care for others. I will then identify some key passages from the Old Testament that place emphasis on the individual. Finally, I will illustrate how aspects of both corporate and individual responsibility function in the New Testament.

Corporate Punishment in the Old Testament

One stream of thought in the Old Testament portrays punishment as corporate in scope, either to include later generations or to include contemporary members of a specified group.

As for transgenerational punishment, a classic text appears in the Ten Commandments: "For I, the LORD your God, am a jealous God, visiting the iniquities of the fathers upon the sons to the third and fourth generations for those who hate me, but exhibiting steadfast love to the thousandth generation for those who love me and keep my commandments" (Exod. 20:5–6; Deut. 5:9–10). Similar language appears in God's revelation to Moses after the incident of the golden calf, where God proclaims, "The LORD, the LORD, a compassionate and gracious God, slow to anger and abounding in steadfast love and faithfulness, keeping steadfast love to the thousandth generation, forgiving iniquity, transgression, and sin; but he does not fail to punish, visiting the iniquities of the fathers upon the sons and upon the sons' sons to the third and fourth generations" (Exod. 34:6–7; see also Num. 14:18). The key phrase in these passages is "visiting the iniquities of the fathers upon the sons (and upon the sons' sons) to the third and fourth generations." The main point of contrast is between God's steadfast love, which abounds to the thousandth generation, and his punishment, which extends only to the third and fourth generations. This formula is meant to convey God's compassion. Still, the idea that God would punish children for what their parents did wrong generated further reflection and clarification, both in these biblical books and elsewhere in the Bible.

The concept of transgenerational punishment in the above passages has sometimes been interpreted in light of the clauses that appear in Exodus 20 and Deuteronomy 5: "for those who hate me" and "for those who love me and keep my commandments." One interpretation of this passage found in ancient Jewish and Christian sources limits the punishment of future generations to those who persist in the iniquity of their parents (i.e., "for later generations who also hate me").[1] This may be a valid reception of this theological concept in the context of Scripture as a whole, as will be discussed below, but in its original context the passage stresses that God's blessing for good (to the thousandth generation) is greater than his punishment for bad (to the third and fourth generations), which does not make sense if each generation is simply evaluated on whether it chooses to continue in its parents' love or hatred for the LORD.[2] Another approach to this passage is to observe that the third and fourth generations constitute the near family units (grandchildren and great-grandchildren) who are most affected by the decisions made by their elders. In Numbers 14:33, for example, it says that the children will have to wander in the wilderness for forty years because of their parents' faithlessness. According to this interpretation, statements about God punishing "to the third and fourth generations" may be a poetic way of saying that the LORD will give abundant blessing for many generations to those who love him and keep his commandments, but he will allow punishment to fall on the generations who must bear the consequences of their parents' sins. In any case, these passages express some concept of divinely sanctioned transgenerational punishment.

In point of fact, the Old Testament is not lacking in what appear to be examples of transgenerational punishment. God's killing of Egypt's firstborns in the book of Exodus could be seen as belonging to this category, although this could also be interpreted as an illustration of how the evil that Pharaoh and his men perpetrated came back on them measure for measure (see Exod. 1:22; 11:4–8; 12:29–30). In the wake of David's sin against Bathsheba and Uriah, the son of David and Bathsheba is killed, whereas David is permitted to live (2 Sam. 12:14). Near the end of David's reign, a three-year famine comes on Israel because of Saul's sin against the Gibeonites, and God cannot be supplicated for the land until seven of Saul's descendants are executed (2 Sam. 21:1–14). In several cases, the wicked behavior of a king is said to bring about divine judgment on his descendants.[3]

As proof that this thinking was part of Israel's consciousness, the rhetoric of transgenerational punishment occasionally surfaces in Old Testament poetic texts. In Isaiah's prophecy against Babylon, for example, sons will be slaughtered for their father's sins (Isa. 14:20–21). At one point, the psalmist

---

1. See Weiss, "Sins of the Parents," 7–10.
2. Still, perhaps punishments initiated by the sins of parents are confirmed by sins committed by the children. In Lev. 26:39–40, for example, reference is made to punishment given because of the people's iniquity and also because of the iniquity of their fathers. See also 1 Kings 11:11; 12:8–15; and the logic of Rom. 5:12.
3. E.g., Ahab (1 Kings 21:29), Hezekiah (2 Kings 20:18), and Manasseh (2 Kings 21:9–16; 23:26–27; 24:3–4). In the case of Judah's fall to Babylon, God's judgment came during the reigns of kings who continued in the evil ways of Manasseh (2 Kings 23:36–24:20).

says, "Do not remember against us the iniquities of our ancestors" (Ps. 79:8), and elsewhere the psalmist wishes of his enemy, "May the iniquity of his fathers be remembered to the LORD" (Ps. 109:14). In Lamentations 5:7, the writer expresses frustration over his generation's suffering after the fall of Jerusalem: "Our fathers sinned and are no more, and we carry their iniquity!" (cf. Job 21:19). Transgenerational punishment was a perceived reality for Old Testament writers and remains part of the theological framework of Scripture.

The Old Testament also contains passages in which punishment is decreed in the present for a whole group. Even here, however, the transgenerational element is normally a factor since children are typically part of the group that is punished. In 1 Samuel 15, as another illustration of measure-for-measure judgment (see Exod. 17:8–16), the LORD commissions Saul to destroy all Amalekites collectively, "man and woman, child and infant, ox and sheep, camel and donkey," in punishment for Amalek's attack against Israel (1 Sam. 15:2–3). This is depicted as collective and transgenerational, as is true for Israel's divinely prescribed wars against the Canaanites.[4] After Achan's sin of taking plunder from the Canaanites, all those in his household are destroyed to avert God's anger and allow the nation as a whole to succeed (Josh. 7:24–26).[5] Similarly, divine judgment against Jeroboam leads to the death of his entire household (1 Kings 15:29–30). In the historical books, the nation as a whole is regularly punished for the sins of its leaders (e.g., 2 Sam. 24:1–17; 1 Kings 14:16), although it should be noted that the people as a whole (even if not every individual) are often mentioned as complicit in the leaders' sins (e.g., 2 Kings 17:11–23). This shows how the corporate punishment of a group because of the actions of a few can sometimes reflect a situation in which the wicked deeds of the few were imitated by many in the group.

Before wrapping up this discussion of corporate punishment, I want to stress that notions of corporate identity can intermingle with recognition of the individual. For example, Rahab represents the individual Canaanite who chose to throw in her lot with the LORD, and yet clemency extends beyond her to her family as well (Josh. 2:8–21; 6:22–23). Concepts of group and individual

4. See Num. 21:34–35; 31:17–18; Deut. 7:2; 20:16–18; Josh. 6:21; 8:22–29; 10:28, 30, 33, 35, 37, 39–40; 11:16–23. On the Hebrew term *ḥrm*, "devoted" (to the LORD by destruction), in the Hebrew Bible, see Kaminsky, *Corporate Responsibility*, 78–95. Within the story line of Israel's possession of the land in the Old Testament, emphasis is placed on the idea that Israel is there not to plunder but to receive an inheritance as part of their divinely ordained mission, and also to bring judgment on the evil represented by the Canaanites (e.g., Lev. 18:1–5, 24–28; Gen. 15:16).

5. See also Josh. 22:20. The death of Daniel's accusers and their families at the hands of Nebuchadnezzar (Dan. 6:24) probably functions in its literary context to illustrate measure-for-measure judgment.

identity are not mutually exclusive. I will say more about the individual in the Old Testament below.

How can we best understand corporate punishment in the Old Testament from a cultural perspective? I will mention just a few common explanations. First, most people groups in the Old Testament world were defined according to factors such as land of residence, religious/ritual practices, and family relations. It was natural in this context for Israel to form as a nation along these lines. The "people" of God was therefore a group who inhabited a specific land (Israel), worshiped a specific deity (the LORD), and perpetuated itself through family (children and grandchildren). When God entered into a covenant with Israel as a people, it was necessary in this setting for the covenant to transfer from one generation to the next through propagation of the family,[6] rather than through some other means, such as missionary activity. This gives some context for the transfer of punishment and blessing from one generation to the next.[7] Second, in the cultural world of the Old Testament, people could be seen as the property of other people (e.g., Exod. 20:17; 21:2–11). In this setting, harm done to one's property could be viewed as punishment meted out to the property owner, without full recognition of the individual status of the one viewed as property (e.g., Exod. 21:20–21). Third, people in the Old Testament world were understood to be blessed in their descendants through whom they lived on after death, because their descendants perpetuated their memory and embodied their identity (e.g., Deut. 25:5–10; Job 42:10–17). Within this framework, to punish an individual's descendants is to punish the individual. Cultural dimensions such as these are important for understanding Old Testament texts in their original contexts. As for theological interpretation and application, I will return to these topics in the third section of this chapter: "Putting the Pieces Together."

Corporate Responsibility as Covenantal Obligation in the Old Testament

Corporate responsibility also finds expression in the Old Testament as the covenantal obligation of community members to care for one another. In the story of Cain and Abel, God asks Cain, "Where is Abel, your brother?" Cain's reply shows his selfishness: "I do not know. Am I my brother's keeper?" (Gen. 4:9). This is clearly the wrong answer. It is not just that Cain acted wickedly

---

6. E.g., Deut. 5:2–3; 29:9–15; 30:19–20.

7. Not only punishment but also blessing can transfer to later generations in the Old Testament, especially in connection with the patriarchs and David. For example, see Gen. 26:3–5; Exod. 20:6; 32:13; Lev. 26:44–45; Deut. 9:27; 2 Kings 13:23; 19:34; 20:2–6; 2 Chron. 6:42; 21:7.

when he killed his brother. More than that, Cain is completely mistaken in how he understands communal responsibility. In the general mindset of the Old Testament, Israelites were expected to be the keepers of their brothers' and sisters' well-being.

The responsibility of Israelites to care for one another is reflected in numerous laws in the Pentateuch. For example, Exodus 23:4–5 requires each Israelite to offer assistance to anyone whose ox or donkey has wandered away or fallen, even if the other person is an enemy (cf. Deut. 22:1–4). Those who built homes were required to make a parapet (protective railing) around the roof so that others would not fall off accidentally (Deut. 22:8). If a member of the covenant community was in financial need, Israelites were obligated to lend money to that person at no interest and sell food to that person for no profit.[8] The Pentateuch forbids people from harvesting their fields and vineyards to the fullest extent so that food will be left for the poor and alien.[9] Other regulations that institutionalized generosity include the third-year tithe for widows, orphans, aliens, and Levites (Deut. 14:28–29; 26:12–13); the seventh-year allocation of fields and vineyards for the poor (Exod. 23:10–11); and the Year of Jubilee (Lev. 25:8–17). Summing up the spirit of the law, Deuteronomy 15:7–11 admonishes Israelites not to be hard-hearted or tightfisted toward one another but instead to show openhanded generosity.

Prophetic books vividly express Israel's obligation to care for those in need. The book of Amos contains several statements to the effect that Israel was failing in its obligation to protect the poor and needy.[10] Isaiah affirms God's demand for justice and care for the vulnerable,[11] condemning those who "add house to house and join field to field" (Isa. 5:8) and thereby violate prescribed land-distribution ideals.[12] Israel as a nation was responsible to see that justice prevailed in courts and commerce, that the vulnerable were protected, that generosity was practiced, and that luxury was moderated. Violations in these areas constitute a major thrust in the prophetic criticism against Israel and Judah.[13] According to Jeremiah 22:13–17, for a king to know the LORD,

---

8. Exod. 22:25; Lev. 25:35–38; Deut. 23:19–20.

9. Lev. 19:9–10; 23:22; Deut. 24:19–22.

10. Amos 2:6–8; 4:1; 5:10–12, 21–24; 8:4–6.

11. E.g., Isa. 1:17, 23; 3:14–15; 10:2; 11:3–4; 14:30; 26:5–6; 32:7; 58:5–7; 61:1–2.

12. Ultimately the land belonged to God and could not be sold permanently (Lev. 25:23). In the Year of Jubilee, families and clans were allowed to return to their allotted land. Relatives were also permitted to buy back property for a family member who became poor and had to sell (Lev. 25:25–31; cf. Ruth 4). Land was initially distributed by the number of names; that is, larger families and clans received more land, smaller groups received less (Num. 26:52–56; 33:54; 35:8).

13. E.g., Hosea 12:7–8; Mic. 2:1–2; 3:9–12; 6:9–12; Jer. 2:34–35; 5:26–28; 7:6; 9:23–24 (cf. 49:11); Zeph. 1:8–9, 11–13; 2:1–3; Ezek. 16:49; 22:7, 29; 45:9; Zech. 7:10; Mal. 3:5.

he must know justice and defend the cause of the poor and needy. As the prophets make clear, the purpose of kingship was not personal entitlement but responsibility for the well-being of the community (cf. Ps. 72).

The book of Proverbs provides another angle on Old Testament communal responsibility. Rather than giving laws or oracles, the book of Proverbs contains pithy sayings that embody values or practical insights. One commonly expressed value is that God looks with favor on generosity to the poor. Whoever is kind to the poor honors God and is blessed,[14] but the one who mistreats the poor shows contempt for God (14:31; 17:5). The righteous are distinguished by their care for the poor (29:7; 31:9). One should not oppress the poor or give to the rich for the sake of one's own well-being (22:16, 22–23). If people shut their ears to the cry of the poor, they will likewise not be answered when they cry for help (21:13). Concern for the poor is the duty of a king (29:14) and a faithful wife (31:20). Whoever is kind to the poor lends to God and will be rewarded (19:17). Righteousness, blamelessness, and the fear of the LORD are better than riches.[15] To be sure, the book of Proverbs does not encourage anyone to seek poverty (e.g., 30:8). In fact, wealth can be a reward for wisdom and righteousness (e.g., 22:4). There are also vices in Proverbs that can lead to poverty, as will be noted below. For the present, however, it suffices to say that the book of Proverbs constructs a value system in which a noble person will show generosity to the poor and needy.

Corporate responsibility in the Old Testament should be seen as more than simply transgenerational or group punishment for wrongdoing. Another dimension of corporate identity is the strong sense of responsibility each member has to help other members of the community. This can be seen as the positive side of responsibility, as understood within a strongly communal context. Of course, the obligation to act on behalf of others falls on the shoulders of individuals. Each Israelite who saw a neighbor's donkey wandering away needed to decide individually whether to give assistance as biblical law requires. I will now discuss a few key passages in the Old Testament that emphasize the role of the individual.

Individual Agency and Accountability in the Old Testament

Although corporate responsibility is a major theme in the Old Testament, threads of individual agency and accountability also figure prominently in certain passages. I will give a few examples from Old Testament law, prophetic literature, Psalms, Proverbs, and the book of Genesis.

14. Prov. 14:21, 31; 22:9; 28:27.
15. Prov. 11:4; 15:16; 16:19; 19:1; 28:6, 11.

The legal material in the Pentateuch is noteworthy for its recognition of individual agency and accountability. Although the Sinai covenant binds God to Israel as a people, the obedience of the individual Israelite is always in view (e.g., "When a man steals an ox . . ."; Exod. 22:1). Priestly laws offer no forgiveness for wrongs against another person unless the individual transgressor first makes recompense to the person wronged (Lev. 6:1–7). Statements on individual agency in Deuteronomy 7:9–10 and 24:16 will be treated below.

Although prophetic books generally emphasize the corporate fate of Israel, some attention is devoted to the individual even in the prophets. Jeremiah and Ezekiel develop this theme most clearly, and I will return to these books in "Inner-Biblical Insights" below. For the present, I will give one example from each. Jeremiah distinguishes between those favored by God, who went to Babylon (e.g., Jer. 24:4–7; 29:4–14), and those rejected by God, who stayed in Jerusalem with the wicked King Zedekiah, ignoring God's words and trusting in false prophecy (e.g., Jer. 24:8–10; 29:15–19).[16] Ezekiel 9:1–11 contains a vision that ends in the destruction of all Jerusalem but also offers an assurance that God recognizes those who sighed and groaned over Jerusalem's sins.

The book of Psalms contains many poems that express the sufferings and hopes of the individual, even in the midst of corporate worship and community lament. Wisdom psalms in particular speak to the choices and consequences that confront individuals (e.g., "Blessed is the man who . . ."; Ps. 1:1). The book of Proverbs also envisions individual people who must make wise decisions for their own personal well-being (e.g., the son in Prov. 13:1 or the woman in Prov. 14:1). Alongside everything the book of Proverbs has to say about the community's responsibility to care for the poor, Proverbs also has much to say about what individuals should do in order to avoid coming to ruin and poverty.[17]

An important text that addresses God's concern for individual accountability is the narrative of Abraham interceding for Sodom. In the passage preceding this account, God explains that he chose Abraham so that he would command his children to observe the way of the LORD by doing righteousness and justice (Gen. 18:19). When God goes down to see the extent of Sodom's sin, Abraham begins to question God as to whether he will indeed destroy the whole city if some righteous people live there (18:22–33). Although Abraham asks with appropriate humility ("I am but dust and ashes"; 18:27), he also challenges God to act in accordance with his divine character by asking,

16. Even within these groups, distinctions are made. The poor who remained in Judah benefited from God's judgment on Zedekiah and his company (Jer. 39:10), whereas two false prophets among the Babylonian exiles were singled out for condemnation (Jer. 29:21–23).

17. E.g., Prov. 6:10–11; 10:4; 13:18; 14:23; 20:13; 21:5, 17; 23:21; 24:33–34; 28:19.

"Shall not the Judge of all the earth do justice?" (18:25). Remarkably, God agrees not to sweep away the righteous together with the guilty, even if fifty, or forty-five, or forty, or thirty, or twenty, or just ten righteous people are found. As it turns out, ten righteous people cannot be found in the city. The only people deemed worthy to rescue are Lot and his family, so they are ushered out of the city before it is destroyed, although Lot's wife falters on the way out (19:1–29). This narrative is important for what it says about Abraham as an intercessor, but it also depicts God as concerned for the just treatment of righteous individuals (cf. Ezek. 22:30–31).

Individual and Corporate Responsibility in the New Testament

In the New Testament, individual responsibility takes on new dimensions in light of the fresh emphasis that New Testament writers place on personal faith, discipleship, and final judgment. At the same time, corporate identity and community responsibility continue to figure prominently.

The Christian message calls for a response of personal faith. Individuals from any background can exhibit this obedient trust in God. In the Gospel of Matthew, for example, Jesus commends the faith of a centurion (8:10), a woman afflicted with sickness (9:22), two blind men (9:29), and a Canaanite woman (15:28). According to the Gospel of Luke, there is great joy in heaven over just one sinner who repents, in the same way that a shepherd would leave ninety-nine sheep in the wilderness to find one that was lost (15:1–7). John 3:16 affirms that anyone who believes in Jesus will not perish but have eternal life. Early Christian preaching taught that everyone who calls on the name of the Lord will be saved.[18] The New Testament church was not composed of people drawn exclusively from this or that group; rather, it consisted of individuals who believed in Jesus, whether Jew or gentile, male or female, slave or free (e.g., Rom. 1:16; Gal. 3:26–29).

Christian discipleship in the New Testament is described in terms that challenge people to individual responsibility. A person cannot become a disciple unless Jesus is the top priority, above self and family; in fact, each person must take up his or her own cross and follow Jesus (Matt. 10:37–39; Luke 14:26–27). God the Father will honor anyone who serves and follows Jesus (John 12:26). The parables imply that God has not entrusted the same level of responsibility to everyone, but each person is accountable to manage well whatever he or she has been given (e.g., Matt. 25:14–30; Luke 12:41–48). It is clear from the New Testament that individuals believed in Jesus despite

---

18. Acts 2:21; 1 Cor. 1:2; 2 Tim. 2:22; cf. Joel 2:32.

restrictive social settings. Slaves might follow Jesus, even though their masters do not; wives might choose to be Christians, even though their husbands are not.[19] On certain pastorally ambiguous points, the conscience of the individual believer plays a role in determining the best course of action, although the concern is not only for the conscience of individuals but also for those affected by their actions.[20]

The fate of individuals comes into focus in the New Testament through its emphasis on final judgment (see chap. 6). In the future divine reckoning described in the New Testament, God will set aside the complexities of the present world and deal with people as individuals according to how they acted in response to God: "For we must all appear before the judgment seat of Christ, so that each one might receive what is due for what he did through the body, whether good or evil" (2 Cor. 5:10). Jesus refers to final judgment that involves separating the righteous from the wicked, where one person is taken and another is left.[21] The Gospel of Luke records a parable that presents a sharp contrast between afterlife punishment for a rich man and afterlife bliss for a poor man (Luke 16:19–31). Paul explains that each person should be careful how he or she builds, because God will test the work of each person (1 Cor. 3:10–15). As Revelation 22:12 states, "Behold! I am coming quickly, and my reward is with me, to render to each person as is his work."

The increased emphasis on individual responsibility in the New Testament converges with the gospel mission to all nations (Matt. 28:18–20; Acts 1:8). In this context, the people of God are composed of all individuals who believe, regardless of their national identities. That this development took place in the Greco-Roman world is no accident. During the Hellenistic period and down into Roman times, cosmopolitan thinkers formed philosophical schools (such as the Platonists, Stoics, and Epicureans) that anyone from any region might adopt as their way of life.[22] Moreover, Roman roads and ships made travel more efficient, and the Greek language served as an international means of communication. In God's providence, this was the environment in which Christianity as "the Way" of Jesus spread throughout the Mediterranean world and beyond,[23] so as to gain adherents from many nations. The

19. E.g., 1 Cor. 7:20–24; Eph. 5:22–6:9; Col. 3:18–4:1; 1 Tim. 2:1–6:2; Titus 2:1–10; 1 Pet. 2:13–3:7. Timothy's mother was a follower of Christ, but his father was not (Acts 16:1; 2 Tim. 1:5).

20. E.g., Rom. 14:1–12; 1 Cor. 10:23–11:1; 2 Cor. 9:6–7; cf. James 4:17. Rom. 14:12 concludes, "Therefore each one of us will give an account of himself to God."

21. E.g., Matt. 13:24–30, 36–43; 24:36–42; Luke 17:26–36.

22. See Hadot, *Philosophy as a Way of Life*.

23. On Christianity as the Way, see Acts 9:2; 16:17; 18:25–26; 19:9, 23; 22:4; 24:14, 22; 2 Pet. 2:2; John 14:6.

New Testament's focus on individual faith and accountability is historically contextual and also fits Christianity's grand narrative of redemption.

Alongside this focus on the individual, the New Testament deepens and expands previous paradigms for understanding the people of God as a chosen community. Those who follow Jesus are members of the "elect" (or "chosen ones") in a manner reminiscent of Old Testament Israel.[24] Christians are chosen by God to be transformed into a holy people.[25] In the Gospel of John, Christians are to be recognized by their love for one another as one community that bears witness to God (13:34–35; 17:20–21). The apostle Paul describes the church as a body with many parts that are united in identity and purpose.[26]

The sense of mutual obligation among Christians in the New Testament is strong. This is depicted vividly in the book of Acts, where the early Christian community is described as sharing all things in common (2:42–47; 4:34–35). The bonds of Christian love were demonstrated by Paul through the offering he collected for needy Christians in Jerusalem.[27] Christians are held responsible for their actions toward one another; for example, leaders in the church are said to be accountable for how they lead (Heb. 13:17; James 3:1). Despite the fact that some members of a household might believe while others do not, in several instances the book of Acts states that entire households converted.[28] This may reflect the predilection of Roman households to adopt the religion of the head of the house, or it may reveal a familial dimension to the theology of conversion.[29]

Overall, the New Testament clarifies the role of individual believers in God's larger plan while also retrieving and renewing the Old Testament's vision for community. Galatians 6:1–10 captures the New Testament's balance on this topic: Christians should gently restore those who transgress and be on guard against sin for themselves (v. 1). They should "bear one another's burdens, and thus fulfill the law of Christ" (v. 2). Christians should humbly

---

24. Matt. 24:22, 24, 31; Luke 18:7; John 10:25–30; 2 Tim. 2:10.

25. Eph. 1:3–14; Col. 3:12; 1 Pet. 2:4–10. The concept of election also has an individual side. Thus, one becomes or shows that one is a member of the elect by believing, whether Jew or gentile (e.g., Rom. 9:22–24), and it seems that individuals can turn away from faith (Heb. 6:4–12; 2 Pet. 2:20–22; 1 Cor. 10:1–13) and are expected to make their election sure (2 Pet. 1:10).

26. 1 Cor. 10:17; 12; Rom. 12:5; Eph. 4:4, 25; Col. 3:15.

27. 1 Cor. 16:1–4; 2 Cor. 8:1–9:15; Rom. 15:25–32; Gal. 2:10; Acts 11:29–30; 24:17.

28. Acts 10:2; 11:14–17; 16:15, 31–34; 18:8; 1 Cor. 1:16.

29. The faith of the household is mentioned explicitly in Acts 16:31–34 and 18:8. In general, baptism was practiced for those who believed (e.g., Acts 2:41; 8:12). Whether young children were among those baptized in these passages is a matter of disagreement. For Christians who see infant baptism in the above household baptism passages, this practice adds another formal aspect of corporate identity to the New Testament—namely, that the children of Christians belong to the fellowship of the baptized.

test their work and not presume to boast against their neighbors (vv. 3–4), "because each one will carry his own load" (v. 5). Those who are taught should share with those who teach (v. 6). "Whatever someone sows, this also he reaps" (v. 7). Christians should sow to the Spirit to reap eternal life, not sow to the flesh to reap corruption (vv. 8–9). "Therefore, as we have opportunity, let us do good to all, and especially to the household of faith" (v. 10).

Inner-Biblical Insights

Both corporate and individual responsibility figure prominently in the Old Testament. Punishment for wrongdoing has both group and personal dimensions. The duty to care for the community's well-being was assigned to individual Israelites and to Israel as a whole. Within the Old Testament, these two major streams of thought typically flowed side by side without self-conscious dialogue. Whereas many readers today may be surprised at the apparent tension between corporate and individual responsibility, most Old Testament writers saw these two dimensions as fitting together naturally within their cultural environment. In a few instances, however, awareness of this tension surfaces in the form of inner-biblical interpretation. The key passages are found in Deuteronomy, Jeremiah, and Ezekiel.[30] Each one addresses the topic of transgenerational punishment with the apparent goal of correcting possible misunderstandings.

Deuteronomy 7:9–10 refers to God as the one who "keeps covenant and steadfast love for those who love him and keep his commandments to a thousand generations. But for those who hate him, he repays to their face by destroying them. He does not delay for the one who hates him. He repays him to his face." This passage echoes Deuteronomy 5:9–10 in its reference to keeping steadfast love for those who love God and keep his commandments, and in dealing with those who hate God. Yet with reference to those who hate God, Deuteronomy 5:9 describes God as "visiting the iniquities of the fathers upon the sons to the third and fourth generations," but Deuteronomy 7:10 says that God "repays to their face by destroying them. He does not delay for the one who hates him. He repays him to his face." The phrase "to his face" does not necessarily mean "immediately," but it does seem to suggest "in his lifetime."[31] The statement in the Ten Commandments (Exod. 20:5–6) already stressed the abounding goodness of God for those who love him and

---

30. See Fishbane, *Biblical Interpretation in Ancient Israel*, 335–47; Kaminsky, *Corporate Responsibility*, 116–78; Levinson, *Legal Revision and Religious Renewal*, 57–88.

31. Levinson, *Legal Revision and Religious Renewal*, 76–77.

keep his commandments (to the thousandth generation) over against the more restricted punishment for those who hate him (to the third and fourth generations). Deuteronomy adopts this language in its recitation of the Ten Commandments (Deut. 5:9–10), but it also seeks to clarify that God will not delay punishment against wrongdoers; rather, he will punish them in their lifetimes (Deut. 7:9–10).

A second key passage in Deuteronomy appears in the collection of miscellaneous laws near the end of the book. According to Deuteronomy 24:16, "Fathers should not be put to death because of their sons, and sons should not be put to death because of their fathers. Each person should be put to death for his own sin." Stated in this way, as a general principle, this passage stands in opposition to transgenerational punishment. With reference to human action, this legal text is cited in 2 Kings 14:5–6 to explain why King Amaziah of Judah does not execute the sons of the servants who killed his father (2 Chron. 25:4). One might suggest that this principle was meant to address human behavior only. Perhaps it was thought that God could punish later generations justly through wisdom and providence in a way that no human could rightly do. Still, to obey God's commandments is to walk in his ways (e.g., Deut. 30:15–16), and we would not expect Deuteronomy to lay down a general principle that does not somehow reflect God's character. The primary concern in Deuteronomy 24:16 seems to be that an innocent individual should not be put to death because of someone else's sin. In fact, many Old Testament texts express the idea that it is wrong to kill the "innocent" (*nāqî*).[32] Deuteronomy 24:16 fits into this stream of thought. The guilty party should be punished appropriately, but an innocent person should not suffer the consequences of the guilty person's wrongdoing.

The prophetic books of Jeremiah and Ezekiel address the topic of transgenerational punishment in connection with the Babylonian exile. In this case, the "fathers" (i.e., the decision makers in the last days of Judah) sinned so grievously that God allowed the Babylonians to destroy Jerusalem and deport many people into captivity. The questions faced by the "sons" in this context are, Is there any point in our returning to the LORD, if our doom is already sealed? And are we not destined to suffer because God is visiting the sins of our fathers on us? Both Jeremiah and Ezekiel encourage the next generation to turn to the LORD with full assurance that they will be received.

In the context of future restoration, Jeremiah promises, "In those days, they will not again say: 'The fathers have eaten unripe fruit, and the sons'

---

32. E.g., Exod. 23:7; Deut. 19:10, 13; 27:25; 2 Kings 21:16; 24:4; Pss. 94:21; 106:38; Prov. 1:11; 6:17; Isa. 59:7; Joel 3:19; Jer. 7:6; 22:17.

teeth are dulled.' Instead, each person will die for his own iniquity. Any person who eats unripe fruit, his own teeth will become dull" (Jer. 31:29–30). Directly following this text comes the "New Covenant" passage (31:31–34). In other words, if anyone were to suggest that the children have no hope of restoration because of the iniquity of their parents, Jeremiah counters by insisting that each person is punished for his or her own iniquity.[33] The similarity of Jeremiah's language to Deuteronomy 24:16 is striking. Even if the "fathers" suffered exile because of their sins, there is still hope for the "sons" to be restored.

Ezekiel makes this same point in even greater detail. He begins by responding to the "unripe fruit" proverb: "The word of the LORD came to me, saying: 'What do you people mean by quoting this proverb about the land of Israel: "The fathers have eaten unripe fruit, and the sons' teeth are dulled." As I live, declares the powerful LORD, this proverb will not be quoted again by you in Israel. Behold, all souls are mine. Both the soul of the father and the soul of the son are mine. The soul that sins is the one that will die'" (Ezek. 18:1–4).

What follows is an extended explanation of how God judges each individual according to his own merits (Ezek. 18:5–32). A righteous man who keeps God's commandments will live (vv. 5–9), but if a man has a wicked son who violates God's commandments, the son will die (vv. 10–13). But if this wicked individual has a righteous child who turns to God and walks in God's ways, the righteous child will live (vv. 14–17), even though the wicked parent died (v. 18). At this point, a question from the people is anticipated: "But you say, 'Why does the son not bear the iniquity of the father?'" Ezekiel responds, "The son has done justice and righteousness; he has kept all my statutes. As he does these, he will live. The soul that sins is the one that will die. The son will not bear the iniquity of his father, and the father will not bear the iniquity of his son. The righteousness of the righteous will be upon himself, and the wickedness of the wicked will be upon himself" (vv. 19–20). From here, Ezekiel elaborates on the potential for each individual to change his ways, both for the wicked to turn away from his sins and live and for a righteous person to turn away from his righteousness and die (vv. 21–29).[34]

---

33. Another allusion to transgenerational punishment occurs at Jer. 32:18–19: "He exhibits steadfast love to the thousandth generation, and he repays the iniquity of the fathers in the lap of their sons after them, . . . whose eyes are open to all the ways of people, to render to each person according to his ways and according to the fruit of his deeds." This passage seems to acknowledge that children experience suffering because of their parents' misdeeds, and yet it also stresses that God reckons to each individual according to what he or she does.

34. On the possibility of crossing from judgment to deliverance or from deliverance to judgment by changing one's actions, see also Ezek. 33:12–20; Jer. 18:7–11; Joel 2:12–14; Jon. 3:6–4:2. Joel 2:13 and Jon. 4:2 allude to the formula found in Exod. 34:6–7.

The chapter concludes with an admonition to the people that they should repent from all their misdeeds and return to the LORD (vv. 30–32). As with Jeremiah 31:29–30, Ezekiel 18 invokes the language of Deuteronomy 24:16 in order to encourage the exiles not to lose hope.

It should be observed that although the proverb ("the fathers have eaten unripe fruit . . .") expresses the basic idea of transgenerational punishment as might be derived from Exodus 20:5–6 or Deuteronomy 5:9–10, neither Jeremiah nor Ezekiel directs his criticism against the precise language of the Pentateuch. One might say that these two prophets are responding to how this concept was being applied in their historical situation. The visitation of parents' sins on their children may stand in the background, but by challenging this idea in the form of a popular saying, Jeremiah and Ezekiel restrict the implications of the earlier biblical tradition without necessarily voiding it of significance.

The key insight we learn from Jeremiah and Ezekiel is that God remains free and willing to receive the sinner who repents and also free to judge the wicked despite previous merit. No one is condemned to divine disfavor because of what his or her parents did. Each person has the opportunity to seek God's favor, just as each person will be held accountable for his or her misdeeds. Whatever reality stands behind the idea of transgenerational punishment, Ezekiel 18 makes a strong case for God's reckoning with people on an individual basis.

Explicit cases of inner-biblical interpretation do not feature prominently in the New Testament's treatment of corporate and individual responsibility. Nevertheless, the New Testament develops its theology on this topic from Old Testament themes. For example, the Old Testament occasionally mentions individuals from outside Israel who chose to honor Israel's God, such as Rahab (Josh. 2), Ruth (Ruth 1–4), and the queen of Sheba (1 Kings 10). In the New Testament, Rahab and Ruth are listed in Jesus's genealogy (Matt. 1:5), Rahab is cited for her faith and works (Heb. 11:31; James 2:25), and the queen of Sheba is commended for respecting Solomon's wisdom (Matt. 12:42; Luke 11:31). References to these figures in the New Testament illustrate that any individual who seeks God will find him. On the negative side, Paul cites the choice of Isaac rather than Ishmael, Jacob rather than Esau, and the faithful remnant of Israel in Isaiah's day to illustrate that not every individual descendant of Abraham participates in God's line of promise (Rom. 9:6–29). As for community obligation, James 5:4 invokes Old Testament legal principles to show that Christians are responsible to pay their workers promptly (Deut. 24:15; Lev. 19:13). In the parable of the good Samaritan, Jesus expands the concept "love your neighbor as yourself" to include anyone in need, not just members of the community (Luke 10:25–37; see Lev. 19:17–18).

As we think about how to interpret each biblical perspective within the context of Scripture as a whole, we should consider what lessons can be learned from our examples of inner-biblical interpretation. The following insights emerge: (1) the wrongdoer should be appropriately punished, rather than leaving punishment to future generations; (2) the innocent should not be punished for the sins of others; (3) a person's standing before God cannot be set in stone on the basis of the sins of his or her parents, but each person can turn to God and find life; (4) the individual has the freedom and responsibility to respond rightly to God, because God acts in freedom to dispense just judgments and abundant mercy; and (5) in Jesus, responsibility to care for others remains in force and expands to include those beyond the community.

Putting the Pieces Together

The insights gleaned from our examples of inner-biblical interpretation suggest a theological framework in which the individual is emphasized with regard to punishment and the community is emphasized with regard to each person's obligations. This framework can be correlated to core Christian theology as embodied in the life and teaching of Jesus. In Jesus's sacrificial death, we see our responsibility to care for the needs of others sacrificially. Jesus will serve as final judge (e.g., Acts 10:42; 17:31) and will render fair and just judgments for each individual in the light of his call to faith and offer of mercy. When we consider the two great commandments, love of God and love of neighbor (Luke 10:27), and also the "Golden Rule" (Matt. 7:12), we should ask ourselves, How can I treat my neighbor as I would treat myself? What would I want someone else to do for me? I suggest the answer is twofold: I would not want to be punished for someone else's crime, and I would want other people to commit themselves to my well-being. We should also remember the careful attention Jesus paid to inner dispositions of the heart (e.g., Mark 7:21–23), which should express themselves in right actions toward others (e.g., Matt. 23:23–24). It is the individual who follows virtue or vice in the heart, and yet these virtues must be lived out (and vices avoided) in fellowship with others. The idea of individual responsibility within community obligations is an expression of the Bible's core teaching on this topic, which in turn helps us to see how each stream of biblical thought contributes to the whole.

A basic outline for putting the biblical pieces together can be sketched along four lines.

First, many biblical texts affirm that people are responsible to care for others. Passages from the Pentateuch, the prophets, and the book of Proverbs illustrate this, and the New Testament offers strong support for this idea and even expands its scope. This idea does not appear to be challenged by other biblical texts. This is a dimension of corporate responsibility that applies in a straightforward way to contemporary times, provided that adjustments are made for culture and context; for example, the principle of generosity expressed by gleaning laws must be appropriated today by Christians whose society is not primarily agrarian and who do not live in a divinely ordered state. That the task of caring for others must be taken up by individuals is also important. It is tragic when few people in a community step up to help because most assume that someone else will get involved. We each, as individuals, have community responsibilities.

Second, a number of important passages stress the role of the individual. These include the Old Testament texts discussed above that exhibit inner-biblical interpretation. We learn from such passages that the guilty and only the guilty should be punished for wrongdoing. We can expect that God will ultimately reckon with each of us as individuals (2 Cor. 5:10), and we should likewise strive to respect individual guilt and innocence when we render judgments. This principle is illustrated well by the narrative of Abraham and Sodom: the Judge of all the earth will do justice (Gen. 18:25) and will not sweep away the righteous with the wicked (Gen. 18:23). Moreover, each person deserves a legitimate opportunity to mend his or her ways. This is expressed in Old Testament texts (e.g., Ezek. 18) and frequently in the New Testament (e.g., Luke 23:43). Individual responsibility comes to prominence in the New Testament through the call to personal faith and discipleship, the preaching of the gospel to each person regardless of nation, and the expectation of final judgment. Biblical texts that address the responsibility of individual believers teach us how to live wisely as part of the Christian community for the benefit of others.

Third, certain passages that emphasize transgenerational punishment illustrate how our sins negatively affect others, and in their immediate contexts these passages teach us important lessons about justice. In the context of Scripture as a whole, we should not take these passages to be teaching that God actively punishes one person for the sin of another. Still, in the outworking of this broken world, where the effects of sin are permitted to unfold, our misdeeds bring negative consequences to the generations that come after us. This is illustrated by the story about the famine caused by Saul's sin and its consequences for his descendants (2 Sam. 21:1–14). Such accounts are narrated in a manner that fits the cultural world of the ancient Near East, according to which this story also illustrates divine judgment against Saul himself through his descendants. In other cases, transgenerational punishment in the Old Testament teaches the principle of measure-for-measure justice—that is, that one reaps what one sows or that the punishment should fit the crime. Thus, just as a pharaoh sought to kill all newly born sons of Israel (Exod. 1:22), so also the firstborn sons of Egypt died because of a pharaoh's sin (Exod. 12:29–30). In light of parallels with ancient Near Eastern texts, it has been suggested that biblical writers sometimes portray historical events using hyperbole and other devices to communicate figurative or symbolic meanings.[35] Perhaps some narratives of measure-for-measure judgment were composed in this way with the goal of teaching this principle of justice. In his treatise *The Life of Moses*, Gregory of Nyssa (fourth century AD) suggests that the narrative of the death of the firstborn is typological rather than historical, in part because of the theological weight of Ezekiel 18:20: "The soul that sins is the one that will die."[36] Interpretive judgments of this kind are admittedly difficult because we lack precise knowledge of the genre conventions of biblical writers. In such cases, historical and theological questions intersect because we are trying to identify precisely what an individual text teaches and also how the Bible fits together as a theological whole.

Fourth, passages that describe the corporate punishment of groups teach lessons similar to those that speak of transgenerational punishment. The corporate fate of Israel and other nations as described in the Old Testament reminds us how interconnected we are to others and that our actions deeply influence those around us. Partly because of what other people do, we often fail to experience true justice in this life. Even if we expect God to pass judgments that are fair and equitable, we know that the world as it currently exists is not always fair, as the book of Ecclesiastes makes clear (e.g., Eccles. 9:11). Narratives of group punishment depict not just total judgment against an individual as the head of the group but also the tragic fate of others who suffer in circumstances beyond their control (e.g., Josh. 7:24–26).

The people of God in the Old Testament were a nation, and as such they did things that nations do, such as fight wars. The idea that God would accomplish anything through human warfare is a challenging concept. But even wars can be conducted according to ethical codes. Biblical ethicists continue to discuss whether God commanded Israel to slay noncombatants in the wars it fought against the Canaanites. The biblical language about killing "men and women"

---

35. Younger, "Figurative Aspect," 157–75. Younger discusses hyperbole and metaphor as literary techniques that operated by a conventional "ideological code" (p. 164) that would have been recognizable to the Bible's first readers.

36. Malherbe and Ferguson, *Gregory of Nyssa*, 75–76. According to Gregory, this element of the narrative is intended to teach that we should completely destroy the first beginnings of evil. In the literary context of the book of Exodus, the concept of measure-for-measure punishment is more likely to be the main point of the passage.

may not be literal; it could be stereotypical language that represents complete destruction of the enemy's forces, or whatever these forces represent.[37] It is worth noting, for example, that even after Saul is said to have destroyed "all the people" of the Amalekites (1 Sam. 15:8), there are still Amalekites living in later times (1 Sam. 27:8; 1 Chron. 4:43).[38] As for how Christians should apply such texts, the narratives about Israel and other nations in the Old Testament provide lessons about trust and blessing, rebellion and judgment. In *On Christian Teaching*, Augustine (fourth to fifth century AD) interprets God's command to Jeremiah that he should uproot and destroy nations (Jer. 1:10) as an admonition for individual Christians to destroy the sin of lust.[39] Although I would not limit the personal application so narrowly, I fully concur that individual Christians can learn lessons for their spiritual lives from reading about how nations in the Old Testament experienced punishment for their corporate sins and blessing for their corporate obedience.

Jesus's life and teachings and our examples of inner-biblical interpretation suggest that the range of biblical texts dealing with corporate and individual responsibility should be interpreted so as to emphasize individual responsibility in the service of community well-being. The interpretive move that emphasizes the individual should promote not self-interest but service to the church and the world. All these biblical texts can be interpreted in conversation with one another and with these greater goals in mind. The result is a balanced, challenging, and inspiring theological account of our corporate and individual responsibilities before God.

---

37. For the idea that these are stereotypical phrases, see Hess, "War in the Hebrew Bible," 29–30. According to Origen of Alexandria (third century AD), the book of Joshua was composed in such a way that the Canaanites represent sin, so that statements that emphasize their total defeat express the total defeat of sin. See Bruce, *Origen*, 94, 120–24. The idea is that God's bringing the people into the land represents the fulfilling of his promise of blessing or salvation (cf. Heb. 3–4; 1 Cor. 10). When the people obey God, they defeat Canaanites (e.g., Jericho), but when they disobey God, they lose to Canaanites (e.g., Ai). According to this line of thought, the biblical writer uses the Canaanites to symbolize what prevents us from experiencing God's blessing—namely, sin. Origen takes the biblical narrative to be generally historical but composed creatively at points in order to highlight certain lessons. See *Philocalia* 1.16; 15.15, 17; *Against Celsus* 1.42; *On First Principles* 4.2.9; 4.3.4–5.

38. For an ancient Near Eastern parallel, the Stela of Merneptah (ca. 1210 BC) celebrates a military victory over Israel by saying, "Israel is wasted, its seed [offspring] is not," but of course they did not literally destroy all the offspring of the Israelites. For the text, see Hoffmeier, "(Israel) Stela of Merneptah," 2:41.

39. Augustine, *On Christian Teaching* 3.11.17 (Green, 77). Augustine cites Jer. 1:10 as an example of his principle that "any harsh and even cruel word or deed attributed to God or his saints that is found in holy scripture applies to the destruction of the realm of lust."

3

Insiders and Outsiders

Outside and Inside Exist,
but Invite the Outsider to Join

In most biblical books, the central narrative or discourse follows a select group of people who are identified as the people of God. These people are set apart from others in that God calls them, gives them promises, enters into covenant with them, and designates them for a purpose. Throughout the Bible, a distinction is made between the people of God on the one hand, and everyone else on the other. In a sense, there are "insiders" and "outsiders" in the Bible. Yet one also finds dynamic interplay between these groups and even fresh thinking about how each group is defined. Not all biblical texts lean in the same direction on this topic. Some passages focus on defining and maintaining boundaries for the people of God, whereas other passages seek to broaden boundaries or reach out to those beyond the community.

Passages that focus on defining boundaries and passages that promote reaching out can be found in both testaments. The specific circumstances being addressed in a given biblical text are key factors in determining which perspective will be emphasized. An underlying issue in many texts is the connection between religion and general culture. In many cases, where specific ideas about God and ethics are closely integrated with fixed cultural identities, biblical texts tend to focus on guarding community boundaries. Where religious values and cultural identity are distinguished, biblical texts often show more readiness to include those who are outside. A major development in the direction of including "outsiders" takes place in the New Testament, but both insider and outsider perspectives remain operative throughout Scripture.

Biblical Perspectives

In the first section of this chapter, I will survey both insider (boundary-defining) and outsider (boundary-broadening) perspectives in the Hexateuch (Genesis–Joshua), the prophetic books, and the New Testament. The goal of this survey is to show the presence and function of both sides of this conversation in the Bible. Ultimately, these perspectives fit together in the New Testament through the proclamation of the gospel.

Insider Themes: Defining and Maintaining Boundaries

The formation of God's chosen people, Israel, from the call of Abraham to Israel's entrance into Canaan, is described in the Pentateuch and the book of Joshua. Old Testament prophets generally affirm God's plan to restore Israel to their land and punish those who afflict them. In the New Testament, membership in the people of God is demonstrated through proper response to Jesus.

Boundaries for God's People in the Pentateuch and Joshua

The origin of Israel as a nation is described in the book of Genesis through stories about their ancestors. After the flood, Canaan is cursed because of his father's imprudence (9:18, 22, 25–27), but blessing is pronounced on Shem (9:25–27), whose family line leads to Abraham (11:10–32). When God calls Abraham and promises him the land of Canaan, many offspring, and expansive blessing,[1] the stage is set for establishing Israel as a chosen people. God's further initiative in forming Israel is indicated by the fact that Isaac is chosen rather than Ishmael (17:21), and Jacob is chosen rather than Esau (25:23). The book of Genesis makes clear that the Canaanites are not God's people. The sins of the Canaanites receive special mention (e.g., 15:16; 18:20–21), Abraham will not accept gifts from Canaanites (14:21–24; 23:3–20), and marriage to a Canaanite is viewed negatively.[2] It is not only the Canaanites, however, who serve as foils for God's chosen people. Israel's other neighbors are also

1. Gen. 12:1–3; 13:14–17; 15:5–7, 18–21; 17:1–8; 22:15–18.
2. Gen. 24:3–4, 37–38; 26:34–35; 28:6–9; 38:2.

portrayed negatively through the misfortune or folly of their ancestors, as with the Ishmaelites (16:11–12; 25:18), the Moabites and Ammonites (19:30–38), and the Edomites (25:23, 30; 36:1, 8). The final chapters of Genesis narrate the remarkable survival of Jacob's sons (chaps. 37–50) and foretell their destiny to become a great nation (chap. 49). From Abraham to the twelve tribes, the book of Genesis provides the backstory for how Israel, among all nations, becomes God's people.

The consecration of Israel as a nation in the book of Exodus solidifies their chosen status. Through the plagues in Egypt, God distinguishes between the Israelites and the Egyptians.[3] The Passover celebration serves to define who is an Israelite and who is not (12:43–49). When the Amalekites ruthlessly attack Israel at a moment of vulnerability (17:8–16), God gives Israel victory and places the Amalekites under a curse.[4] God offers a special covenant to Israel at Sinai, which they accept (19:8; 20:1–2; 24:8). Even after the incident of the golden calf, God graciously renews his covenant with Israel (chap. 34). In the context of this covenant relationship, God warns Israel not to worship Canaanite deities (23:23–28) but promises that he will drive out the Canaanites when Israel enters the land.[5]

The remainder of the Pentateuch contains laws and narratives that reinforce Israel's unique position as God's chosen people. The priestly regulations of Leviticus show Israel how to devote themselves in holiness to the LORD (e.g., 1:1–2; 19:1–2) and avoid imitating the wicked practices of the Canaanites (18:1–5, 24–30). Specific laws in Leviticus differentiate Israel from other nations. Thus, as representatives of Israel's holiness, priests are not allowed to marry foreigners but can only marry other Israelites (21:14). Furthermore, in view of the family bond that unites all of God's people, an Israelite cannot take another Israelite as a permanent slave, even though a foreigner can be enslaved permanently (Lev. 25:39–46; Deut. 24:7).[6]

In their journey from Sinai to the plains of Moab in the book of Numbers, the Israelites experience hostility from various foreign nations and peoples, such as Edom (20:14–21; 21:4), Arad (21:1–3), and the Amorites (21:21–32). The Moabites attempt to curse Israel (chaps. 22–24), and they later seduce many Israelites to sin (chap. 25). These narratives foreshadow later hostilities between the nation of Israel and its near neighbors (cf. Midian in chap. 31).

Deuteronomy maintains strict boundaries between Israel and other nations. As Israel prepares to enter the land, Deuteronomy places the Canaanites under

---

3. Exod. 7:3–4; 8:22–23; 9:4–7, 25–26; 10:22–23; 11:6–7.
4. Cf. Num. 24:20; Deut. 25:17–19; 1 Sam. 14:48; 15:2–3.
5. See Exod. 23:28–32; 33:2; 34:11; cf. Josh. 24:12, 18; Judg. 2:3; etc.
6. Cf. Num. 31:11–12; Deut. 20:10–14; 1 Kings 5:13–14; 9:15; 2 Chron. 8:7–9.

the complete ban of destruction.[7] The law of centralization in Deuteronomy aims to prevent the Israelites from worshiping as the Canaanites do (12:1–4, 29–31). Deuteronomy forbids exacting interest from fellow Israelites, even though foreigners can be charged interest.[8] Because of past conflicts with Ammon and Moab, Deuteronomy 23:3 states that no Ammonite or Moabite may enter the LORD's assembly, even to the tenth generation.

God's requirement that Israel must remain separate from the Canaanites finds fulfillment in the book of Joshua. Particular Canaanite cities are devoted to the LORD under the ban of destruction.[9] Furthermore, Joshua issues a stern warning not to intermingle with the Canaanites who remain in the land (chap. 23). The fundamental concern is that Israel should not serve Canaanite gods but should serve the LORD alone (24:14–24). To be clear, the Old Testament's portrayal of severe judgment against the Canaanites does not represent Israel's normal relationship with other nations. The picture in these books of divine punishment against Canaan is unique. Nevertheless, it is indicative of Israel's identity as God's chosen people that they are given the strictest possible orders to reject Canaanite religious influences and devote themselves entirely to the LORD.

Boundaries for God's People in the Prophets

The prophets in the Old Testament pronounce judgments against Israel, but they also announce future blessing. Whenever they present pictures of national restoration on a grand scale, they affirm the continuing status of Israel as God's people. For example, Hosea predicts great prosperity for a united Israel and Judah ruled by a Davidic king.[10] Micah foresees the regathering of Israel, the forgiveness of sins, and the vindication of God's people before the nations, in fulfillment of oaths that God swore to Abraham and Jacob (Mic. 7:8–20). Isaiah describes a remnant that will survive God's judgment and return to Jerusalem, some of whom will serve as priests and Levites.[11] Jeremiah affirms the restoration of Israel and Judah to the land, accompanied by material prosperity, renewed priestly worship, and eternal Davidic kingship, all of which will come to pass as surely as God brings about day and night.[12] Ezekiel's symbolic action of joining two sticks that represent Israel and Judah vividly illustrates the prophetic promise of national renewal.[13]

7. E.g., Deut. 2:34; 3:6; 7:1–6, 16–26; 13:15; 20:10–20.
8. Deut. 23:19–20; Exod. 22:25; Lev. 25:36–37.
9. Josh. 2:10; 6:18, 21; 8:26; 10:1, 28, 35, 37, 39–40; 11:11–12, 20–21.
10. Hosea 1:10–11; 3:5; 14:4–7; cf. Amos 9:11–15.
11. E.g., Isa. 6:11–13; 10:20–25; 27:12–13; 66:19–22.
12. Jer. 30:1–3; 31:1–6, 23–28, 35–40; 32:42–44; 33:6–26.
13. Ezek. 37:15–28; cf. 11:16–25; 20:39–44.

Israel's unique status as the people of God can also be seen in how the prophets deal with foreign nations. Although Israel's God is the Lord of every nation, the prophets typically do not mention what God is doing with other nations unless the action or fate of a given nation has direct bearing on God's plan for Israel—for example, to punish the Israelites (e.g., Jer. 25:9) or to restore them (e.g., Isa. 44:28–45:3). Some possible exceptions will be mentioned below. The most extensive discussions of foreign powers in prophetic literature are found in the collections of oracles against the nations.[14] These oracles demonstrate the LORD's sovereignty over all humanity, but their primary function is to assure God's people that justice will be meted out against the nations that have afflicted them.

Israel's insider status becomes especially evident when we consider something familiar from the New Testament that is generally absent from the Old Testament—namely, missionary activity. The God of Israel does not send prophets to other nations to convert them to biblical Yahwism. Perhaps this reflects God's policy of allowing the nations to walk in their own ways (cf. Acts 14:16; 17:30). To be sure, idolatry is always regarded as folly (e.g., Isa. 44:6–20; Jer. 10:1–16), and God holds the nations accountable for their wicked deeds (e.g., Amos 1:3–2:3). But the nations are not condemned for violating the Torah, which was never given to them. In fact, Deuteronomy 4:19 suggests that God apportioned the stars as symbols of the divine realm to the nations. The worship of heavenly bodies is erroneous (Ps. 19:1–6; Rom. 1:20), but perhaps it is less foolish than worshiping human-made idols. Regardless of how God dealt with the nations during this period, the general lack of missionary activity in the Old Testament shows the extent to which God entrusted unique responsibility to Israel as his chosen people.

Boundaries for God's People in the New Testament

In terms of ethnic identity and land of origin, the New Testament broadens the scope of God's people, but it does not eliminate the distinction between insiders and outsiders. The identifying mark of the people of God becomes trust in Jesus and obedience to Jesus's teaching.

In the Sermon on the Mount, for example, Jesus tells his listeners that they are "the salt of the earth" and "the light of the world." He warns them not to lose their saltiness lest they be thrown out, and he tells them to let their light shine before others, who are presumably not "light" themselves but may become "light" if they learn to glorify God (Matt. 5:13–16). Later in

---

14. E.g., Isa. 13–23, 34; Jer. 46–51; Ezek. 25–32; Zeph. 2:4–15.

the sermon, Jesus says that we should not be like hypocrites, who act piously in front of others just to be seen (6:2), and we should not pray like gentiles, who babble without understanding (6:7). All of this suggests that there is an outsider path and an insider path, the characteristics of which Jesus explains in Matthew 5–7. The intended outcome is that those who listen will choose the insider path by believing and putting into practice what they have believed. As Jesus explains at the end of the sermon, not everyone who says, "Lord, Lord" will enter the kingdom of heaven, but only those who do the Father's will (7:21–23).

The Gospel of John makes clear that God loves the world (3:16), but the world as a whole did not receive him, in that they did not receive Jesus, the divine Word (1:10–11). Yet those who receive him and believe in his name are given the right to become children of God (1:12–13). The world does not know God (17:25). But Jesus has sheep who hear his voice and follow him, and he gives them eternal life (10:25–30). In fact, the world hates Jesus's disciples just as it hates Jesus, but Jesus has chosen his disciples out of the world (15:18–19). The contrast between the world and the followers of Jesus in the Gospel of John shows the potentially hostile relationship between the New Testament people of God and those who hold them in contempt.

Several key passages that discuss the two opposing ways to live indicate that God will not separate the good from the bad until after this life. In Jesus's narrative about the rich man and Lazarus, it is only after death that the rich man suffers torment, while the poor man (Lazarus) enjoys blessing in the company of Abraham (Luke 16:19–31). In the parable of the weeds, the good seed (the sons of the kingdom) are separated from the weeds (the sons of the evil one) at the end of the age when the Son of Man returns.[15] Similarly, the sheep (those who cared for the least of their brothers) are separated from the goats (those who did not) in a final judgment scene in which all the nations appear before the Son of Man on his throne (Matt. 25:31–46). According to these accounts, people who follow either path exist side by side on earth, but each one receives a just reward or punishment directly from God at the end of life or at the end of the present age.

This does not mean, however, that no divisions should exist between people on earth. When sin is present in the church, differences necessarily emerge between sinners and those who follow God's ways (1 Cor. 11:19). According to the apostle Paul's instructions, Christians should break off fellowship with a member of the church who persists in sin, yet the purpose of this separation is the eventual restoration of the wayward individual (2 Thess. 3:14–15;

15. Matt. 13:24–30, 36–43; cf. 13:47–50.

1 Cor. 5:4–5). The church should not rush into judgment against an err-ing member but should pursue friendly correction and reconciliation (Matt. 18:15–17; James 5:19–20). Furthermore, the directive not to associate with immoral people applies strictly to those who call themselves Christians. It is not necessary to effect total separation from non-Christians who sin, because this would require Christians to leave the world entirely (1 Cor. 5:9–11; John 17:15). Nevertheless, in the case of a Christian who persistently engages in sin, the New Testament recognizes the practice of excommunication, whereby sinful church members are treated as outsiders so that they will feel remorse and return to the community.

Outsider Themes: Broadening and Reaching Out

Despite its overall emphasis on Israel as the people of God, the Hexateuch begins with a universal creation story and contains important inclusive themes throughout. God's plan to reach the nations receives greater attention in the prophets and comes to fruition in the New Testament.

Broadening the Scope of God's People in the Hexateuch

The book of Genesis begins not with the call of Abraham but with the creation of all humanity. Genesis is not simply about the origin of Israel as a nation. The subject of the Old Testament is the whole world, which God made good (Gen. 1–2) but which suffers the effects of human sin (chaps. 3–11). God's selection of Abraham in Genesis 12 is the response to a worldwide problem. Whereas human sin brought curses into the world,[16] all families of the earth will find blessings through Abraham's descendants.[17] Consequently, the story of Israel is also the story about how God plans to restore blessing to all people.

A few passages in Genesis hint at God's wider concern for humanity. God blesses Noah and his sons, from whom all nations of the world come (9:1, 19). God's covenant with Noah is a covenant with all life on earth (9:8–11, 17). In Genesis 14:18–20, Melchizedek, the king of "Salem" (i.e., Jerusalem, see Ps. 76:2), who was also a priest of "God Most High" ($'\bar{e}l$ $'ely\hat{o}n$, a Canaanite title), blessed Abraham and presented him with bread and wine, and Abraham paid Melchizedek a tithe. Although Ishmael is not the child of promise, God nevertheless blesses him and cares for him and his mother.[18] When Abraham conceals from Abimelech of Gerar that Sarah is his wife, Abimelech is

---

16. Gen. 3:14, 17; 4:11; 5:29.
17. Gen. 12:3; 18:18; 22:18; 26:4; 28:14.
18. Gen. 16:10, 13–14; 17:18, 20, 23–27; 21:11–21.

presented as upright in his dealings, and Abraham is directed to intercede on his behalf (Gen. 20:4–7, 17). Later, Abimelech recognizes that God is with Abraham, and he makes a treaty with him (21:22–34). When Joseph goes to Egypt, he brings blessing on the house in which he serves (39:5), and Jacob blesses Pharaoh (47:7, 10). Remarkably, Joseph marries Asenath, the daughter of an Egyptian priest (41:45). Although marriage to a Canaanite would be problematic, Joseph's marriage to the Egyptian Asenath receives no negative comment. Overall in Genesis, Israel's ancestors take center stage and some of Israel's later rivals (especially the Canaanites) are censured, but the possibility of positive relations with other nations is left open. In connection with the patriarchs, it is worth noting that Job, from the land of Uz, is not an Israelite (Job 1:1).

Occasional indications can be found in the rest of the Pentateuch that God's interests extend beyond Israel. In the book of Exodus, for example, Moses marries the daughter of a Midianite priest, a man who eventually acknowledges the LORD's greatness, advises Moses on appointing judges, and then returns to his own country.[19] Moses also marries a Cushite woman (Num. 12:1). Through the plagues in Egypt, God's name is declared in all the earth (Exod. 9:16). After the sin of the golden calf, one of Moses's arguments that God should not destroy Israel is that if Israel does not survive to inherit the land, God's reputation among the nations will suffer.[20] Some of Pharaoh's servants fear the LORD (Exod. 9:20), and a mixed multitude of people come out of Egypt with the Israelites (Exod. 12:38). Thus, even in Exodus, where the narrative centers on Moses and Israel, other peoples do not fall entirely out of focus.

When Israel arrives at Sinai to receive the Torah, God tells them that if they will obey the LORD and keep his covenant, they will be God's "special possession" (səgullâ) among all peoples because all the world belongs to God (Exod. 19:5). If all the world is God's, why does he need a "special possession"? The answer comes in the next verse: "You will be to me a kingdom of priests and a holy nation" (Exod. 19:6). Just as priests within Israel serve to mediate between God and the Israelites as a whole, the nation of Israel is meant to serve as a kingdom of priests to mediate between God and all people. This statement in Exodus 19 shows how the covenantal stipulations between God and Israel in the Pentateuch relate to God's broader concern for other nations. Old Testament laws that relate to outsiders include (1) commands to care for resident foreigners,[21] (2) gleaning and other practices of generosity that extend

19. Exod. 2:18, 21; 3:1; 4:18; 18:1–27.
20. Exod. 32:12; cf. Num. 14:13–17.
21. E.g., Exod. 22:21; 23:9; Lev. 19:33–34; Deut. 10:18–19; 27:19.

to foreigners,[22] (3) rules that treat foreigners and Israelites alike,[23] and (4) the command not to return foreign runaway slaves to their masters (Deut. 23:15–16).

In the book of Joshua, Rahab of Jericho is presented as the paradigmatic Canaanite who believes in the LORD and binds herself to the Israelites (Josh. 2:8–21; 6:22–25). Deuteronomy describes a procedure whereby foreign women captured in war can be taken as wives by Israelite men. The procedure involves shaving the woman's head, cutting her nails, and getting rid of her previous clothes (Deut. 21:10–14), which probably symbolizes the renunciation of her Canaanite identity. As for Rahab, she remains among the Israelites (Josh. 6:25). Assuming that Rahab married an Israelite man (cf. Matt. 1:5), she no doubt relinquished her Canaanite identity and became "Israelite."

The Gibeonites represent another example of Canaanites who make peace with Israel (Josh. 9). Unlike Rahab, the Gibeonites make peace through deception. They claim that they are not Canaanites so that Joshua will make a treaty with them. When it is discovered that the Gibeonites actually come from Canaan, Joshua honors the treaty and spares them. Yet they do not relinquish their Canaanite identity. For this reason, the Gibeonites are reduced to the status of servants (Josh. 9:26–27). Israel cannot integrate with Canaanites because of the wicked practices that the Canaanites follow.[24] Still, Canaanites can become part of God's people, if they give up the practices that mark them as Canaanites.

Broadening the Scope of God's People in the Prophetic Books

The prophetic books of the Old Testament contain passages that question Israel's unique status or else expand the category of God's people to include nations beyond Israel.

The book of Amos, for example, sometimes treats Israel as one of the nations as part of its rhetoric of prophetic condemnation. Amos begins with oracles against foreign nations that do not signal the vindication of God's people but, on the contrary, set the stage for judgments against Israel and Judah (Amos 1:3–2:16). Near the end of the book, Amos asks Israel rhetorically, "Are you not like the Cushites to me? . . . Did I not bring Israel up from the land of Egypt? And the Philistines from Caphtor? And the Arameans from Kir?" (Amos 9:7). In other words, Israel should not expect special treatment just because God brought them up from Egypt, since all nations are wherever they are because God brought them from somewhere else. At the same

22. E.g., Lev. 19:10; 23:22; Deut. 5:14; 14:29; 24:19–22; 26:13.
23. E.g., Lev. 17:8–16; 20:2; Num. 9:14; Deut. 16:14.
24. Lev. 18:1–5, 24–28; Deut. 12:29–31.

time, Amos can also embrace Israel's chosen status for the sake of prophetic critique. For example, "You only have I known from all families of the earth; for this reason, I will punish you for all your iniquities" (Amos 3:2). Another type of boundary blurring occurs in Jeremiah, where the prophet predicts restoration not only for Israel and Judah but also for other nations, such as Egypt and Moab.[25] As a general rule, the prophets affirm Israel as God's unique people among the nations, but on occasion they deal with Israel as they do with other nations.

In some prophetic passages, God's domain expands beyond the borders of Israel through the exile of God's people or through Israel's military conquests. Isaiah 11:10–16 promises that Israelites who were scattered into exile will be gathered to the LORD when a Davidic king is exalted as a banner to the nations. Along these lines, Zephaniah 3:10 says that God's people who were dispersed will bring offerings from distant lands. As for military conquest, the prophet Isaiah says that nations and kings will come to the brightness of God's rising (Isa. 60:3). These foreign powers will come to worship the LORD, to be sure, but they will also come as conquered peoples.[26] A similar scenario is depicted in Amos 9:11–12, where God rebuilds the fallen booth of David so that Israel might possess the remnant of Edom and all the nations over whom God's name is called. In passages such as these, true worship of the LORD reaches the nations either because Israel was sent into exile or because God establishes a Davidic king who brings all people into submission to Israel's God.

In other passages, foreign nations come to know and worship the LORD, so it seems, by their own choice. Thus, the gentle servant in Isaiah is appointed by God to be "a light to the nations."[27] In Isaiah 2, not only do the nations stream into Jerusalem, but they also learn the LORD's ways so that by God's righteous mediation they experience everlasting peace (Isa. 2:2–4; Mic. 4:1–3). Isaiah 19:19–25 describes true worship of the LORD that will take place in Assyria and Egypt, and Malachi 1:11 states that God's name will be great among the nations. In a surprisingly clear passage on the inclusion of outsiders, including foreigners and eunuchs, Isaiah 56:3–8 says that foreigners who join themselves to the LORD, observe the Sabbath, and hold fast to his covenant will be included among God's people. These foreigners will experience joy in the temple and make acceptable offerings to the LORD because "my house will be called a house of prayer for all peoples" (Isa. 56:7). Whether by witness,

25. Jer. 46:26; 48:47; 49:6; 49:39.
26. Isa. 60:11–12; cf. 14:1–2; Zeph. 2:11.
27. Isa. 42:6; 49:6; cf. 51:4.

conquest, or some supernatural means, the prophets predict that many people from other nations will join Israel in worshiping the one true God.

Broadening the Scope of God's People in the New Testament

In the New Testament, Jesus and the apostles build on their Jewish foundations to implement God's plan to bring light to the nations. The outworking of this plan is evident in the Gospels whenever the faith of outsiders is highlighted. Whereas King Herod does not recognize the birth of the Messiah, the magi come from the east to worship him (Matt. 2:1–12). In response to a Roman centurion who shows faith, Jesus says, "I have not found such great faith in anyone in Israel" (Matt. 8:10; Luke 7:9). He adds, "Many will come from the east and the west and will recline with Abraham, Isaac, and Jacob in the kingdom of heaven, but the sons of the kingdom will be cast out to the outer darkness" (Matt. 8:11–12; Luke 13:29). When approached by a Canaanite woman, Jesus begins by telling her that he was sent only to the lost sheep of Israel (cf. Matt. 10:5), but after her humble supplication, he says to her, "O woman, great is your faith! Let it be done to you as you wish" (Matt. 15:21–28). On one occasion, after Jesus heals ten lepers but only one, a Samaritan, returns to praise God, Jesus wonders aloud, "Were none found who came back to give glory to God, except this foreigner?" (Luke 17:18).

The theological basis for Jesus's openness to outsiders comes through clearly in his teaching. For example, according to the Beatitudes, the kingdom of heaven belongs to the poor in spirit, and peacemakers will be called children of God (Matt. 5:3, 9). Anyone can pursue these ideals, not just Israelites. As Jesus says elsewhere, all who humble themselves before God will be exalted (Luke 18:13–14). Again, this path is open to all people. Jesus himself lived as a pious Jew, but his deeds and message offer a road map for anyone, Jew or gentile, to seek God and pursue righteousness.

The parables of Jesus sometimes depict a reversal of fortunes in God's reckoning between insiders and outsiders. In the parable about workers in a vineyard (Matt. 20:1–16), those who work just an hour at the end of the day (i.e., recently included outsiders) receive the same wage as those who work the full day (i.e., insiders of long standing). The latter are told not to begrudge the wage paid to the former, and the lesson is that "the last will be first, and the first will be last."[28] In other instances, such as the parable of the vineyard rented to tenants (Matt. 21:33–46; Luke 20:9–19) and the parable of the banquet (Matt. 22:1–14; Luke 14:15–24), those who were initially chosen

---

28. Matt. 20:16; cf. 19:30; Mark 9:35; 10:31; Luke 13:30.

are rejected because of their evil behavior, and others are invited to replace them.[29] Jesus elaborates on this theme in his rebuke of certain leaders who refused to repent at the preaching of John the Baptist, even though they saw tax collectors and prostitutes repent (Matt. 21:28–32). Because the sinners turned to God when these leaders did not, Jesus says to the latter, "Tax collectors and prostitutes are entering ahead of you into the kingdom of God" (Matt. 21:31). This shows that the outsiders in Jesus's parables might be sinful people who were regarded as unworthy of God. In some cases, however, the outsiders might include gentiles. This is supported by Jesus's final command in the Gospel of Matthew, that his followers are to "make disciples of all nations" (28:19).

The book of Acts tells the story of how the early church bore witness to Jesus "in Jerusalem, in all Judea and Samaria, and to the end of the earth" (Acts 1:8; cf. 26:20). After Jesus ascended, the Holy Spirit empowered the Jewish disciples through the sign of speaking in tongues (2:1–12), and the Spirit gave the same sign to signify God's acceptance of the gentiles when they first believed.[30] In keeping with the paradigm established by Jesus, the apostle Paul often began his ministry by preaching to the Jews. Only after most Jews in an area rejected Paul's message did he turn to the gentiles.[31] Ultimately, gentiles became the primary focus of Paul's ministry (e.g., Gal. 2:7; 1 Tim. 2:7). By the end of the book of Acts, Paul is preaching Christ without hindrance in Rome (Acts 28:16–31). A major theme of Acts is how the Holy Spirit guides the ministry of the apostles so that the gospel is preached to all people everywhere.[32] A fundamental principle that drives this ministry is that "God does not show favoritism."[33]

A core element of the gospel as preached by Paul is that, because of Christ, gentiles are heirs of God's promises together with Israel (Eph. 3:6). Christ is the wisdom and power of God for both Jews and Greeks (1 Cor. 1:24) so that in Christ there is no distinction between Jew and Greek, slave and free, or male and female, in that all are reckoned as Abraham's descendants and heirs according to the promise (Gal. 3:26–29). Paul develops this theme extensively in the book of Romans, explaining that the gospel of Christ is the power of God for salvation for everyone who believes, first for the Jew, then for the Greek (Rom. 1:16). All are guilty of sin, the Jews for violating the written commandments and the gentiles for breaking the law written on

29. Matt. 21:41; 22:8–10; Luke 14:21–24; 20:16.
30. Acts 10:44–46; cf. 11:1, 18.
31. Acts 13:46; 18:6; 28:28.
32. See Acts 17:30–31; cf. Col. 1:6, 23.
33. Acts 10:34; cf. Gal. 2:6; Eph. 6:9.

their consciences; consequently, both Jew and gentile stand in need of forgiveness, which God provides through faith in Jesus (Rom. 2–3). On one level, to be a member of the true "Israel" of God is not a matter of ethnicity or race; instead, it depends on the condition of the heart and spirit (e.g., Rom. 2:28–29; 9:1–29). In Christ, therefore, everyone stands on the same footing before God, and the division between outsiders and insiders is abolished (cf. Eph. 2:11–22). This does not mean, however, that there is no special role for the physical descendants of Abraham (Rom. 11:25–29). I will return to this topic in the next section.

Inner-Biblical Insights

Both insider and outsider perspectives are represented in passages that exhibit inner-biblical interpretation. Within the Old Testament, early biblical traditions on Israel and the nations were redeployed in the postexilic period to address the challenge of outside influences on God's people. In the New Testament, the ministry of Jesus had transformative implications for Israel's relationship to other groups. In this section, I will first discuss contrasting uses of inherited biblical material in the Old Testament, both to maintain boundaries (Ezra, Nehemiah) and to broaden perspectives (Ruth, Jonah). Then I will show how the New Testament employs the Old Testament to articulate its gospel mission to include the gentiles within the people of God.

Old Testament

When the Judeans who had been deported to Babylon returned to their land, they faced challenges as to how they should interact with others who were living in and around Judea. How should the returning exiles keep their religious identity intact? Does God have any plans for those who are not Israelites? As we consider the divergent perspectives evident in different Old Testament books, it is important to keep in mind the particular question each text is seeking to answer.

Ezra and Nehemiah

The books of Ezra and Nehemiah interpret Mosaic legal traditions so as to strengthen the boundaries that distinguish God's people from other nations. After many years of exile in Babylon, the Judeans were granted permission to return to their land, restore temple worship, and rebuild the walls around Jerusalem. The land to which they were returning, however, was not totally

vacant. In and around Judea there lived Israelites with foreign religious practices, as well as people of non-Israelite origin who began worshiping the God
of Israel, perhaps alongside other deities, when the Assyrians settled them
in the land two hundred years earlier (Ezra 4:2; cf. 2 Kings 17:24–41). In this
context, Ezra and Nehemiah emphasize various measures that were taken to
maintain the purity of Israelite religion.

The return of the exiles to Judea is portrayed in the book of Ezra as God's
work accomplished for religious purposes. Permission to return is granted because the LORD stirs up the spirit of King Cyrus of Persia (1:1–2). The sacred
vessels that were in Solomon's temple are sent back for use in the new temple,
thus linking the postexilic people of God back to the great Davidic-Solomonic
tradition of ancient Israel (1:7–11). In another connection to Solomon's temple
(1 Kings 5:1–12), the returnees trade with Tyre and Sidon to acquire cedars
of Lebanon to build the new temple (Ezra 3:7). The first task for the exiles on
arrival is to rebuild the altar and make offerings to the LORD (3:1–6). Sacrificial
worship and festival observance also accompany the completion of the temple
(6:16–22). When Ezra returns, worship and piety again take center stage, as
Levites are commissioned to perform their duties, and the people fast, pray, and
humble themselves before God (8:15–23; cf. 10:6). The leaders of the reform are
identified as those who "tremble" (*ḥārēd*) at the words of the God of Israel.[34]
The religious nature of the return is highlighted at every point.

Nevertheless, despite God's help, the returning exiles face opposition when
they attempt to restore proper worship. They succeed in establishing the altar
on its foundation, but they must do so in fear of the surrounding peoples
(Ezra 3:3). In Ezra 4:1–5, some of those who were settled in the land by the
Assyrians offer to assist in rebuilding the temple, but the returning exiles do
not want the local people's syncretistic practices to corrupt temple worship.
Therefore, they refuse help from these "people of the land" (4:4), who consequently harass the returnees and actively oppose their efforts to rebuild.
When the temple finally reaches completion, God's people hold a Passover
celebration that includes both "those who returned from exile" and "all those
who separated themselves from the uncleanness of the surrounding nations
in order to seek the LORD" (6:21). In other words, the returnees do not limit
participation to those who were in exile; rather, they allow others to join,
provided that they separate themselves from the nations. The ultimate goal
of this building project was correct worship of the LORD. In practical terms,
however, this meant keeping strict boundaries around the people of God
vis-à-vis other peoples.

34. Ezra 9:4; 10:3; cf. Isa. 66:2, 5.

The problem of intermarriage is addressed in Ezra 9–10. Our clearest examples of inner-biblical interpretation occur in this section of the book. The issue is introduced at Ezra 9:1–2: "As soon as they finished these things, the leaders approached me, saying: The people of Israel, the priests, and the Levites have not separated themselves from the surrounding peoples who act according to their abominations, even the Canaanites, the Hittites, the Perizzites, the Jebusites, the Ammonites, the Moabites, the Egyptians, and the Amorites. For they have taken some of their daughters as wives for themselves and for their sons, so that the holy seed is mixed together with the surrounding peoples. In fact, the leaders and officials have been foremost in this treachery."

Ezra and those faithful to the LORD are appalled at this situation (Ezra 9:3–5), and Ezra offers a prayer of confession and repentance (vv. 6–15). As part of this prayer, Ezra makes the following comment (vv. 10–12):

> And now, our God, what shall we say after this? For we have forsaken your commandments, which you commanded by the hand of your servants the prophets, saying: The land, which you are entering in order to possess it, is an impure land because of the impurity of the surrounding peoples through their abominations, by which they have filled the land from one end to the other with their uncleanness. And now, do not give your daughters as wives to their sons, and do not take their daughters as wives for your sons, and do not seek their peace or their welfare forever, so that you may be strong, and eat the goodness of the land, and leave it for your sons as an inheritance forever.

Ezra states explicitly in verses 10–11 that he is hearkening back to God's commandments, which God gave through his servants the prophets. Although no single commandment in the Pentateuch matches what Ezra says here, three biblical passages appear to stand behind the perspective on intermarriage expressed in these chapters: Deuteronomy 7:1–6, Deuteronomy 23:3–8, and Leviticus 18.[35]

First, Deuteronomy 7:1–6 instructs the Israelites not to make covenants with other nations in "the land which you are entering there to possess it" (v. 1) but to break down their altars and destroy them completely. Marriage alliances are also forbidden: "Do not give your daughter as a wife to his son, and do not take his daughter as a wife for your son" (v. 3). Radical separation is necessary because Israel is a "holy people" (v. 6). The specific nations listed in Deuteronomy 7:1 are the Hittites, Girgashites, Amorites, Canaanites, Perizzites, Hivites, and Jebusites. Several details connect this passage with Ezra 9.

---

35. On the inner-biblical connections in this chapter, see Fishbane, *Biblical Interpretation in Ancient Israel*, 114–20.

Thus, Ezra 9:11 alludes to Deuteronomy 7:1 when it speaks of "the land, which you are entering in order to possess it." The language against intermarriage in Ezra 9:12 ("Do not give your daughters as wives to their sons, and do not take their daughters as wives for your sons") echoes Deuteronomy 7:3. The statement in Deuteronomy 7:6 that Israel is a "holy people" finds expression in Ezra 9:2, "so that the holy seed is mixed together with the surrounding peoples." Moreover, five out of the eight nations listed in Ezra 9:1 appear in Deuteronomy 7:1—namely, the Hittites, Amorites, Canaanites, Perizzites, and Jebusites. These verbal similarities suggest that the condemnation of foreign marriage in Ezra 9 is based on the prohibition against intermarriage in Deuteronomy 7:1–6.

Second, Deuteronomy 23:3–8 accounts for several details in Ezra 9. Deuteronomy 23:3 says, "No Ammonite or Moabite may enter the assembly of the Lord, even to the tenth generation. None of them shall enter the assembly of the Lord forever." Verse 6 adds, "Do not seek their peace or their welfare throughout all your days forever." Moreover, verses 7–8 establish a lesser prohibition directed at Edomites and Egyptians. The appearance of Ammonites, Moabites, and Egyptians in Ezra 9:1 probably stems from their presence in Deuteronomy 23:3–8, and the command in Ezra 9:12 not to seek the welfare of the surrounding nations ("Do not seek their peace or their welfare forever") clearly refers to Deuteronomy 23:6. It appears that Ezra 9 has included Deuteronomy 23:3–8 alongside Deuteronomy 7:1–6 as part of its scriptural case against intermarriage.

Third, Leviticus 18 provides much of the language that Ezra 9 uses to describe how foreign marriages corrupt God's people. Leviticus 18 begins with a general admonition not to imitate the practices of the Egyptians or Canaanites. After a series of negative commandments, many of which deal with illicit sexual relations, such as intercourse with a woman during the uncleanness of her menstrual "impurity" (niddâ; v. 19), the chapter ends with further admonitions for the Israelites not to render themselves or the land "unclean" (ṭm'; vv. 24–25) by following any of the "abominations" (tô'ēbōt; vv. 26–30) of the Canaanites. When we turn to the book of Ezra, we see that Ezra 9 employs the terms "impurity" (v. 11), "uncleanness" (v. 11), and "abominations" (vv. 1, 11, 14) to describe the people's sin and the effects of their sin on the land. With its themes of separating from foreign influence and avoiding sexual transgressions, Leviticus 18 made an important contribution to Ezra's efforts to address the problem of intermarriage.

How can we sum up the inner-biblical interpretation that takes place in Ezra 9–10? The prohibition against intermarrying with peoples of the land in Deuteronomy 7:1–6 served as the foundation for Ezra's condemnation of intermarriage. Especially important was the concern to maintain Israel's holiness (Deut. 7:6; Ezra 9:2). The allusion to Deuteronomy 23:3–8 deepened the level of exclusion (e.g., "Do not seek their peace or their welfare forever"). Moreover, when the community responds to Ezra's prayer, the people commit themselves to send away not only their foreign wives but also the children born from these unions (Ezra 10:3). This is not strictly required by any biblical law, but the prohibition against any Ammonite or Moabite entering the assembly to the tenth generation (Deut. 23:3) may have been interpreted so as to exclude both foreign wives and their children from the community.[36] In Ezra 10, the people respond in agreement with Ezra's prayer and agree to separate themselves (*bdl*; v. 11) from their foreign wives and children. On this occasion, the desire to keep Israel pure in its practices led to extreme social exclusivity.[37] As the language borrowed from Leviticus 18 makes clear, the core concern was religious purity, not simply cultural elitism for its own sake. Still, it is perplexing that no mention is made of the possibility that a foreigner might join God's people. This differs from what Isaiah 56:3 envisions: "Let not the foreigner who has joined himself to the LORD say: The LORD will surely separate [*bdl*] me from his people."[38]

The book of Nehemiah focuses on rebuilding the wall around Jerusalem. Like the book of Ezra, Nehemiah gives special attention to the topic of intermarriage. After the completion of the city wall (6:15–16), Ezra reads the Torah before all the people (chap. 8), who respond with repentance, worship, and prayer (9:1–38). The participants in this religious renewal are described as "the seed of Israel" who "separated themselves from all foreigners" (9:2). Eventually, many in the community, including religious leaders and "all those who separated themselves from the surrounding peoples for the sake of God's law" (10:28–29), make an agreement to fulfill their religious obligations. These

36. Fishbane, *Biblical Interpretation in Ancient Israel*, 117–18.

37. The heightened expectation of exclusivity can be seen in the fact that, whereas in Lev. 21:14 only priests are forbidden to marry non-Israelites, in Ezra and Nehemiah all Judeans are forbidden to marry non-Israelites.

38. The perspective on this topic in Isa. 56 differs from what we find in the priestly prophet Ezekiel. In contrast to Isa. 56:3–8, which affirms that foreigners will offer acceptable sacrifices on God's altar (v. 7), Ezek. 44:7–9 says, "No foreigner uncircumcised in heart and uncircumcised in flesh will enter my sanctuary, even the foreigner who lives among the Israelites." Ezekiel's rule seems even more stringent than the Pentateuch (cf. Lev. 17:8; Num. 15:14–16, 27–31). Nevertheless, although they lean in different directions, Isa. 56 and Ezek. 44 do not fundamentally contradict each other. Ezekiel restricts from the altar any foreigner who is "uncircumcised in heart." The foreigner in Isaiah who makes offerings on the altar has joined himself to the LORD, loves the LORD, keeps the Sabbath, and holds fast to the covenant. Isaiah and Ezekiel are clearly describing different categories of people. It should also be noted that in Ezek. 47:22–23 land is set aside for sojourners (resident foreigners) who have children.

obligations include avoiding intermarriage with the "people of the land" (10:30), observing Sabbath laws (10:31), and assuming financial responsibility for temple worship (10:32–39). Later, at the dedication of Jerusalem's wall (12:27), another reading of Torah inspires further reforms. These reforms address intermarriage (13:1–3, 23–27), failure to support the Levites (13:10–14), and Sabbath violations (13:15–22). The discussion of intermarriage in Nehemiah 13 constitutes another case of inner-biblical interpretation.

According to Nehemiah 13:1–2, the people read in the book of Moses that "no Ammonite or Moabite may enter the assembly of God forever" because these nations would not help with food and water when Israel came out of Egypt—on the contrary they hired Balaam to curse Israel. The reference to Deuteronomy 23:3–5 is unmistakable. Yet the manner in which Nehemiah applies this passage to his context is somewhat surprising. Some Judeans have married women from Ashdod, Ammon, and Moab (Neh. 13:23). Great distress is caused by the fact that "half of their children spoke the language of Ashdod or the language of this or that people, and they did not know how to speak the language of Judea" (13:24). In response, Nehemiah brings charges against the transgressors, curses them, beats some of the men, pulls out their hair, and makes them take oaths not to intermarry (13:25). Although this goes beyond anything in Deuteronomy 23:3–8, it is certainly in the spirit of Deuteronomy that Nehemiah "purifies" the priests and Levites from everything foreign (Neh. 13:30). What is striking about this passage is Nehemiah's harsh application of Deuteronomy 23 to the postexilic issue of intermarriage with foreigners.[39]

The overriding concern for the books of Ezra and Nehemiah is that God's people should remain separate from the nations around them. The emphasis in these books on maintaining boundaries can be likened to the similar emphasis in Deuteronomy and Joshua. Just as the Israelites needed to shun foreign influence when they first entered the land, the exiles need to guard against foreign influence when they return to the land. The underlying issue that stands behind this controversy in Ezra and Nehemiah is the threat of turning away from God. As Nehemiah 13:26 explains, even

---

39. Another possible inner-biblical connection occurs at Neh. 13:3. According to Exod. 12:38, a great "mixture" ('*ēreb*) of people came out of Egypt with the Israelites. These non-Israelites do not feature in the rest of the Pentateuch, although some have suggested that the "rabble" ('*āsapsup*) who cause trouble in Num. 11:4 should be identified as the "great mixture" of people from Exod. 12:38. The word '*ēreb*, "mixture," does not occur frequently in the Hebrew Bible (cf. Jer. 25:20; 50:37; Ezek. 30:5). But Neh. 13:3 says, "As soon as they heard the Torah, they separated from Israel all the mixture ['*ēreb*]"—that is, the foreign people who were mixed together with the Israelites. If Neh. 13 is alluding to the Exodus narrative, the inclusion of this great mixture of people in Exodus is being viewed in a negative light.

Solomon fell into sin through marriages with foreign women. In the post-exilic context, however, lines between religion and general culture were not easy to draw. For the authors of Ezra and Nehemiah, such lines could not be drawn. Belief, ritual practice, ethics, and local custom were seen as so inextricably bound together that there was no way to preserve one without guarding the others, and any faltering in one area threatened the others. Therefore, preserving purity in peoplehood became a mechanism for preserving purity in devotion.

Ruth and Jonah

The books of Ruth and Jonah both reference traditions known from the Pentateuch in order to highlight God's openness to outsiders. Neither of these books rejects the idea that Israel is God's chosen people. But each in its own way illustrates God's concern for nations beyond it.

The book of Ruth tells the story of a noble Moabite woman whose deeds of steadfast love (*ḥesed*) bring blessing to a family of Israelites. At one level, the story of Ruth simply extols the virtue of steadfast love. This is a time-less lesson that requires no special occasion within the Old Testament. On another level, however, the identity of Ruth and the genealogy at the end of the book suggest another dimension of meaning that intersects with previous Old Testament traditions.[40] As noted above, Deuteronomy 23:3 says, "No Ammonite or Moabite may enter the assembly of the LORD, even to the tenth generation. None of them shall enter the assembly of the LORD forever." The goal of Deuteronomy 23 is to keep Israel separate from Moab and Ammon because of their past behavior. Still, if an Ammonite chose to believe and act like an Israelite, would that make a difference? If a Moabite

---

40. There is no clear indication of when the book of Ruth was written. Ruth presupposes legal customs known from the Pentateuch, such as levirate marriage (Deut. 25:5–10) and land redemption (Lev. 25:24–34), although they are practiced in a distinctive way in Ruth (see chap. 1, n. 14). The events of the story take place in the period of the judges, and the genealogy at the end of the book ends with King David. The book in its present form, therefore, must come from the time of David or later. Since Ruth starts with the words, "In the days when the judges ruled" (Ruth 1:1), it has been suggested that Ruth was composed at a time when the book of Judges already existed, which might be after the deportation of the Northern Kingdom or even after the Babylonian exile (cf. Judg. 18:30). The fact that the writer of Ruth needs to explain the custom of establishing transactions through the transfer of a shoe (cf. Deut. 25:9), as was practiced "formerly" in Israel (Ruth 4:7), suggests that considerable time has elapsed between the events of the story and the composition of the book. According to a recent linguistic analysis, "all the relevant data *suggest* (but not strongly) that Ruth was written during a period of Aramaic ascendancy but not dominance and thus it may come from the early Persian period." Holmstedt, *Ruth*, 39. In light of linguistic, source, and thematic features, many scholars today assign Ruth to the early Persian period, although the evidence is not conclusive. See Schipper, *Ruth*, 20–22.

switched allegiance from Moab to Israel, would that change anything? The book of Ruth can be seen as a response to these questions.

Both the virtue of Ruth and her status as a foreigner are highlighted throughout the book. In the first chapter, Naomi testifies that Ruth and her sister-in-law, Orpah, have shown steadfast love (ḥesed). Even when reason dictates that the two daughters-in-law should return to their Moabite homes, Ruth persists in her devotion to Naomi, returns to Judah with her, and supports her by gleaning in the fields. Ruth is surprised at the kind treatment she receives from Boaz, since she is a foreigner (Ruth 2:10). The text often reminds us of her status by calling her "Ruth the Moabite."[41] Boaz, however, explains that he has heard about her good deeds and how she gave up her father, mother, and homeland in order to live with a people she did not know (2:11). Later, Ruth again shows steadfast love to her mother-in-law by seeking marriage with Boaz (3:10), which benefits Naomi in relation to her family line and the redemption of her land.[42] For his part, Boaz offers Ruth a blessing and assures her that she is known as a "woman of valor" (3:10–11; cf. Prov. 31:10). Indeed, Ruth's steadfast love is the catalyst that initiates God's acting in steadfast love through Boaz (Ruth 2:20; 4:1–12, 14). Ruth's commitment to Naomi and Naomi's people, land, and God is expressed with absolute clarity in the declaration of loyalty she makes to her mother-in-law before they leave Moab (1:16–17). By the end of the book, when Ruth gives birth to an heir for Naomi's family, the women of the town proclaim that Ruth is better to Naomi than seven sons.[43] As the book as a whole makes clear, Ruth is a Moabite whose allegiance and actions make her a model Israelite.

Special attention is given at the end of the book to the connection between Ruth and David. When Ruth's son is born, the women name him Obed, who is the father of Jesse, the father of David (Ruth 4:17). To emphasize the point, the story appends a formal genealogy that begins with Perez and ends with David. It is evidently important to see that David is the climax of the narrative. Why is this significant? One possibility is that the narrator wants to praise David. Although many Israelites in the judges period were wicked, some people displayed steadfast love (ḥesed), and it is from such people that King David descended. If this is the reason for the emphasis on David, the book could be a political work intended to justify David's rule. This is not

41. Ruth 1:22; 2:2, 21; 4:5, 10. Ruth is not identified as "the Moabite" when Naomi speaks to her in Ruth 2:22 ("Then Naomi said to Ruth, her daughter-in-law"), nor is she called a Moabite when Boaz takes her as his wife (Ruth 4:13).

42. On the apparent connection between the levirate marriage duty and land redemption in Ruth 4, see Younger, *Judges and Ruth*, 474–78.

43. Ruth 4:14–15; cf. 1 Sam. 2:5; Job 42:13.

impossible, but would a story tracing David's ancestry back to a Moabite woman make for good propaganda if the legitimacy of David's kingship were in doubt? Instead, I suspect that when the book of Ruth was composed, David's reputation was already firmly established, and the figure who stood to benefit most from this connection was Ruth the Moabite.

If the book of Ruth was composed at a time when the memory of David was held in high regard, the point of emphasizing the connection to David would be to validate Ruth the Moabite and potentially Moabites (or foreigners) in general. Near the end of the book, the people wish for God to allow Ruth to become like Rachel and Leah, who built the house of Israel (Ruth 4:11). With the genealogical link to David, Ruth's credentials are confirmed. Deuteronomy 23:3–6 states that no Ammonite or Moabite may enter the assembly of the LORD, even to the tenth generation. According to the book of Ruth, however, David is only four generations removed from a Moabite. Perhaps the book of Ruth addresses the question, Could a Moabite be accepted into the assembly of the LORD if she joins herself to the LORD and displays steadfast love? It would seem that the book of Ruth interprets the prohibition of Deuteronomy 23 as not applying to a foreigner who chooses to become part of God's people.

The book of Jonah offers an ironic critique of the kind of self-centered attitude that could result from being chosen by God. Jonah the son of Amittai is mentioned in 2 Kings 14:25 as a prophet who gave a favorable word of the LORD in the days of King Jeroboam II of Israel, who was a wicked ruler. The writer of 2 Kings makes clear that God blessed Israel in those days not because of Jeroboam's disobedience but as an act of mercy to preserve Israel (2 Kings 14:26–27). Still, Jonah stands in 2 Kings as a prophet who gave good news to a bad king. This often signifies false prophecy in the Old Testament. On the basis of this reference in 2 Kings, Jonah looks like a perfect figure to appear in a satire on the presumptuous mindset that underlies false prophecy. The book of Jonah recounts the story of Jonah's initial disobedience, and later obedience, in response to God's command to prophesy against Nineveh, which is followed by lessons from how Nineveh and Jonah respond to God. Jonah is not a straightforward hero. In fact, he is held up as a somewhat negative example. In other words, the book makes its point at the expense of the prophet Jonah. Near the end of the book, Jonah makes an ironic reference to a Pentateuchal tradition that provides important commentary on that tradition.

The book of Jonah is made up of four sections, which essentially match the four chapter divisions in modern Bibles. The first two chapters narrate God's initial call to Jonah, the prophet's attempt to flee, and his dramatic rescue from the sea. The final two chapters describe God's second call to

Jonah, the response of the Ninevites to Jonah's warning, and God's lesson for the prophet.

In chapter 1, God summons Jonah to go to Nineveh and call out against it because of its evil (Jon. 1:2). Nineveh was a major city in the Assyrian Empire, which was a menacing superpower well known to the book's audience. Jonah flees from God and boards a ship going away from Nineveh. God, in turn, casts a great storm on the sea that puts the entire ship in peril. The pagan sailors on the ship act commendably toward Jonah, initially not wanting to throw him overboard, even to save themselves (1:12–14). After the sea calms, these pagans fear the LORD and make sacrifices and vows to him (1:16). Jonah, by contrast, is found sleeping on the ship during the crisis (1:5). Once he is woken up, Jonah makes a declaration that is theologically correct ("I fear the LORD, the God of heaven, who made the sea and the dry ground," 1:9) but that does not match his behavior (i.e., he is trying to escape from God on the sea). When Jonah is finally thrown into the sea, God rescues the prophet by sending a great fish to swallow him (1:17). Chapter 2 consists primarily of Jonah's prayer of thanksgiving from the belly of the fish, which makes extensive use of poetic phrases and imagery from the Psalms.[44] Jonah never actually expresses repentance, however. At the end of this prayer, God tells the fish to vomit Jonah out onto dry land (2:10).

In chapter 3, God again commands Jonah to go to Nineveh to "call out to it the message that I will tell you" (Jon. 3:2). Previously God said that Nineveh was a "great city" (1:2; 3:2), but now we are told that Nineveh is "a great city to God" (3:3).[45] This time Jonah goes, and the message he proclaims is "in yet forty days, Nineveh will be overthrown" (3:4). The Ninevites respond by believing in God and supplicating him by fasting and wearing sackcloth. By royal decree, all Ninevites, from the nobles to the cattle, participate in these acts of supplication. Each person is commanded to cry out to God and turn away from evil and violence (3:8). The king expresses his hope thus: "Who knows? God may turn and relent, and turn away from his burning anger so that we do not perish" (3:9). As it turns out, God does relent, so the city is not destroyed (3:10; cf. Jer. 18:7–10).

44. For parallels to the prayer in Jon. 2, e.g., on v. 2, see Pss. 18:6; 116:3; 120:1; cf. Job 20:15. On v. 3, see Pss. 42:7; 88:6. On v. 4, see Ps. 31:22. On v. 5, see Pss. 18:4–5; 69:1–2. On v. 6, see Pss. 22:29; 30:3; 103:4. On v. 7, see Pss. 88:2; 138:2–3; 142:2; 143:4–5. On v. 8, see Ps. 144:4. On v. 9, see Pss. 3:2, 8; 50:14, 23; 116:17–19. For detailed discussion, see Sasson, *Jonah*, 168–201.

45. Some translations render the phrase "great city to God" as equivalent to "a very great city," on the grounds that this was an idiom that pertained to the size of the city without any intended reference to God. However, linguistic evidence for such an idiom in Hebrew is not strong, and an intentional reference to "God" in chapter 3 fits the story since the Ninevites believe in God (Jon. 3:5) and God expresses concern for the city (Jon. 4:11).

As for Jonah, he is so angry about Nineveh being pardoned that he asks God to take his life (Jon. 4:1–3). In response, God teaches Jonah a lesson by raising up a plant to protect him from the sun, making Jonah happy, only to destroy the plant on the next day, leaving the prophet bitter (4:4–9). The book concludes with God's explanation of this object lesson: "You took pity on this plant, although you neither labored for it nor made it grow, and it grew in a night and perished in a day. And I, should I not have pity on the great city Nineveh, in which are more than 120,000 people who do not know their right hand from their left, and also many cattle?" (4:10–11). In the end, we learn that God has pity on the Ninevites, even if Jonah does not. The prophet showed concern for the plant because it met his own personal need. God, however, shows concern for the welfare of Nineveh, perhaps because he did labor for it and make it grow, even though the Ninevites are oblivious to what God expects from them. God even cares for the cattle. The book of Jonah does not suggest that the Ninevites converted to biblical Yahwism, nor does it deny that Israel is God's chosen people. Nevertheless, the book clearly affirms that God's compassion extends beyond Israel to include other nations, even a known enemy such as Assyria.

In explaining why he fled from God, Jonah uses inherited scriptural language about God in an unexpected way. After the narrator informs us that Jonah is angry (Jon. 4:1), the prophet says to God, "Isn't this what I said when I was in my own land? That is why I first fled to Tarshish, because I knew that you are a compassionate and gracious God, slow to anger and abounding in steadfast love, who relents from disaster" (4:2). In other words, Jonah did not want to announce God's judgment against Nineveh because he knew that God is merciful and would spare them if they repented. The descriptor of God as "a compassionate and gracious God, slow to anger and abounding in steadfast love" is known especially from Exodus 34:6–7, which concludes, "abounding in steadfast love *and faithfulness*," and then continues with statements about transgenerational reward and punishment (see chap. 2). These latter statements are not relevant to the present context in the book of Jonah, so they are omitted. Elements of this description of God appear in numerous passages in the Old Testament,[46] but the way Jonah employs this

---

46. E.g., Num. 14:18; Pss. 86:15; 103:8; 145:8; Nah. 1:3; Neh. 9:17. A description of God that matches Jon. 4:2 is found in Joel 2:13: "Your God, because he is compassionate and gracious, slow to anger and abounding in steadfast love, relenting from disaster." Because Joel 2:14 ("Who knows? He may turn and relent") resembles Jon. 3:9, and *ḥws*, "to have mercy," occurs in Joel 2:17 and Jon. 4:10–11, there is probably a direct literary connection between the two books, whether one borrowed from the other or they both followed a common source. The precise nature of the connection, however, is difficult to determine.

traditional language is unique. Just as with his statement to the sailors (Jon. 1:9), Jonah articulates correct theology, but with an ironic twist: God's gracious compassion, which should be a source of comfort, is a source of grief for Jonah because it extends to his enemies. Jonah would rather die than see God show mercy to the Ninevites (4:3, 9). The book of Jonah employs the formula of God's compassion to highlight the hypocrisy of delighting in God's mercy for oneself while begrudging it to outsiders.

The book of Ruth interprets the legal tradition found in Deuteronomy 23:3–6 by permitting an individual Moabite to join herself to Israel and Israel's God. The book of Jonah interprets the description of God's compassion found in Exodus 34:6–7 by applying it to nations beyond Israel. Both of these books respond to earlier biblical traditions by broadening the horizon of God's concern. On the basis of these texts, one would not be surprised by future acts of God that show compassion to the nations and include non-Israelites among God's people. These themes find fulfillment in the early church, as seen in the New Testament's use of relevant Old Testament passages.

New Testament

In some instances, the New Testament employs the Old Testament to clarify and strengthen the boundaries that make God's people distinct. More often, however, New Testament writers interpret Old Testament texts as part of their theology of gentile inclusion. In all cases, the New Testament's interpretation of the Old is shaped by the ministry of Jesus.

Defining and Maintaining Boundaries

A few examples will suffice to show how the New Testament interprets the Old Testament to define and maintain boundaries. To begin with, some New Testament writers quote an Old Testament text about the nations and apply it to the "nations" of their own day—that is, gentiles. We see this in the quotation of Psalm 2:1–2 in Acts 4:25–28, where the passage beginning with "Why do the nations rage?" is applied to Herod Antipas, Pontius Pilate, and the gentiles who conspired to crucify Jesus.

Furthermore, even when old categories such as Jew and gentile are broken down, Old Testament concepts are often used to shape new boundaries. For example, in Colossians 3:11 Paul says, "Here there is no Greek or Jew, circumcision or uncircumcision, Barbarian, Scythian, slave, or free, but Christ is all and is in all." Then, after dissolving these boundaries, he says, "Therefore, as the chosen of God, holy and beloved, put on compassion, the kindness of mercy, humility, gentleness and patience" (3:12; cf. Gal. 6:16; 1 Pet. 2:9–10).

An especially interesting boundary is drawn in 2 Corinthians 6:14–7:1, which involves the combination of several Old Testament texts: "Therefore, come out from among them and be separate. Do not touch anything unclean, and I will receive you. I will be father to you, and you will be sons and daughters to me, says the Lord Almighty" (6:17–18).[47] By "come out from among them," Paul does not mean "come out from among the [literal] gentiles," but "come out from those whose teachings and actions are contrary to Christ." Likewise, by "anything unclean," Paul does not mean ritually unclean in the Levitical sense but metaphorically unclean due to contamination from immorality, idolatry, and false teaching. Here, Paul uses the Old Testament to differentiate God's people from outsiders in a distinctively Christian way.

Confirming God's Plan to Expand the People of God

Following Jesus's death and resurrection, New Testament writers found passages in the Old Testament that confirm God's plan to enlarge his people by reaching out to the nations. Many of these Old Testament passages have the nations explicitly in view in their original contexts. In other cases, the core idea of an Old Testament text allowed for its application to the inclusion of the gentiles.

The Gospel of Matthew identifies a number of Old Testament passages that speak to God's concern for the nations. For example, when Jesus withdraws to Galilee and stays in the regions of Zebulun and Naphtali (Matt. 4:12–16), this is said to "fulfill" (i.e., bring to its fullest realization) the prophecy of Isaiah that God would honor Zebulun and Naphtali and the whole area known as "Galilee of the nations," as announced with the statement "The people who walk [or "sit" in Matt. 4:16] in darkness have seen a great light" (Isa. 9:1–2).

Another citation of Isaiah appears in Matthew 12:17–21, when Jesus heals many and tells them not to reveal his identity. This fulfills Isaiah 42:1–4, which describes God's "servant" as one who will not cry aloud or make his voice heard but will bring justice to the nations. In the Old Testament, this passage concludes, "Until he sets justice in the earth, and the coastlands await his Torah" (Isa. 42:4). But Matthew 12 reads, "Until he brings justice to victory, and the gentiles will hope in his name" (vv. 20–21). Matthew's wording is adjusted to highlight God's outreach to the gentiles through the servant himself (i.e., his "name").[48]

---

47. See Isa. 43:6; 52:11; 2 Sam. 7:14; Jer. 31:1, 9.
48. On Isa. 42 and the servant as a light to the nations in the New Testament, see Luke 2:32; Acts 26:23; cf. Isa. 42:6; 49:6. See also Acts 13:47; cf. Isa. 49:6.

The Gospel of Matthew includes several outsiders in Jesus's genealogy (Tamar, 1:3; Rahab and Ruth, 1:5), and it cites the "queen of the South" (the queen of Sheba, 1 Kings 10:1) as one who came from the ends of the earth to hear Solomon's wisdom (Matt. 12:42). God's intention to include gentiles among his people is expressed early in the Gospel of Matthew also through John the Baptist's reference to Abraham. In rebuking certain hypocrites from among his own people, John says, "Do not think you can say to yourselves, 'We have Abraham as our father.' For I say to you, God is able to raise up children for Abraham out of these stones" (Matt. 3:9).

Jesus's parable of the good Samaritan in Luke 10:25–37 illustrates how the core idea of an Old Testament passage can be expanded. When a certain teacher of the law asks Jesus, "What must I do to inherit eternal life?" Jesus answers with a question: "What is written in the law? How do you read it?" Jesus seems to be probing not only the teacher's basic knowledge of the law but also his interpretation of its core values. The teacher responds by quoting Deuteronomy 6:4 ("Love the Lord your God . . .") and Leviticus 19:18 ("Love your neighbor as yourself"), which elicits positive feedback from Jesus: "You answered correctly. Do this and you will live." But the teacher, wishing to justify himself (as Luke tells us), asks Jesus, "Who is my neighbor?"—as if to excuse himself for not applying this principle in his dealings with all people.

In the immediate context of Leviticus 19, this teacher's question is not absurd. Rules addressing how to treat one's neighbor appear in Leviticus 19:13–18. Interspersed in this section are commands not to go about slandering "among your people" (v. 16) and not to hate "your brother" in your heart (v. 17). And in verse 18, "You should not take vengeance or hold a grudge against the sons of your people, but you should love your neighbor as yourself." In its original context, therefore, this verse seems to be describing how to relate to a fellow Israelite. Does this principle apply more broadly? If we look a few verses later, we find that it does. Concerning the sojourner who lives in the land, Leviticus 19:34 says, "You should love him as yourself." Already in Leviticus 19, the application of this principle is extended from Israelites to sojourners. So, should the interpreter stop there? Through the parable of the good Samaritan (Luke 10:30–37), Jesus indicates that we should not stop at the sojourner; rather, we should extend the principle of "loving the other as oneself" to anyone in need of a neighbor. Jesus's interpretation broadens the application of Leviticus 19:18 by following a trajectory already present in Leviticus.

Old Testament regulations dealing with ritually "unclean" food served as boundary markers for ancient Israel vis-à-vis other nations (see Lev. 11; Deut. 14:1–21). As part of the New Testament's mission to the gentiles, this boundary is removed. The first stage of this removal occurs in the teaching of Jesus. After discussing a traditional (but not scriptural) practice of ritually washing one's hands before eating, Jesus says that "nothing outside a person that enters him can defile him, but what comes out of a person defiles him" (Mark 7:15). When asked to elaborate, Jesus explains that evil thoughts and deeds come from within, and these are what truly defile (Mark 7:20–23; Matt. 15:10–20). Although Jesus did not apply this principle to food explicitly, the Gospel writer, looking back on these events, comments, "Thus he declared all foods clean" (Mark 7:19).[49] Another stage of this boundary removal is described in Acts 10, when God reveals to Peter that all food is "clean." Peter sees a vision of "unclean" animals and is told to eat. When Peter objects, a heavenly voice tells him, "Do not regard as defiled what God has made clean" (Acts 10:15). This results in Peter's visit to the house of Cornelius and the coming of the Holy Spirit on the gentiles (Acts 10:44–48). Finally, in Acts 15 it is discussed whether gentiles can be saved apart from obedience to the law of Moses. Part of the argument in favor of gentile inclusion is Amos 9:11–12 ("I will rebuild the fallen booth of David . . ."), which is interpreted as confirmation that God will receive gentiles who turn to him through faith in Christ, apart from strict adherence to the external regulations of the Pentateuch (Acts 15:12–21). This goes beyond the specific wording of Amos 9, but the idea of gentile inclusion through the restoration of Davidic kingship finds its ultimate fulfillment in the gospel of Jesus. The setting aside of the distinction between "clean" and "unclean" food is a new development in the New Testament, but even this new development is grounded in the hope of Old Testament prophecy.

As a final illustration, Romans 9–11 offers a discussion of God's plan for Jews and gentiles in light of the gospel, in which Old Testament passages feature prominently. In Hosea 1:11 and 2:23, God pledges to restore Israel as his people, even after he has called them "not my people" in judgment for their sins. Paul takes the idea of God making a nonpeople (Israel under judgment) into a people (Israel restored) and applies it to God's ministry in Christ to bring gentiles (a nonpeople) into the people of God (Rom. 9:25–26). In Romans 10:12–13, Paul cites Joel 2:32—"Anyone who calls on the name of the Lord will be saved"—as evidence that "there is no distinction between Jew and Greek, for he is the same Lord of all, who gives richly to all who call on him." Once the issue of gospel proclamation has been raised, Paul quotes

---

49. This phrase—literally, "cleansing all foods"—can be identified as a comment made by the Gospel writer, rather than as part of Jesus's discourse, partly by its grammar (participle referring all the way back to Jesus as the speaker) and partly because the continuing validity of "clean/unclean" foods is a point of contention among some in the book of Acts, which suggests that Jesus did not speak with absolute clarity on this topic in his earthly ministry.

Isaiah 53:1—"Who has believed our message?"—to show that some (including Israel) did not respond to the gospel (Rom. 10:16). Then he cites Psalm 19:4—"Their sound went out to all the earth . . ."—to prove that everyone (including Israel) heard the gospel (Rom. 10:18). Finally, he uses Deuteronomy 32:21—"I will make you jealous by what is not a nation . . ."—to demonstrate that Israel understood the gospel (Rom. 10:19), since the point of preaching to the nations was to make Israel jealous. Each link in Paul's argument is supported by a passage from the Old Testament.

Having shown that both Israel and the nations have received the good news, Paul appeals to Isaiah 65:1–2 to explain why many gentiles believed but many Jews did not. In Isaiah 64, the prophet asks God to do a mighty act ("If only you would rend the heavens!") to correct the people and thus avert judgment. In Isaiah 65, God responds by pointing out that it is not he who has failed to act but Israel who has failed to seek: "I let myself be sought by those who were not asking. I let myself be found by those who were not seeking" (v. 1). The image of God making himself known to those who were not seeking him is applied to the gentiles (Rom. 10:20). Paul applies God's declaration—"I held out my hands all day to a disobedient people" (Isa. 65:2)—to Israel (Rom. 10:21). At the same time, the story of Elijah illustrates that God preserves a faithful remnant for Israel (Rom. 11:2–5; see 1 Kings 19:18), even if some have been hardened.[50]

In a passage that has been discussed often, Paul uses Isaiah 59:20–21 and 27:9 to corroborate that once the fullness of the gentiles has come in, "thus all Israel will be saved" (Rom. 11:26). This might mean that "all Israel"—that is, gentiles and Jews who believe in Jesus—will be saved by the inclusion of the gentiles. Alternatively, it might mean that after the fullness of the gentiles, the hardening of national Israel will be reversed, and then "all Israel"—that is, all physical descendants of Abraham—will be saved. In either case, a key principle for Paul with regard to Israel is that "the gifts and the call of God are irrevocable" (Rom. 11:29).

Not every text cited by Paul to support gentile inclusion spoke to the issue of gentile inclusion in its original context, and none of these texts in their historical sense were literally about Christian gospel preaching. Still, each Old Testament passage contains a core theological idea that serves as a building block for Paul's argument. Numerous other Old Testament texts are quoted by Paul in the book of Romans.[51] Each quotation reveals some special facet

50. Rom. 11:7–10, citing Deut. 29:4; Isa. 29:10; Ps. 69:22–23.
51. Especially relevant to this chapter is Rom. 15:9–12, which cites 2 Sam. 22:50 (Ps. 18:49); Deut. 32:43; Ps. 117:1; and Isa. 11:10 to confirm God's plan to be glorified among the nations.

of Paul's use of the Old Testament, which is a subject that greatly rewards deeper study.[52]

The examples of inner-biblical interpretation discussed above indicate both an expansion of God's people to include outsiders and an abiding distinction between insider and outsider characteristics. In the Old Testament, Ezra and Nehemiah emphasize the need to keep insiders pure in their religious identity, whereas Ruth and Jonah focus on God's concern for outsiders and the possibility that outsiders might become insiders. The major thrust of the New Testament is the inclusion of all nations through the gospel, with Jesus serving as the criterion for differentiating between inside and outside.

Five key insights can be derived from these examples: (1) The ultimate reason for distinguishing God's people from outsiders is maintaining purity in devotion to God. (2) God's compassion extends to all people. (3) Those who choose to follow God can become part of God's people. (4) God calls everyone to join his people through Jesus. (5) As the gospel reaches all nations, the defining characteristic of God's people is faith in Christ and obedience to his teaching.

Putting the Pieces Together

The theological framework suggested by these inner-biblical insights preserves an inside identity, and by necessity an outside identity, but the major task of insiders is to show God's compassion to all and invite outsiders to join. There is an abiding distinction between what is characteristic of God and what is not. Because we often judge matters wrongly, what we consider inside is sometimes outside, and what we deem to be outside is sometimes inside. Therefore, godliness in human beings manifests itself in humility. Because we are saved *from* "abominations" (what is contrary to God) and *for* "holiness" (what is like God), insider identity is not a privileged status but a life of discipleship that teaches us to become more like Christ. We learn from Jesus (and Ruth) that no person is inherently outside. To follow Jesus means to express God's concern for all people and to welcome everyone as Christ welcomed us (Rom. 15:7).

This theological framework is consistent with Scripture's core values. Through the incarnation, Jesus shows that God reaches down to bring those who are outside (all humanity) into his kingdom. The "weightier matters of the law" (justice, mercy, and faith; Matt. 23:23–24) can be practiced by

52. See the books recommended in chap. 1, n. 25.

anyone, and yet all people fall short of God's glory (Rom. 3:23). This reflects a distinction between godliness and sin and makes clear why everyone should be invited to join. As for the Golden Rule (Matt. 7:12), if I were not part of God's people, I would want to be included, so I should seek to include others. Just as the works of the flesh differ from the fruit of the Spirit (Gal. 5:19–25), so there is a sharp distinction between outside and inside. But the gospel of Jesus, although incompatible with the works of the flesh, calls and empowers the outsider to abandon the works of the flesh and live by the spirit. Inner-biblical insights converge with core Christian beliefs, and these interpretive guides help us to see the particular contribution each passage makes to the Bible's coherent teaching on this topic.

Passages from the Old Testament that highlight God's broad concern for humanity can be interpreted as looking forward to the Christian gospel mission. In their original historical contexts, of course, these Old Testament texts do not envision a worldwide community of faith made up of many nations with diverse customs that differ from the customs of ancient Israel. The formation of the people of God in the New Testament on the basis of Jesus's death and resurrection constitutes a new movement in God's plan for the world. This movement, however, fits coherently with the aspirations and themes of the Old Testament and thus serves as their authentic fulfillment. Without claiming that the entire Christian gospel is contained in any single Old Testament passage, Christians can recognize in many Old Testament texts the conceptual building blocks that make up God's ultimate plan to reach those outside through Jesus. This means interpreting key passages, such as Genesis 12:1–3, Exodus 19:4–6, and Isaiah 42:1–7 with an eye toward what they contribute to the theological framework of the Christian gospel message. Other key themes that can be highlighted through interpretation include kindness to all people, as seen in laws that mandate generosity toward outsiders, and the idea that God graciously receives even small steps in the right direction, as seen with the Ninevites in Jonah.

As we interpret (in the applied sense) the Old Testament, we should be careful to let the details of each passage inform how we think it contributes to the Bible's overall message. For example, both Jethro and Rahab are presented as outsiders who come to acknowledge the greatness of Israel's God (Exod. 18:8–12; Josh. 2:9–13). Yet this does not mean that these two stories should be interpreted simply as Old Testament tokens for the same Christian lesson. Jethro's role as Moses's father-in-law, the advice he gives to Moses about judges, and the fact that he returns to his land (and so is not trying to make himself a judge) give his story a distinctive message. The same level of distinctiveness is true for Rahab, who is introduced as a "harlot," conceals the spies through deception, and eventually joins the Israelites. The fact that both characters are non-Israelites who acknowledge the LORD makes them valid paradigms for God's openness to outsiders, but the specific details of each passage should shape how their stories are interpreted as part of Scripture's overall teaching.

Passages from the Old Testament that focus on maintaining boundaries can be interpreted as teaching how we should distinguish between good and bad, between righteousness and evil. Even when these texts combine diverse elements in their condemnation, such as foreign clothing, idolatry, and child sacrifice, the Christian interpreter should derive lessons related to faith and morals by developing themes such as opposition to idolatry and child sacrifice. As for cultural elements such as the problem of foreign clothing or language, these dimensions of the text should not be applied literally, but they do remind us to consider how our religious and moral choices intersect with other aspects of our lives. Laws in the Pentateuch that emphasize boundary maintenance should not be interpreted in ways that disadvantage those who are outside the faith, but they should instead teach lessons about how to guard against immorality in human interactions. In general, Old Testament passages with insider themes should be used to differentiate the fruit of the Spirit from the works of the flesh in a way that speaks in different cultures to the inner person.

Moreover, beyond notions of abstract right and wrong, the Old Testament's concreteness in dealing with insiders and outsiders encourages us to take responsibility for our beliefs and actions. Yes, we should "love the sinner and hate the sin," but we also embody sinfulness in a way that we need to acknowledge. We all need forgiveness through Christ. As for interpersonal relationships, there may be times when some manner of separation between people is prudent for the sake of preserving holiness. Yet we should not think of ourselves as above others, because Jesus himself came to seek and save the lost. In some circumstances, we should cross boundaries to bring others to God, as did Jesus, who was called a friend of sinners (Luke 7:34; cf. 15:2; 19:7). In other circumstances, we should avoid walking with sinners so as to shun their influence, as wisdom texts advise (e.g., Prov. 1:10–15; Ps. 1:1). The best course of action depends on the specific situation and the likely outcome. The Bible provides wisdom to equip Christians to make such decisions.

In the New Testament, we are told that God does not wish that any should perish (2 Pet. 3:9). Through the gospel, all are invited to come inside the community of faith. Because the LORD opposes the proud, we who are Christians should apply New Testament warning passages first to ourselves (e.g., 1 Cor. 10:12) so that we do not imagine ourselves to be first (insiders) when we are actually last (outsiders). Then, we can invite others to enter through repentance, faith, and discipleship. The categories of inside and outside persist, and although the invitation to join is extended to all, those who do not accept remain outside not because they are unwelcome but because they decide not to belong. If it is true that God does not show favoritism (e.g., Acts 10:34), every person will somehow be given the good news of salvation.[53] This good news comes with the ultimate love and power of God to save all people, but it does not eliminate our free will in responding to God, if we choose to remain outside.

53. I believe this to be true, even if we do not know how or when God accomplishes this. For discussion and alternative views on this topic, see Sanders, *What About Those Who Have Never Heard?*

4

Marriage, Polygamy, and Divorce

Human Well-Being Now, Closeness to God as the Ultimate Goal

I n the ancient societies surrounding Israel and the early church, marriage existed as a recognized union between a man and a woman with special interest in producing "legitimate" children; related concerns included economic stability, community bonds, and interpersonal relationships. In the Old Testament, no instructions are given on how people get married. Biblical writers assume that they do, but the marriage ceremony, like the institution of marriage itself, is presupposed as part of the broader culture.[1] Aspects of marriage in the Old Testament that belong culturally to the ancient Near Eastern world are a period of formal betrothal,[2] the payment of a bride gift from the groom to the bride's family,[3] the practice of a wife joining her husband's

---

1. The Jacob narrative presupposes a formal wedding custom (Gen. 29:22–30), as does the story of Samson (Judg. 14:10–13). Our earliest evidence for written marriage contracts among Jews is the Elephantine (Egypt) papyri of the fifth century BC. In the third or second century BC, Tobit 7:13–14 mentions a Jewish marriage document. Some sense of what a marriage ceremony in ancient Israel might have included can be gleaned from parts of the Song of Songs and Ps. 45. On marriage in the Old Testament, see King and Stager, *Life in Biblical Israel*, 54–57; Borowski, *Daily Life in Biblical Times*, 81–83.

2. E.g., Deut. 28:30; 2 Sam. 3:14; Hosea 2:19–20.

3. E.g., Gen. 24:53; 34:12; 1 Sam. 18:25. In Exod. 22:16–17, a man who entices a virgin to have sexual relations with him must pay her father the bride gift, whether or not the young woman's father allows him to marry her. According to Deut. 22:28–29, a man who takes a virgin woman by force and has sexual relations with her must pay her father the bride gift, marry her,

household, and the general concern for having children.[4] The New Testament likewise reflects assumptions about marriage that were current in its cultural context, which was both Jewish and Greco-Roman.[5] The betrothal process is featured in Matthew's infancy narrative (Matt. 1:18–25; cf. Luke 2:4–6), and Jesus attends a wedding with his mother at Cana in Galilee (John 2:1–11). In his teaching Jesus uses a royal wedding banquet to describe the kingdom of heaven (Matt. 22:1–14; cf. 25:1–13), gives advice on how to behave at a wedding feast (Luke 14:7–11), and refers to himself figuratively as a bridegroom.[6] The marriage practices we see in both testaments were largely inherited from the surrounding cultures, although these practices are often presented by biblical writers in a way that communicates specific values.

Ultimately, modern-day interpreters should look for core ideas expressed through the various biblical perspectives on marriage. Given the strong cultural dimension of this topic, we cannot expect that the assumptions and values embedded in the world of the Bible will be the same as what we recognize today. For example, Old Testament society was patriarchal in a way that is not practiced in any contemporary Western society. Women were often treated as if they were the property of their fathers or husbands.[7] In the commandment against coveting, wives are listed among the items of property that men should not covet (Exod. 20:17).[8] Laws in the Pentateuch are directed at the

---

and provide financial support for her indefinitely. The concern in these texts is for the woman's long-term financial welfare, but they do not address the wrong done to her psychologically or otherwise. In the Middle Assyrian Laws §55, the wife of the sexual assaulter is handed over to be sexually assaulted as punishment for her husband's crime, and the assaulter must pay triple the bride gift, whether or not the victim's father gives her to the assaulter as a wife; see Roth, "Middle Assyrian Laws," 2:359.

4. In many ancient cultures, and perhaps in Old Testament Israel, the bride's family supplied a dowry to the groom. This dowry had to be returned if the husband repudiated the marriage. For example, see the Elephantine Jewish marriage documents; see Porten, "Egyptian Aramaic," 3:154–55, 172, 183–84. For earlier examples outside of Israel, see the Middle Assyrian Laws §29 (Roth, "Middle Assyrian Laws," 356), and the Code of Hammurabi §137–38, 162–64 (Roth, "Laws of Hammurabi," 2:344–45, 356).

5. Kraemer, "Typical and Atypical Jewish Family Dynamics," 130–56, cautions against assuming major differences between typical Jewish and general Roman practices in relation to marriage.

6. Matt. 9:15; Mark 2:19–20; Luke 5:34–35; cf. John 3:29.

7. In the Old Testament, some words and phrases used in describing the marital relationship are baʿal ("owner, lord," referring to the husband; Exod. 21:3; Deut. 22:22), "takers of daughters" (Gen. 19:14; cf. Num. 12:1), and "to (belong) to a man" (Lev. 22:12; Num. 30:6). The New Testament also assumes that a man marries, and a woman is given in marriage (Matt. 22:30; Mark 12:25; cf. Luke 14:20). In Old Testament historical narratives, royal wives and concubines are reckoned as property of the king (e.g., 2 Sam. 3:7; 12:8, 11; 16:21–22; 1 Kings 2:13–25).

8. In Deut. 5:21, however, the wife is distinguished from the man's property in the list of items that men should not covet.

male head of the household. Thus, whereas men are prohibited from coveting their neighbors' wives, there is no explicit prohibition against women coveting their neighbors' husbands. In Ezekiel 16:1–22, God's choice of Israel as his people is likened to a man who finds an abandoned female infant, raises her as a daughter, and then marries her when she comes of age. The cultural reality that stands behind this analogy presents serious ethical problems. In short, the specific narratives and laws covered in the section below communicate divine truths, but they are expressed in problematic cultural contexts.

Biblical Perspectives

Many important aspects of marriage in the Bible could be discussed. I will address three that figure prominently in Scripture, reflect some diversity of practice, and involve significant elements of inner-biblical interpretation: (1) the purpose of marriage, (2) polygamy, and (3) divorce.

The Purpose of Marriage

The Old Testament

In the Old Testament, marriage is the divine means for multiplying people on the earth, a representation of the human need for companionship, an important societal bond, and a potential source of physical delight.

The multiplication of offspring is a key function of marriage in the Old Testament. In Genesis 1, God makes human beings (*'ādām*) in his own image and gives them dominion over the other living creatures (v. 26). This dominion is exercised by humans, created as male and female, when they "are fruitful and multiply" through sexual union (vv. 27–28). After the creation of humanity, all that God made is deemed "very good" (v. 31). Sexual reproduction (which implies marriage) is God's mechanism for filling the earth with people who will rule benevolently on his behalf. In the rest of the book of Genesis, reproduction through marriage is portrayed as a great blessing.[9] As the psalmist says, blessed is the man whose quiver is filled with "the sons of youth" (Ps. 127:4–5). Philip King and Lawrence Stager sum up the main purpose of marriage in ancient Israel as follows: "The chief goal of marriage was to have and raise children, especially boys."[10]

In the garden of Eden (Gen. 2), because it is not good for the "man" (*'ādām*) to be alone, God creates the woman to be a "help" who corresponds to him

9. E.g., Gen. 9:1, 7; 16:10; 17:2, 6, 20; 22:17; 26:4; 28:3; 35:11; 47:27; 48:4.
10. King and Stager, *Life in Biblical Israel*, 54.

(vv. 18–23). The marriage relationship is clearly in view, but the focus is on the need for human companionship. God first tried to meet this need with animals, but they could not serve as suitable companions. The man is to forsake his father and mother in order to "cleave" to his wife (v. 24). This probably refers to sexual union but also symbolizes the priority of marriage over other relationships.[11] In their pristine state, the man and woman are not ashamed of their nakedness (v. 25). After disobeying God, however, they come to recognize their nakedness and feel shame (3:7, 10–11).[12] Did they not previously know that they were naked? What does this say about reproduction and sex? Did rebellion against God damage human sexuality? Were people supposed to reproduce without fully recognizing their "nakedness"? The answers to these questions are not fully clear. Among the curses that result from human disobedience are pain in childbirth, the woman's "desire" being directed at her husband, and the husband's rule over his wife (v. 16). Whereas Genesis 2 depicts marriage as embodying perfect companionship, Genesis 3 shows how human rebellion ruins relationships and seemingly corrupts sexuality.

A primary function of marriage in the Old Testament is the establishment of social and economic well-being. "In marriage the economic motivation was more important than the romantic."[13] The book of Ruth and Proverbs 31:10–31 illustrate the societal blessings of marriage apart from romantic sentiment or sexual desire. For the male authors of Proverbs the most desirable traits in a wife are those that ease the hardships of life and enhance the husband's standing in the community, traits such as noble character, diligence, prudence, and affability.[14] Individuals were encouraged to marry within their own group (e.g., clan or tribe) so as to keep family wealth within the family.[15] The practice of levirate marriage served to preserve the family name and inheritance of the deceased.[16] Several narratives describe alliances between prominent individuals that were created through marriage.[17] Such alliances probably took place among people of lesser means too, albeit on a smaller scale. Because marriage was primarily a family concern with social and

11. In the Old Testament, the wife typically joins the husband's household, rather than the husband literally forsaking his parents. With Jacob (Gen. 28–29) and Moses (Exod. 2–3), the husband joins the household of his wife because he previously fled from his own home.

12. The Hebrew word ʿerwâ, "nakedness," refers to the male or female genital area, and it is often used in idioms that express indecency or something shameful (e.g., Deut. 23:14; 24:1; Hosea 2:9; Lam. 1:8).

13. King and Stager, *Life in Biblical Israel*, 54.

14. Prov. 12:4; 18:22; 19:13–14; 21:9, 19.

15. E.g., Num. 26:33; 27:5–11; 36:5–9; Josh. 17:3–6.

16. Deut. 25:5–10; cf. Gen. 38; Ruth 4.

17. E.g., Judg. 1:12–13 (Josh. 15:16–17); 1 Sam. 18:21, 27; 2 Sam. 3:3, 14; 1 Kings 9:16; 16:31.

economic implications, parents were often instrumental in arranging marriages.[18] In the world of the Old Testament, practical aspects of marriage took precedence over personal feelings.

Although love and desire were not prioritized in the cultural world of the Old Testament, people still experienced these feelings. The Sumerian composition Courtship of Inanna and Dumuzi (ca. 2250 BC) and Egyptian love songs from the second millennium BC (ca. 1300 BC) testify to the fact that people felt romantic love and sexual desire even in ancient cultures that did not rely primarily on such feelings to guide choices about marriage.[19] Proverbs 5:18–19 shows that sexual delight was encouraged within marriage in ancient Israel (cf. Eccles. 9:9). We are told that Isaac loved Rebekah and was comforted by her after his mother's death (Gen. 24:67) and that Jacob's seven years of service for Rachel seemed like only a few days because he loved her (Gen. 29:20). In Deuteronomy 24:5, a newly married man is exempt from military and related service for a year so that he can make his wife glad. And feelings of love and desire are expressed in Psalm 45 as part of a wedding scene (e.g., vv. 10–15).

The best-known Old Testament text that highlights romantic love and sexual desire is the Song of Songs. Until recently, the standard way of interpreting the Song in both Jewish and Christian traditions was as a symbolic depiction of God's love for his people (or the individual soul) and of human devotion for God.[20] It was not until two hundred years ago that a literal reading of the Song gained wide acceptance in the church. I will revisit the possibility of a symbolic interpretation of the Song of Songs in the final section of this chapter. For the present, it suffices to say that nothing in the Song indicates an underlying figurative meaning, and traditional attempts to allegorize the text's specific details result in idiosyncratic flights of fancy. In all likelihood, the Song of Songs was originally composed as a collection of love poems that celebrate sensual human love. Male and female voices take turns expressing longing for one another and extolling each other's physical desirability using an array of images such as fruit, gardens, precious stones, spices, flora, and

18. E.g., Gen. 21:21; 24:1–4; 34:4; 38:6, 8; Exod. 2:21; Judg. 1:12–13 (Josh. 15:16–17); Judg. 14:2. Nevertheless, a powerful man such as David could acquire wives on his own (e.g., 1 Sam. 25:42–43; 2 Sam. 3:2–5; cf. Gen. 38:2).

19. See Matthews and Benjamin, *Old Testament Parallels*, 357–65.

20. For brief overviews of the interpretation of the Song of Songs, see Beaton, "Song of Songs 3," 760–69; Norris, *Song of Songs*, xvii–xx; and Pope, *Song of Songs*, 89–192. See also Matter, *Voice of My Beloved*; and Kaplan, *My Perfect One*. The original King James Version (1611) provides the words "Christ, and his Church" as a heading for the Song of Songs. The Scofield Reference Bible (1917) proposes a twofold interpretation of the Song: first as an expression of pure marital love as ordained in creation and second as describing the relationship between Christ and his heavenly bride, the church.

fauna. Along the way, a word of restraint is spoken to the "daughters of Jerusalem" not to "arouse or awaken love until it pleases" (Song 2:7; 3:5; 8:4). Near the end of the book, a reflective statement on sensual love in the context of marriage ("Place me as a seal over your heart") declares that "love is as strong as death," that "many waters cannot quench love," and that love is more desirable than all the wealth of one's house (Song 8:6–7). The Song of Songs in its historical sense establishes within the Old Testament a positive disposition toward human sexual desire within marriage.

In discussing the erotic imagery of the Song of Songs, it is important to remember that sex outside of marriage is viewed negatively in the Old Testament. It harms individuals, destroys the social order, and leads people away from God. Old Testament laws forbid adultery and associate sex with marriage.[21] In narrative texts, sex outside of marriage leads to personal harm, community conflict, and alienation from God.[22] The negative consequences of adultery for young men are vividly portrayed in the book of Proverbs.[23] Metaphorically, Hosea describes idolatry as a kind of adultery (Hosea 1–3), and Jeremiah condemns Judah's love of false worship by likening it to unbridled sexual passion.[24] The Old Testament recognizes human sexual desire, but the only proper outlet for this desire is marriage.

Overall, marriage in the Old Testament benefits society, provides offspring for family well-being, and represents the fulfillment of our need for human companionship. In Genesis 2–3 we can see marriage as divinely ordained and yet, like everything human, damaged by sin. Romantic love and sexual desire were not the primary structuring elements of marriage in the Old Testament world, but they found a legitimate context for expression in marriage. Occasionally, sexual activity is a cause of ritual impurity,[25] but this does not necessarily imply a negative moral assessment. The Old Testament does not imagine that anyone would choose to live a celibate life. "In Israel celibacy had no status, and not to be married was considered a humiliation."[26]

The New Testament

The New Testament offers a picture of marriage that fits within the first-century Jewish and Greco-Roman world but has been shaped by the teaching

21. E.g., Exod. 20:14; Deut. 5:18; 22:13–21, 22–24; Lev. 20:10.
22. E.g., Gen. 19:4–5; 34:2–3; Num. 25:1–3; Judg. 14:1–2; 16:1–3, 4–21; 19:22–30; 2 Sam. 11:1–15; 13:1–22.
23. E.g., Prov. 5:3–20; 6:24–29, 32–35; 7:4–27.
24. E.g., Jer. 2:20, 23–25, 33; 3:1–3, 6–11, 20.
25. E.g., Exod. 19:15; Lev. 15:16–18; 1 Sam. 21:4–5.
26. King and Stager, *Life in Biblical Israel*, 56.

of Jesus and the apostles. In general, New Testament texts affirm marriage as a divinely ordained relationship. Jesus says that a man and woman united in marriage have been joined together by God (Matt. 19:6). Hebrews 13:4 states, "Let marriage be honored among all, and let the marriage bed be undefiled, for God will judge those who are sexually immoral and adulterers." In other words, the sexual parameters created by marriage should be respected. New Testament writers consistently uphold the prohibition in the Ten Commandments against adultery.[27]

In the "household codes" found in the New Testament,[28] proper behavior in marriage is encouraged according to culturally recognized standards with specific Christian applications, as part of the general respect that should be given to all human institutions.[29] Motives for such behavior include reverence for Christ (Eph. 5:21), concern not to give outsiders occasion to malign God's word (Titus 2:5),[30] and the desire for all people to be saved (1 Tim. 2:2–4). Some of the admonitions that appear in New Testament household codes resemble advice given by Greco-Roman writers on marriage.[31] However, significant differences also exist. For example, whereas Plutarch advises a wife to overlook her husband's sexual misdeeds if he sins with a courtesan or maidservant,[32] Paul insists that no sexual immorality of any kind should be present among God's people (Eph. 5:3). In the household codes, wives are to submit to their husbands, and husbands are to love and care for their wives, all out of a sense of mutual submission, love, and respect.[33] For the sake of Christian edification and witness, marriage provides beneficial order for the household and community.

The New Testament does not emphasize the importance of marriage for propagating the human race or multiplying the size of one's family.[34] In the New Testament, the people of God expand primarily through conversion, rather than through progeny. In fact, discipleship to Jesus takes precedence over family relationships, including marriage.[35] Early Christians likely fol-

27. E.g., Matt. 5:27–28; Mark 10:19; Luke 18:20; Rom. 13:9; James 2:11.

28. Eph. 5:21–33; Col. 3:18–19; 1 Pet. 2:13–17; 3:1–7. See also 1 Tim. 2:9–15; 5:1–16; Titus 2:3–5.

29. 1 Pet. 2:13–17; 1 Tim. 2:1–4; Titus 3:1–2; cf. Matt. 17:24–27; Rom. 13:1–7.

30. Cf. Titus 2:8; 1 Pet. 2:15; 1 Tim. 5:14; 6:1.

31. See Boring, Berger, and Colpe, *Hellenistic Commentary*, 478, 488–90, 530–34. According to the Hellenistic Jewish writer Philo, public affairs of state are entrusted to men, whereas home matters are proper to women (*Questions and Answers on Genesis* 1.26).

32. See Plutarch, *Advice to Bride and Groom* 16; see Babbitt, *Plutarch*, 309.

33. Eph. 5:21–33; Col. 3:12–19; 1 Pet. 2:13–17; 3:1–7.

34. A slightly different emphasis is found in the writings of the first-century Jewish historian Josephus, who says that divine law permits sexual intercourse only within marriage, and this only for the sake of procreation (*Against Apion* 2.199; cf. *Antiquities* 3.274).

35. See Mark 3:31–35 (Luke 8:19–21); Mark 10:29–30 (Matt. 19:29; Luke 18:29–30); Luke 9:59–62 (Matt. 8:21–22); Luke 12:53 (Matt. 10:21); Luke 14:26 (Matt. 10:35–37). Following

lowed standard marriage customs pertaining to bride gifts, dowries, and inheritance. Unlike the Old Testament, however, the New Testament does not devote special attention to the economic aspects of marriage. Although generosity with money and wise stewardship are themes in the New Testament, Jesus did not set down specific rules for the management of family property.[36]

The physical delights of marriage are not particularly celebrated in the New Testament; nothing in the New Testament corresponds to the Song of Songs. In 1 Timothy, for example, the proper adornment for women is good deeds rather than fine clothing (2:9–10). This concern for public modesty is not balanced by any encouragement of private intimacy within marriage. Moreover, it is said that younger widows wish to marry when their pursuit of sensuality leads them away from Christ (1 Tim. 5:11). Another fresh development in the New Testament is the positive place created for certain holy people to live a celibate life.[37] Examples include the widowed prophetess Anna (Luke 2:36–37), Philip's four virgin daughters who prophesy (Acts 21:9), and the apostle Paul (1 Cor. 7:7–8). Jesus himself seems never to have married, and a significant aspect of his miraculous birth is his conception in the womb of the virgin Mary, apart from sexual intercourse (Matt. 1:18–25; Luke 1:26–38). In the book of Revelation, the 144,000 who are redeemed from the earth and follow the Lamb wherever he goes are described as "those who were not defiled with women, for they are virgins" (14:4). In comparison with the Old Testament, the New Testament lessens the emphasis on sexual delight in marriage, and it also establishes the sacred status of celibacy.

An important statement of permission and qualification on marriage is given by the apostle Paul in 1 Corinthians 7. Several points in Paul's argument are not entirely clear, but I will attempt to summarize the main ideas.[38] Paul begins by indicating that he is responding to a question asked by the Corinthians ("concerning the issues about which you wrote"). Paul's initial statement is "It is good for a man not to touch [sexually] a woman" (v. 1).

Jesus is given priority over the marital relationship explicitly in Luke 14:20, 26; 18:29 (cf. Deut. 24:5). Of course, one must still honor one's father and mother (Matt. 15:3–6 [Mark 7:9–13]; Matt. 19:19 [Mark 10:19; Luke 18:20]; Eph. 6:2).

36. See Luke 12:13–15; cf. Mark 12:13–17; Matt. 22:15–21; Luke 20:20–25.

37. Affirmations of celibacy fit within the New Testament's Greco-Roman and Jewish context. Philosophers warned against excessive desire for sex, even with one's spouse. See Dixon, "Sex and the Married Woman," 122–25. Philo describes ascetic Jewish communities in which people renounce sex for the sake of closeness to God—namely, the Therapeutae (*On the Contemplative Life* VIII [68]) and the Essenes (*Hypothetica* 11.14–17). On the Essenes, see also Josephus, *Antiquities* 18.21; *Jewish War* 2.120–21.

38. A useful presentation of the various issues involved in the interpretation of this passage can be found in Loader, *New Testament on Sexuality*, 182–220.

Some take this to be Paul's own formulation, while others argue that Paul is quoting back a statement made by someone in the Corinthian church (cf. 1 Cor. 6:12–13). In either case, Paul's discussion both affirms and qualifies this viewpoint. Paul allows that each person should have his or her own spouse "because of sexual immoralities" (7:2), thus showing that he approves of the basic principle expressed in 7:1. Husband and wife should fulfill each other's sexual needs so that they do not succumb to Satan's temptations and commit sexual immorality outside of marriage (vv. 3–5). But this is merely a concession, not a command (v. 6). Paul wishes that all people would be unmarried, as he is, but he also recognizes that each person has his or her own gift (v. 7). One might take this to mean that Paul regards both celibacy and marriage as gifts. Yet Paul seems to view marriage as a concession, not a gift. Paul is more likely saying that some people have the gift of celibacy, while other Christians have other gifts, such as healing, tongues, or prophecy (see 1 Cor. 12), and that only those with the gift of celibacy will be able to follow Paul's example on this issue.

The rest of Paul's argument in 1 Corinthians 7 follows this same line of thought, applying the general perspective expressed in verses 1–7 to specific cases. Paul advises the unmarried to remain unmarried but encourages them to marry if they cannot practice self-control (cf. Acts 24:25; Gal. 5:23), because it is better to marry than to burn with sexual desire (1 Cor. 7:8–9).[39] To the married, Paul passes along the command of the Lord (Jesus) that the wife should not separate from her husband and the husband should not divorce his wife (e.g., Mark 10:2–12), but if the wife (and perhaps the husband) separates, she (or he) must remain unmarried or be reconciled (1 Cor. 7:10–11). Other topics addressed in this chapter are what a believer should do when married to an unbeliever (vv. 12–16) and how the Christian calling should influence one's station in life (vv. 17–24). In verses 25–35, Paul expands on his advice that Christians should remain unmarried. He is clear that it is no sin to marry (v. 28), but he wants to spare them the trouble in the flesh that comes from marriage (v. 28), because of the "present distress" (v. 26) and because "the time is short" (v. 29). Married people are divided in their concerns between God and their spouse, whereas an unmarried person can be singularly concerned for God.[40] Only the unmarried person is truly holy in spirit and body (v. 34).

39. In Tob. 8:7, Tobias assures God in prayer that he is not taking his wife simply because he is overcome by sexual desire, but rather he is taking her "in truth."

40. According to the first-century-AD Stoic philosopher Epictetus, in light of present circumstances, where so few people devote themselves to wisdom, the Cynic philosopher will probably choose not to marry and have a family so that he can avoid distractions and be entirely given to the service of God (*Discourses* 3.22.67–76). See Oldfather, *Epictetus*, 153–57. Cf. 2 Tim. 2:4: "No

Marriage creates a distraction from full service to the Lord (vv. 32–35). Paul allows a man to marry his intended virgin (or else give in marriage his virgin daughter), but he who has authority over his own will does better if he does not marry (or else give in marriage) his virgin (vv. 36–38). Lastly, Paul grants that a widow may remarry "in the Lord," but he says that she will be happier if she remains unmarried. He acknowledges that this is not a divine command but his own view, and yet he adds, "And I think I also have the Spirit of God," as if to affirm that his advice is indeed spiritually sound (v. 40). Paul permits Christians to marry, but the purpose of marriage is to prevent unbridled desire from leading to adultery or fornication. Celibacy is preferable.

The lukewarm approval of marriage in 1 Corinthians 7 should not be construed as complete rejection. Paul clearly states that marriage is not a sin (vv. 28, 36), and elsewhere he says that to forbid marriage is to engage in false teaching (1 Tim. 4:3). Moreover, Paul affirms Peter's right to have a believing wife.[41] According to Titus 2:5, a woman can be married and also "pure," which means that sexual union in marriage does not constitute impurity.[42] Paul's important discussion of marriage in Ephesians 5 will be addressed in the next section.

In sum, the New Testament affirms marriage as a relationship established by God and as a culturally recognized institution that deserves respect. Although generating offspring is not a major theme, marriage does present an occasion for building up someone else in the faith and bearing witness to Christ. Marriage creates a relationship in which respect and love are conveyed, but it also serves as a defense against the temptation to commit sexual sin. The New Testament places special emphasis on the dangers of sexual desire, and it introduces celibacy as a preferred Christian calling.

Polygamy

The Old Testament

Polygamy is a notorious aspect of marriage in the Old Testament. The specific type of polygamy reflected in biblical texts is "polygyny"—that is,

---

one who serves as a soldier entangles himself in the affairs of this life, so that he can please the one who enlisted him as a soldier."

41. 1 Cor. 9:5; cf. Matt. 8:14; Mark 1:30; Luke 4:38.

42. In 1 Thess. 4:3–5, Paul says that Christians should abstain from sexual immorality and not act out of the passion of desire like gentiles who do not know God. As part of this admonition, Paul says that each man should know how to "obtain" or "control" (*ktaomai*) his own "vessel" (*skeuos*) in holiness and honor. Some take the word "vessel" to refer to his wife, in which case Paul is saying that instead of engaging in sexual immorality, each man should obtain a wife in purity and honor. Others take the word "vessel" to refer to the man's own body, in which case Paul is saying that men should practice self-control.

the practice of a husband having multiple wives. I will offer here only a brief overview of polygamy in the Old Testament, and I will revisit some of the key texts when I address the phenomenon of inner-biblical interpretation on this topic.

The Old Testament assumes polygamy as part of the ancient Near Eastern world in which it was written.[43] Not every adult male could afford more than one wife, but having multiple wives helped provide more children to work the land and also communicated a certain status. Deuteronomy 21:15–17 ("If a man has two wives . . .") protects the rights of the firstborn son in a situation where the mother of the firstborn is not the favored wife. Levirate marriage represents a specific mechanism by which a man might acquire an additional wife (Deut. 25:5–10). Legally, only a man can be the victim of adultery, because a married man who has sexual relations with an unmarried (and unbetrothed) woman can simply take her as another wife.[44] This is why the law against adultery states, "When a man commits adultery with another man's wife."[45] This also explains in part why only the husband can initiate a test for adultery against his wife, but the wife cannot initiate a test for adultery against her husband (Num. 5:11–31).[46] These legal texts illustrate polygamy as the cultural norm that is presupposed by the Old Testament.

Numerous Old Testament narratives show that polygamy was practiced both in the patriarchal period and in later times. Alongside marrying multiple wives of full legal status, men could also take concubines, who were essentially wives without the same legal status or rights of inheritance for themselves or their children. Examples show that polygamy was most common among men of financial means.[47] Polygamy played an important role

43. For examples of laws dealing with polygamy, concubines, and sexual intercourse with maidservants in the ancient Near East, see the Code of Hammurabi §144–47, 170, and the Middle Assyrian Laws §40–41 (Roth, "Laws of Hammurabi," 344–46; and Roth, "Middle Assyrian Laws," 357–58).

44. E.g., Exod. 22:16; Deut. 22:28–29.

45. Lev. 20:10; cf. Deut. 22:22, 23–24.

46. The test for adultery in Num. 5 offered some protection to a wife within a system that strongly favored the interests of the husband. Rather than taking his jealous anger out on his wife through violence, social abuse, or economic oppression, a jealous husband was required to take his wife to the priest, make an offering, and request that the priest subject her to this test for adultery. If God deemed her guilty, it was God who punished her, not the husband. Otherwise, apart from the obvious emotional pain and public humiliation, the innocent woman would be spared harsh treatment from her husband. The procedure restrained worse evil, but it did not reflect perfect justice.

47. E.g., Gen. 4:19, 23; 16:1–16; 21:8–14; 22:20–24; 25:1–6; 28:9; 29:30; 30:3–13; 36:11–12; Judg. 8:30; 10:4; 12:14; 1 Sam. 1:2; 25:42–43; 2 Sam. 2:2; 3:2–5, 7, 13–16; 5:13–16; 12:8, 11;

in Israel's history: the heads of the twelve tribes of Israel—that is, Jacob's twelve sons—were born from their father's multiple wives.[48]

Still, other Old Testament passages place some restrictions on polygamy or present a picture of marriage that fits best with monogamy. For example, Deuteronomy 17:17 states that Israel's king should not marry many wives "lest his heart turn aside," showing that polygamy is not without problems. Certain wisdom texts encourage a man to find contentment with the wife of his youth, which suggests a preference for monogamy (e.g., Prov. 5:18; Eccles. 9:9). Encouragement in the direction of monogamy may be found in the creation account of Genesis 2, in that God meets the man's need for companionship by creating one woman, not many (vv. 18–25). Additionally, the man leaves his father and mother to cleave to his wife, and they become one flesh (v. 24). Perhaps a husband could become one flesh with more than one woman, but the picture of fellowship and intimacy suggested by Genesis 2:24–25 favors an exclusive relationship between one man and one woman.

The New Testament

The New Testament does not presuppose polygamy and does nothing to encourage it. None of its characters are involved in polygamous relationships. At the same time, polygamy is never explicitly condemned for all Christians. The general tenor of the New Testament, however, does not support the practice of polygamy.

At the time of the New Testament, Roman law did not legally recognize polygamy. Sexual promiscuity was common, if poets and historians are to be believed. Augustan legislation of 18 BC sought to strengthen Roman marriage by punishing men who committed adultery with a married woman and punishing women who had sex with anyone other than their husband.[49] Despite the supposedly monogamous nature of Roman marriages, Roman men could have sex with male and female slaves as desired.

Polygamy was not common among Jews in the Roman world, but some evidence exists for polygamous Jewish marriages. In speaking of Herod's many wives, Josephus notes that polygamy was permitted to Jews from early times and that the king was glad to take advantage of this allowance.[50] A Jewish woman named Babatha (second century AD), whose legal documents

---

15:16; 16:21–22; 19:5; 20:3; 1 Kings 11:1–8; 20:3, 7; 2 Kings 24:15; 1 Chron. 1:32; 3:9; 4:5; 7:4; 8:8; 14:3; 2 Chron. 11:21, 23; 13:21; 21:17; 24:3.

48. Gen. 29:31–30:24; 35:16–18.

49. MacDonald, "Marriage, NT," 3:813–14.

50. Josephus, *Jewish War* 1.477; *Antiquities* 17.19–22. Josephus describes levirate marriage in his summary restatement of Mosaic legislation (*Antiquities* 4.254–56). It is not clear whether

were preserved in the Judean desert near the Dead Sea, is known to have married a man (Judah) who already had a wife (Miriam).[51] It is possible that the alarm expressed by Ben Sira over one woman being jealous of another is speaking about the jealousy of rival wives (Sir. 26:6; 37:11). Through their condemnation of polygamists, the Dead Sea Scrolls offer indirect evidence for polygamy among certain Jews. The Damascus Document cites the "principle of creation" from Genesis 1:27 ("Male and female he created them"), Deuteronomy 17:17 (the king should not marry many wives), and the fact that animals went two by two into the ark as proof that God intended for a man to have only one wife, so that those who take two wives are guilty of fornication.[52] There is no reason to think that polygamy was widespread among Jews in the first century AD, but if marriage to more than one woman was possible for a Jewish man in the time of Peter and Paul, it was also possible for a Christian man during this period.

There are no blanket condemnations of polygamy in the New Testament, but the qualifications established for certain leadership roles exclude polygamists. An overseer or elder should be "a man of one woman" (1 Tim. 3:2; Titus 1:6), and deacons should be "men of one woman" (1 Tim. 3:12). It is possible to take these texts as saying that an elder/overseer or deacon must be married (see 1 Tim. 3:4–5), although this runs counter to Paul's example (1 Cor. 9:5) and his advice in 1 Corinthians 7. These passages might simply mean that elders and deacons, if they are married, must be faithful within their marriages (e.g., they should not have sex with slaves).[53] This is a plausible interpretation, although if this were the intent, why do these texts not simply forbid "sexual immorality" or "adultery"? These passages might also refer to second marriages. According to 1 Timothy 5:9, a widow should not be enrolled for church support unless she is "a woman of one man"; that is, she did not remarry after her husband's death. Based on this parallel, Paul might be saying that a man who remarries after his first wife's death cannot serve as an elder or deacon.[54] If so, this requirement for leadership matches

---

this was still being practiced in the first century AD. Philo does not mention the law of levirate marriage. See Feldman, *Flavius Josephus*, 428–29.

51. Kraemer, "Typical and Atypical Jewish Family Dynamics," 137–40.

52. CD 4.20–5.2. See Martínez and Tigchelaar, *Dead Sea Scrolls Study Edition*, 1:557.

53. This view is supported by many modern commentators, for example Marshall, *Critical and Exegetical Commentary*, 156–57; and Knight, *Pastoral Epistles*, 157–59.

54. Most early Christian sources reflect this view, for example Tertullian (ca. 155–225), *To His Wife* 1.7. Hippolytus (ca. 170–235), *Refutation of All Heresies* 9.7. Athenagoras (ca. 135–190), *A Plea for the Christians* 33. Origen (ca. 185–250), *Against Celsus* 3.48; *Commentary on Matthew* 14.22. The Apostolic Constitutions (ca. 400) 6.17; 8.47(17). Augustine (354–430), *On the Good of Marriage* 21. Tertullian, in his later works, *Exhortation to Chastity* 7 and *On*

Paul's personal recommendation in 1 Corinthians 7:8, although he permits Christians in general to remarry if they cannot control themselves (1 Cor. 7:9). In any case, even if polygamy was not the primary issue, these passages certainly disqualify polygamists from serving as elders or deacons.

Given the New Testament's condemnation of sexual immorality and disapproval of earthly status and power, we would not expect any New Testament writer to encourage Christians to acquire multiple wives. But in view of Paul's advice that Christians should normally remain in the life condition in which they were called (1 Cor. 7:20–24), it is unclear what instructions were given to lay Christians who already had more than one wife when they first believed in Jesus.

Divorce

The Old Testament

Divorce does not figure prominently in Old Testament narratives, probably because it was uncommon due to the economic complications it caused. But Old Testament laws assume that divorce happens, and one law in particular focuses on a situation involving divorce (Deut. 24:1–4).

As the syntax of Deuteronomy 24:1–4 makes clear, this law was not given to establish the practice of divorce, but instead it presupposes divorce and regulates one possible scenario. This is described in verses 1–3: A man marries a woman, and she does not find favor in his eyes because he finds in her "something indecent" (*'erwat dābār*). He writes for her a certificate of separation and sends her away, and when the woman marries again, this second husband either divorces her or dies. This scenario serves as the backdrop for the law itself, which is given in verse 4. "When a man takes a woman and marries her, . . . her first husband, who sent her away, is not permitted to take her again as a wife, after she has been deemed unclean, because this would be an abomination before the LORD, and you should not cause sin upon the land which the LORD your God is giving to you as an inheritance" (vv. 1–4). In other words, the point of the law is to prevent the first husband from marrying the woman a second time, not to create divorce as a new category. In fact, the practice of divorce is already presupposed in earlier Old Testament

---

Monogamy 11–12, argues (contrary to 1 Cor. 7) that the prohibition against second marriages extends to all Christians. This clearly was not a standard view, but in his arguments he assumes that all Christians agree that those who marry more than once cannot serve as clergy. Theodore of Mopsuestia (ca. 350–428), *Commentary on 1 Timothy* 3:2, acknowledges that many interpret 1 Tim. 3:2 as excluding from the clergy any man who has married twice, but he favors applying the passage in keeping with the "faithful in marriage" view.

laws.[55] Furthermore, a major concern for ancient Near Eastern divorce law is the resolution of economic complications—for example, whether the divorced woman or her ex-husband gets to keep the dowry.[56] Deuteronomy 24 does not discuss these issues. This further highlights the fact that Deuteronomy 24:1–4 presupposes an existing practice of divorce. To be sure, this passage offers our best glimpse into Old Testament divorce customs, but it is not a charter for divorce.

In order to understand what Deuteronomy 24:1–4 was saying in its original context, several exegetical issues need to be clarified. First, the woman does not find favor in the man's eyes because he found in her "something indecent," 'erwat dābār—literally, "nakedness of a thing." What does this mean? The word 'erwâ, "nakedness," can refer to literal exposure of one's private parts (e.g., Exod. 20:26), exposure meant to shame someone (e.g., Gen. 9:22–23; Isa. 47:3), or illicit sexual relations such as incest (e.g., Lev. 18:6). It is unlikely, however, that the indecency in question is the sexual misdeed of adultery, because the penalty for adultery is death (Lev. 20:10; Deut. 22:20–24). The woman in Deuteronomy 24 does not die but lives to remarry.[57] The exact phrase 'erwat dābār occurs at Deuteronomy 23:14, where it refers to shameful bodily excretions (such as nocturnal emissions or excrement) that God should not see. The idea of nakedness as something shameful can be seen in passages where it is used metaphorically—for example, "nakedness of the land" (Gen. 42:9, 12) or "the shame of your mother's nakedness" for Jonathan's alleged disloyalty to Saul (1 Sam. 20:30). Apparently, the husband divorces his wife in Deuteronomy 24 because he has found something in her that he deems shameful—probably shameful in some sexual sense, although not adulterous. Perhaps she has behaved in a way that he regards as immodest or lewd. In any case, his judgment in the matter gives him the right to initiate a divorce. The text does not necessarily suggest that he is in the wrong, but neither does the woman lose her right to remarry. If she were considered guilty

55. E.g., Lev. 21:14; 22:13; Num. 30:9; Deut. 22:19, 29.

56. See the Code of Hammurabi §137–43 and the Middle Assyrian Laws §37–38 (Roth, "Laws of Hammurabi," 344; Roth, "Middle Assyrian Laws," 357). In the Code of Hammurabi, if the man initiates the divorce, a woman of particular status who has provided her husband with children keeps her dowry and receives other economic compensation. Other scenarios are less favorable for the divorced woman. If the wife is the one who leaves her husband, she is subject to harsh penalties unless it can be demonstrated that her husband refused to have marital relations with her, in which case she receives no penalty and retains her dowry.

57. It is not impossible that a woman who committed adultery might survive because a male adulterer pays a ransom for their lives (cf. Prov. 6:35), or because two witnesses could not be found to confirm the adultery charge (cf. Deut. 17:6). But I doubt any such circumstance stands behind Deut. 24:1–4 because Deut. 24 assumes that the woman remains desirable for marriage, which is unlikely if she has been divorced because of an adultery charge.

of immodest behavior, perhaps she would lose her dowry, but this aspect of divorce is not discussed.

Second, what is the meaning of the phrase "after she has been deemed unclean" or "after she has been defiled" (Deut. 24:4)? Was she "defiled" simply because she married twice? There is no reason why this would be so. What the law seeks to avoid is her first husband marrying her again. The sense, therefore, seems to be that her first husband cannot marry her again after she has already been deemed "unclean" by him.[58] In other words, after he has rejected her once, he cannot get her back.

Third, why is this an "abomination," and how does it bring sin on the land? In Leviticus 19:29, the land is filled with wickedness because of harlotry, and in Exodus 23:33, Israel must be careful lest the Canaanites cause Israel to sin in the land (cf. Lev. 18 on Canaanite sexual sin). Perhaps remarriage after a divorce as described in Deuteronomy 24:1–4 was viewed as a form of harlotry because such an arrangement would allow the husband to lend or rent his wife out to someone else and later take her back. This would have been seen as a form of sexual immorality and therefore strictly forbidden.

Even if these exegetical questions cannot be answered with absolute certainty, the preceding discussion can serve as the basis for some tentative conclusions. I propose that Deuteronomy 24:1–4 functioned in its context to protect the woman's right to remarry, to discourage divorce, and to prevent sexual immorality. If the divorced woman was of the proper age, she would probably remarry for the sake of her own economic survival. The certificate of separation proves to the community that she is free to do so. A husband should not divorce his wife for a trivial reason because he will not be able to remarry her. This discourages divorce. This law also stops a man from using the divorce procedure to profit himself by giving his wife out for "rent" to another man and then taking her back. This prevents sexual immorality that would defile the land. On this difficult passage, two general observations can be made in conclusion: First, Deuteronomy 24 assumes the practice of divorce rather than creating it. Second, the thrust of the passage is to prevent the husband from harming the woman or the community.

The slave law in Exodus 21:9–11 describes another possible divorce scenario and raises an important question about how divorce worked in ancient Israel. If a father sells his daughter as a maidservant, and the man who acquired her designates her as his son's wife, the man who acquired her must treat her as a daughter, not a maidservant. If the son obtains a second wife, he cannot

---

58. This verb in Deut. 24:4 is the *hotpaal* of *ṭmʾ*. Cf. the *piel* use of this verb in Lev. 13:3, "declare him unclean."

reduce his first wife's food, clothing, or marital rights. If he reduces any of these, the first wife (the former maidservant) is permitted to depart from her husband, and her family will not need to pay the debt that caused her to be sold in the first place. In other words, she is granted a divorce. The question this text raises is this: If the woman reports that her rights have been reduced, who compels the man to release her? Presumably, Israel's judges settled disputes of this kind.[59] This suggests that the woman could petition the judges (through a male representative—e.g., her father) to require the man to divorce her. To push this one step further, if a woman who entered marriage with free status had the same rights as a former maidservant, a free woman would also be entitled to petition the judges to compel her husband to divorce her if he was unwilling to fulfill his basic marital duties.[60] Although Deuteronomy 24:1–4 grants the right to initiate divorce to the man alone, Exodus 21:9–11 raises the question of whether women might have had some legal recourse in the case of a wayward husband. Although the situation presupposed by Exodus 21 is negative toward women, the law itself was meant to offer some measure of protection to the woman within this system.[61]

Other Old Testament examples of divorce show the many situations and outcomes that were possible. For example, in Genesis 21:8–14 Sarah tells Abraham to divorce his concubine Hagar, and God commands Abraham to do as Sarah said and divorce her. Yet God also cares for the divorced Hagar and her son (Gen. 21:15–21). King Saul gives his daughter Michal to David as a wife (1 Sam. 18:27), but when conflict arises between the two men, Saul takes Michal away from David and marries her to Paltiel the son of Laish (1 Sam. 25:44). Later, after Saul has died and David has come to power, David demands that Michal be taken away from Paltiel and returned to him (2 Sam. 3:13–16). Powerful men such as Saul and David seem to do as they wish with regard to marriage and divorce. In the book of Ezra, God requires the people to divorce their foreign wives (Ezra 9–10), but in Malachi 2:10–16 God rebukes the people for divorcing their Judean wives. I will discuss these passages below.

The New Testament

The topic of divorce is addressed by several New Testament passages. Each of these presents interpretive difficulties in terms of cultural background,

---

59. E.g., Exod. 18:13–26; 21:22; Num. 35:24; Deut. 1:16; 16:18; 17:12; 25:1.

60. See Tigay, *Deuteronomy*, 221.

61. For another divorce case where the practice regulated is brutal and hostile toward women, but the law itself was meant to offer some measure of protection, see Deut. 21:14.

language, and purpose. Below, I survey the evidence and highlight major points of discussion.

In Mark 10:2–12, some Pharisees test Jesus by asking him if it is lawful for a man to divorce his wife. Because Deuteronomy 24:1–4 clearly allows divorce, some assume that the Pharisees are asking Jesus about the proper grounds for divorce.[62] Alternatively, perhaps they have heard that Jesus takes a stringent position against divorce, so they ask him this question to show publicly that his strict view contradicts Deuteronomy 24. Jesus asks them, "What did Moses command you?" (Mark 10:3). The Pharisees reply that Moses allowed a man to write a certificate of separation and thereby divorce his wife. In his response to them, Jesus asserts that Moses wrote this commandment because of the people's "hard-heartedness" but that at the beginning God made them male and female (Gen. 1:27). Then, citing Genesis 2:24 as proof, he concludes, "What God has joined together, let no one separate" (Mark 10:9). In other words, the reality of marriage as defined by God's work in creation takes precedence over Deuteronomy 24:1–4. Later, when the disciples ask about this, Jesus explains, "Whoever divorces his wife and marries another woman commits adultery against her [his first wife, to whom, in God's eyes, he is still married], and if a woman divorces her husband and marries another man, she commits adultery" (Mark 10:11–12). In this passage, a woman divorced by her husband is identified as the victim of adultery ("against her"), and it is assumed that a woman can divorce her husband. These points reflect the broader Roman context.[63]

The same conversation between Jesus and the Pharisees is reported in Matthew 19:3–12 with some notable variations. First, the Pharisees ask Jesus specifically about the grounds for divorce: "Is it lawful for a man to divorce his wife *for any reason*?" (v. 3, emphasis added). Second, Jesus makes his statements based on Genesis 1:27 and 2:24 ("What God has joined together, let no one separate") in direct response to this initial challenge. The Pharisees follow up with another question, in which they (not Jesus) refer to Moses's "command" to write a certificate of separation. It is Jesus (not the Pharisees) who introduces the concept of permission—namely, that Moses "permitted" them to divorce because of their "hard-heartedness." Jesus's wrap-up statement, which is not given later to the disciples but concludes his discussion

62. Later rabbinic texts report discussions on the proper grounds of divorce that range from very restrictive views to very permissive views. See Mishnah Gittin 9:10 (Danby, *Mishnah*, 321); and Sifre Deuteronomy 269 (Hammer, *Sifre*, 263–64).

63. By the time of Jesus, some provision was made for Jewish women to initiate a divorce process, but the assumption that a woman could carry through a divorce reflects the influence of Roman practice. Loader, *New Testament on Sexuality*, 56–57, 254, 257.

with the Pharisees, is as follows: "Whoever divorces his wife, except for 'sexual immorality' [*porneia*], and marries another woman commits adultery" (Matt. 10:9). In this statement, the wife is not identified as the victim of adultery, no indication is given that a woman can divorce her husband, and "sexual immorality" (probably sex outside of marriage) is introduced as an exception to Jesus's restrictive position on divorce. The addition of the phrase "except for sexual immorality" likely alludes to Deuteronomy 24:1 and directly answers the Pharisees' initial question in Matthew 19:3. Each of these elements points to a distinctively Jewish setting for Matthew's report, rather than to the more general Roman setting of Mark's version. Later, the disciples declare that, if this is true, it is better not to marry. Jesus answers with a statement about people who make themselves eunuchs for the kingdom of heaven (Matt. 19:11–12). The inner-biblical dimensions of these texts will be discussed in the next section.

Two other passages in the Gospels report sayings of Jesus on divorce. In the Sermon on the Mount, Jesus comments on Deuteronomy 24:1–4: "It was said: Whoever divorces his wife, let him give to her a [certificate of] separation. But I say to you: Anyone who divorces his wife, with the exception of a matter of sexual immorality [*porneia*], causes her to commit adultery, and whoever marries a divorced woman commits adultery" (Matt. 5:31–32). As with Matthew 19, Matthew 5 includes an exception for sexual immorality ("matter of *porneia*"). Matthew 5 focuses on what the man's sinful action does to the woman. If a man subjects his wife to an illegitimate divorce and she marries another man, she is made to commit adultery because her first marriage was not properly ended. As a result, the other man who marries this divorced woman commits adultery. Luke 16:18 is worded similarly, although there is no exception clause: "Anyone who divorces his wife and marries another woman commits adultery, and the one who marries a woman who was divorced by a man commits adultery." Here, the text focuses on how the man's actions affect him. Whereas Mark 10:11–12 and Luke 16:18 lack exception clauses, both Matthew passages (Matt. 5:31–32; 19:9) allow for divorce in the case of "sexual immorality."

In 1 Corinthians 7, the apostle Paul offers counsel on divorce based on the teachings of Jesus and Paul's own pastoral wisdom. For Christians who are married, Paul says in the name of the Lord (Jesus) that a wife should not depart from her husband—and that if she has departed, she should remain unmarried or be reconciled to her husband—and that a husband should not forsake his wife (vv. 10–11). The language assumes a Roman cultural setting where either the man or the woman could carry out a divorce by leaving.[64] After this, Paul gives his own counsel that a believer should not divorce an unbelieving spouse who consents to stay (vv. 12–13). One reason given is that the believer brings a sanctifying witness to the marriage and provides a holy presence for the children (v. 14).[65] However, if the unbelieving spouse abandons the marriage, the believer is permitted to let them go. In such a case, the believer "has not been bound" to the marriage because "God has called you in peace" (v. 15). Paul's comments on divorce fit within his broader set of instructions on marriage in 1 Corinthians 7.

Inner-Biblical Insights

Whereas the above survey of biblical perspectives focused on giving the range of ideas present in Scripture, the discussion below attempts to explain passages where some form of inner-biblical interpretation takes place. I pay special attention to examples that offer interpretive insights for our own reading of Scripture.

The Purpose of Marriage

I will discuss two passages in the New Testament that speak to the purpose of marriage with reference to previous biblical traditions. In the Gospels, Jesus touches on the future of marital unions in response to a question about levirate marriage and the resurrection. In his letter to the Ephesians, Paul cites Genesis 2:24 to elaborate on the relationship between husband and wife in comparison with Christ's relationship to the church.

Jesus makes an important statement on marriage when a group of Sadducees ask him about levirate marriage and the afterlife.[66] What would happen, ask the Sadducees, if a woman married seven brothers in succession because each brother died childless after taking her as a wife? If this woman was married to all seven men, whose wife would she be at the resurrection? For the Sadducees, this conundrum highlights the implausibility of the resurrection. The major thrust of Jesus's reply is a scriptural defense of bodily resurrection (Mark 12:26–27; see chap. 6). But he also addresses the topic of marriage. According to the account given in Mark, Jesus says, "When people

64. See Instone-Brewer, *Divorce and Remarriage*, 72–74, 190–91.
65. Cf. 1 Pet. 3:1; Mal. 2:15.
66. Mark 12:18–27; Matt. 22:23–33; Luke 20:27–40. On levirate marriage, see Deut. 25:5–10. Levirate marriage is a clear example that is grounded in Scripture. The basic issue is remarriage in general.

are raised from the dead, they neither marry [men do not marry] nor are given in marriage [women are not given in marriage], but they are as angels in the heavens" (Mark 12:25). In other words, the issue raised by the Sadducees will not present any problems because marriage will not exist at the resurrection. The Gospel of Matthew records Jesus's statement in much the same words (Matt. 22:30).

In the Gospel of Luke, however, Jesus's explanation is given in a longer form that gives deeper insight into the purpose of marriage. In Luke 20:34–36, Jesus says, "The sons of this age marry and are given to marry, but those who have been deemed worthy to attain that age and the resurrection from the dead neither marry nor are given in marriage; for they are no longer able to die, because they are equal to angels and are sons of God, being sons of the resurrection." Several aspects of this passage are illuminating for our topic. First, people no longer marry at the resurrection because "they are no longer able to die." The implication is that people marry in this age because they need to procreate to preserve the human race. But since people will not die in the future age, procreation will not be needed, and therefore marriage will be obsolete.[67] In other words, procreation to preserve humanity is a fundamental purpose of marriage. Second, the "sons of the resurrection" are "equal to angels" and "sons of God."[68] This suggests that people at the resurrection will not need to marry for the sake of identity, livelihood, fellowship, or any other need that is presently met through marriage. Every person at the resurrection will be a child of God, and that will be sufficient. Third, "those who have been deemed worthy to attain that age and the resurrection from the dead neither marry nor are given in marriage." The wording of this statement could easily mean that anyone who wishes to be considered worthy of the future age should abstain from marriage in the present age. This interpretation is unlikely, however, because people will not become immortal until the next age, so marriage remains necessary while procreation is still needed. Still, Jesus's words appear to encourage celibacy.[69] There is no reason to conclude that Luke 20:34–36 teaches that Christians are forbidden to marry in this life.

67. This notion finds a parallel in the early Jewish text 1 Enoch, where fallen angels are rebuked for behaving like humans and taking wives, whereas formerly they were spiritual and immortal, possessed eternal life, and therefore did not need wives (1 En. 15:6–7). See Charlesworth, *Old Testament Pseudepigrapha*, 1:21.

68. The "sons of God" obviously include women, as indicated by the phrase "given in marriage."

69. According to Cyprian (ca. 200–258), for example, Christians who dedicate themselves to lifelong virginity possess now the glory of the resurrection and already are what the rest of us someday will become (*On the Dress of Virgins* 22). See also Methodius of Olympus (ca. 250–311), *The Banquet of the Ten Virgins* 2.7. Both of these authors clearly affirm the validity

But Jesus's answer reveals that someday the institution of marriage will no longer be needed.

The teaching of Jesus on the purpose of marriage receives further clarification from his final remark in Matthew 19:1–12 on divorce. After Jesus states his restrictive view on the topic (vv. 8–9), the disciples propose that if what Jesus says is true, perhaps it is better not to marry at all (v. 10). Jesus responds to them: "Not all people are able to receive this statement, but only those to whom it has been given. For there are some eunuchs who were born this way from their mother's womb, and there are some eunuchs who were made eunuchs by people, and there are some eunuchs who made themselves eunuchs for the sake of the kingdom of heaven. Let the one who is able to receive it, receive it" (vv. 11–12). Although some in the early church took Jesus's statement to mean that Christians should castrate themselves to become literal eunuchs, the mainstream interpretation in preserved Christian sources is that Jesus was speaking metaphorically.[70] In other words, just as some people are born with a physical disability that renders them a eunuch, and some are castrated by others, some Christians will choose to live as if they were eunuchs by renouncing sex and marriage. Jesus encourages this behavior by saying "Let the one who is able to receive it, receive it" and by indicating that those who choose a celibate life do so "for the sake of the kingdom of heaven" (v. 12). This agrees with what Jesus says about marriage at the resurrection in Luke 20:34–36. At the same time, Jesus also says, "Not all people are able to receive this statement, but only those to whom it has been given" (Matt. 19:11). Only those to whom God has given this gift are able to become "eunuchs for the kingdom of heaven" (cf. 1 Cor. 7:7). What Jesus teaches about marriage, both in response to the Sadducees' question about levirate marriage and in Matthew 19, affirms marriage for this life but also relegates marriage to the status of a temporal (not eternal) good.

As for Paul, the apostle interprets Genesis 2:24 as a model for marriage in Ephesians 5:21–33. Like Jesus, Paul looks to this model to derive a principle for practical instruction.[71] In Ephesians 4–5, Paul urges the Christians in Ephesus not to live as the gentiles do but to conduct themselves as imitators of God. They should not be foolish or drunk with wine (Eph. 5:15–18) but instead should be filled with the Spirit (v. 18). The command to be filled with the Spirit is followed by a series of participles that elaborate on this idea: "speaking to each other in psalms, hymns, and spiritual songs" (v. 19); "singing and making

---

of Christian marriage in the present age. This affirmation is defended against critics of marriage by Clement of Alexandria (ca. 160–215), *Stromateis* 3.6.45–49.

70. See Loader, *New Testament on Sexuality*, 442.

71. Cf. Matt. 19:4–6; Mark 10:6–9.

music in your heart to the Lord" (v. 19); "giving thanks always" (v. 20); and "submitting to one another out of reverence for Christ" (v. 21). This leads to a series of household instructions addressing wives (5:22–24, 33), husbands (5:25–33), children (6:1–3), fathers (6:4), slaves (6:5–8), and masters (6:9).[72]

As the series begins with the general admonition to submit to one another (5:21), the overall tone of the passage is that each person fulfills his or her role out of reverence for Christ in a spirit of mutual submission. Nevertheless, the duties prescribed follow standard expectations for the Roman world, albeit with specifically Christian motives. The section addressed to wives borrows its verb from the initial participle in 5:21: "submitting to one another . . ." "Wives, [submitting] to their own husbands as to the Lord" (v. 22). In keeping with the practice of instructing everyone according to their assigned roles, the section addressed to husbands begins with a new finite verb: "Husbands, love your wives" (v. 25).

The key to understanding Paul's use of Genesis 2:24 is his metaphorical description of the church as Christ's body. In this analogy, Christ is the "head," and the church is the rest of the "body." Wives are to submit to their husbands, just as the church, the "body," submits to Christ, the "head" (Eph. 5:22–24). Paul's first words directed to husbands focus on the Christ-church aspect of this complex analogy. Husbands are to love their wives as Christ loved the church and gave himself up for it (v. 25), so that he might sanctify and purify it with the washing of water by the word, so as to present the church to himself as glorious, holy, and unblemished, without stain or wrinkle (vv. 26–27). Then Paul returns to speaking directly about husbands and wives, and he also comes back to the body metaphor: Husbands should love their wives as they love their own bodies. To love one's wife is to love oneself. People do not typically mistreat their own bodies; rather, they take care of their bodies, as Christ did for the church (vv. 28–29). A core theological idea is then stated that justifies this analogy: We Christians are members of Christ's body (v. 30). Paul seems to press this point home because he is about to quote a biblical prooftext that deals with human bodies, and he wants to make clear its application both to human marriage and also to Christ's relationship to the church.

Paul quotes Genesis 2:24 to demonstrate that the husband and wife are one body (Eph. 5:31). The important phrases for Paul are that the husband "will be joined to his wife" and that the two "will become one flesh."[73] In terms of human marriage, the fact that the husband and wife become one

---

72. For New Testament household codes, see n. 28.

73. In 1 Cor. 6:15–16, Paul uses Gen. 2:24 to argue that a Christian man should not have sex with a prostitute, because by doing so, he would become one flesh with her, whereas his body is already a member of Christ.

flesh, which is the equivalent of their sharing one body (v. 30), means that they should care for each other as they care for themselves. This is the principle that Paul derives from Genesis 2:24. In the context of this household code, a husband will care for his wife (as he cares for himself) by loving her, and a wife will care for her husband (as she cares for herself) by showing reverence for him (Eph. 5:33). This is how Paul applies this principle to the situation of his first-century church. In addition to this practical application, Paul says that Genesis 2:24 contains a great "mystery" in that it reveals the oneness of Christ and the church (Eph. 5:32).

The intermingling of these two interpretations of Genesis 2:24, the mystical and the practical, enriches the picture of marriage that emerges. Paul charges husbands to love their wives "thus" (Eph. 5:28): as Christ loved the church. This divine love is described not only as Christ giving himself up for the church (v. 25) but also as the cleansing and sanctification of the church to make it an offering that Christ presents to himself (vv. 26–27). By this analogy, a husband should love his wife by setting aside his own needs to help her live a holy life. The primary focus of this passage is not companionship but drawing closer to God. In Ephesians 5:21–33, marriage is a unique context for spiritual ministry in the life of another person.

Polygamy

Polygamy is generally presupposed in the Old Testament. It is essentially absent from the New Testament. There is no explicit commentary on polygamy anywhere in Scripture. But consistently negative portrayals of polygamy in Old Testament narratives function as implicit criticism. In the New Testament, the translation of a key Old Testament passage into Greek reveals a subtle shift of thinking in the direction of monogamy.

In the Old Testament, polygamy is highlighted as the cause of conflict with such regularity and consistency that we cannot help but conclude that biblical narrators disapprove of it. The first character in Genesis who is said to have taken two wives is Lamech, the near descendant of Cain. A particular point is made of his polygamy: "And Lamech took to himself two wives" (Gen. 4:19). Like Cain, Lamech is implicated in violence, saying to his wives, "I killed a man for wounding me, a youth for striking me. If Cain will be avenged sevenfold [see v. 15], Lamech will be avenged seventy-seven-fold" (vv. 23–24). This initial story sets the stage for what follows.

The practice of taking multiple wives generates conflict at key moments throughout Genesis. For example, Abraham takes Hagar as a concubine alongside his wife, Sarah, and this leads to hostility between the two women and the expulsion of Hagar and her son, Ishmael, who is to become a nation hostile to Israel (Gen. 16:1–12; 21:9–21). Conflict likewise arises in connection with Jacob's polygamous behavior (30:15). The LORD gives Leah children to compensate for the fact that Jacob prefers Rachel (29:30–31). This leads to competition between the sisters to see who can bear more children, which involves each wife giving a handmaid to Jacob as a concubine (30:1–24). Jacob favors Joseph, his son by Rachel (37:3), along with Rachel's other son, Benjamin (42:4; 44:30–34). As a result, Joseph's half brothers resent Joseph and eventually sell him into slavery. Joseph's exploits in Egypt and his eventual reconciliation with his brothers take center stage for the rest of the book. Even after they have made peace, however, Joseph continues to favor Benjamin (Gen. 45:22). Although Jacob's polygamy helped create the nation of Israel, his multiple marriages produced bitterness between his wives and conflict among his children.

References to polygamy follow this same pattern in later Old Testament narratives. After Gideon turns down kingship for ostensibly pious reasons (Judg. 8:23), he immediately takes for himself the wealth of a king (8:24–26), builds a golden ephod that promotes idolatry (8:27), and acquires many wives (8:30). It seems that Gideon wants the privileges of kingship without the prescribed responsibilities (see Deut. 17:14–20). The outcome of Gideon's polygamy is that one of his sons, Abimelech, slaughters his half brothers in order to make himself king (Judg. 9:5–6), causing many deaths during his wicked rule (9:6–57). Conflict caused by polygamy likewise opens the tragic tale of Jephthah (Judg. 11:1–3). In the story of Samuel's birth, discord between the wives of Elkanah drives Hannah to the temple, where she dedicates her son to the LORD's service (1 Sam. 1:2–11). David's acquisition of wives appears to pass without criticism at first,[74] but the text's negative assessment of David's behavior becomes apparent when his kingdom nearly collapses after his sin against Bathsheba and Uriah (2 Sam. 11). The immediate cause of this near collapse is Absalom's rebellion (2 Sam. 15), which is precipitated by an act of hostility by a son of David by one wife (Amnon, son of Ahinoam) against a daughter of David by another wife (Tamar, daughter of Maacah), who is avenged by her full brother (2 Sam. 13). Conflict and ultimately death surround the accession of Solomon to the throne, because his half brother Adonijah (son of Haggith) claims the right to kingship against Solomon, son of Bathsheba (1 Kings 1:5–53; 2:13–25). Eventually, Solomon worships false gods in connection with his marrying multiple foreign wives (1 Kings 11:1–8). Other examples could be given.

74. 1 Sam. 25:42–43; 2 Sam. 3:2–5, 13–16; 5:13–16.

In sum, the writers of Old Testament narratives make a point to highlight the destructive effects of polygamy on Israel's ancestors and leaders. Although the practice of polygamy is allowed and even used by God (as, e.g., a wayward Samson was used), biblical writers consistently show its negative impact on families and societies. When a man marries more than one woman, conflict arises between the wives, and seeds of hostility are planted among the children. Without offering an explicit condemnation, Old Testament writers criticize polygamy in the way they portray it. The problem with polygamy is not just unchecked sexual desire but also lust for power and status.

While not forbidding polygamy outright, the New Testament speaks of marriage in a way that fits best with monogamy, and the values of the New Testament discourage men from seeking more than one wife. This shift in the direction of monogamy is probably reflected in the translation of Genesis 2:24 as it appears in the Gospels and Paul's Letters. In Hebrew, Genesis 2:24 says, "Therefore a man will leave his father and mother and cleave to his wife, and they will become one flesh." In the ancient (pre-Christian) Greek translation of the Old Testament known as the Septuagint, the conclusion of this verse was rendered into Greek as "and *the two* will become one flesh." This text is quoted four times in the New Testament,[75] and in each case the translation follows the wording of the Septuagint: "*the two* will become one flesh." Perhaps without giving the matter much thought, by using "the two" (i.e., the man and the woman) instead of simply "they," the Greek translator of the Septuagint revealed his assumption that marriage joined "two" people together, not a husband plus many wives. This seems to be the concept of marriage that underlies the New Testament. In a subtle way, the consistent adoption of this translation supports the New Testament's general orientation away from polygamy and toward marriage as the union of two people.

Divorce

Passages that exhibit inner-biblical interpretation illustrate both the situational nature of divorce in the Bible and some of the core ideas associated with marriage.

Legal traditions and early narratives that deal with marriage and faithfulness to God were applied to the topic of divorce in the postexilic period. The major issue at stake was the preservation of Israel's religious identity. Two different perspectives on divorce emerged from these scriptural traditions in postexilic books.

75. Matt. 19:5; Mark 10:7–8; 1 Cor. 6:16; Eph. 5:31.

On the one hand, the campaign against intermarriage reported in Ezra and Nehemiah required that the Judeans divorce their "foreign" wives.[76] The "holy seed" was being intermingled with the surrounding peoples.[77] This was taking place through intermarriage with non-Judean women, which caused the people to turn away from God.[78] Foreign marriages corrupted God's "covenant" with the priests and Levites (Neh. 13:29). In response, Ezra led the people to make a "covenant" to divorce their foreign wives and send them away, along with their children (Ezra 10:3).

On the other hand, in Malachi 2:10–16 the prophet condemns those who have divorced their Judean wives in order to marry the daughters of a "foreign" god (v. 11). These Judean men have profaned the Lord's "holiness" (v. 11), in part because they have acted treacherously against the wives of their youth, who are described relationally as "your companion" and theologically as "the wife of your covenant" (v. 14).[79] God made them "one" with their Judean wives (cf. Gen. 2:24) and left a remnant of his Spirit in their union (cf. Gen. 2:7; 3:16–21) because he sought from these marriages godly "seed"—that is, offspring (Mal. 2:15).[80] Because the men of Judah are divorcing godly wives to marry idolatrous women and yet have covered the altar with tears because God has rejected their offerings (v. 13), the prophecy concludes, "For if someone hates his wife and sends her away, says the Lord God of Israel, then he covers his clothing with violence, says the Lord of hosts" (v. 16).[81]

The primary concern for these passages is keeping God's people faithful to their sacred covenant. Intermarriage threatened the covenant by creating strong cultural links to foreign worship. In Ezra, it is necessary for the Judeans to divorce their foreign wives to keep faith with God. In Malachi, it is an act

76. Ezra 10:3–5, 10–11, 14–16.

77. Ezra 9:2; Neh. 9:2; cf. Deut. 7:6.

78. Neh. 9:2; 13:30; cf. 1 Kings 11:1.

79. Judah's sin is also described as profaning the covenant of their fathers (v. 10); see Exod. 23:32; 34:12; Deut. 7:2.

80. The Hebrew text for v. 15 is difficult. For an interpretation similar to what I am proposing, see Petterson, *Haggai, Zechariah & Malachi*, 344–45, 352–54.

81. The Hebrew text is unclear. The word "if" (lacking in the Masoretic Text) appears in both the Septuagint and the Dead Sea Scroll fragment 4QXII[a]. The Hebrew word for "hates" (*śnʾ*) in the Masoretic Text is vocalized as a third-person perfect, but it could also be construed as a participle or infinitive. Some translations read the participle and add the subject "I" ("I hate divorce"). The Septuagint gives "send away," as a second person, and 4QXII[a] reads "hate," as a second person. Each text was probably trying to resolve the syntactic obscurity. I am reading *śnʾ* as a participle in view of the third-person "covers," and I am taking "if" in combination with *waw* + "cover" as a conditional clause, with the sense: "If a man divorces his wife, it is like he covers my altar, not with his hypocritical tears, but with violence." The word "hate" is often used for a husband's decision to divorce his wife (Deut. 21:15–17; 22:13, 16; 24:3). On divorce as "sending away," see Deut. 24:1, 3, 4.

of faithlessness to divorce one's Judean wife to marry a foreigner. In the end, both texts draw on previous biblical traditions and both deal with divorce. But neither is fundamentally about divorce. Each one emphasizes faithfulness to God as the first priority, which determines whether divorce is required or condemned. Still, Malachi 2:10–16 offers a theologically rich concept of marriage in which the husband and wife are joined by God in covenant and companionship, and marriage serves covenant purposes.

The book of Jeremiah invokes the divorce law found in Deuteronomy 24:1–4 to impress on Judah the seriousness of their sin. Jeremiah 3:1 begins a series of reflections on Judah's turning away and possible repentance with the following word of the LORD: "If a man sends away his wife and she goes from him, and then she is joined to another man, can he return to her again? Would not the land be polluted? You have committed adultery with many lovers. Can you return to me?" The implied answer is no. When a man divorces his wife and she marries another man, even if she becomes available again for marriage, her first husband can never remarry her. In the same way, the people of Judah have turned away from the LORD and joined themselves to foreign gods, thus showing that they are "divorced" from the LORD and "married" to another deity (cf. Jer. 3:8 for Israel). According to Deuteronomy, the husband cannot take the wife back; or, as Jeremiah says, the LORD cannot return to Judah. Such an act would defile the land (Jer. 3:1; Deut. 24:4). The point of this analogy is that Judah's unfaithfulness has created an irreparable breach with the LORD. At least, this is the logical conclusion based on the principle of Deuteronomy 24. What is remarkable about Jeremiah's use of this analogy is that the LORD plans to restore Judah.[82] Similar analogies of unfaithfulness, divorce, and restoration appear in the books of Isaiah (50:1; 54:5–7) and Hosea (2:2, 16–23). In these prophetic books, God's compassion for his people supersedes the rule that prevents the "divorced" nation from being restored to the LORD.

As for the New Testament, Jesus's teaching on divorce establishes the trajectory for how this topic is approached. Rather than addressing divorce primarily as a legal problem, Jesus recenters the conversation so that marriage itself is the primary issue. If we understand marriage correctly, a proper attitude toward divorce will follow.

Both Mark 10:11–12 and Luke 16:18 condemn divorce without any stated exceptions. The major theme of Jesus's teaching is that marriage creates a bond between husband and wife that people should not break. Still, these statements should probably be taken with a measure of hyperbole, as when

82. E.g., Jer. 3:14–18; 23:3–8; 30–33.

Jesus forbids public prayer (Matt. 6:5–6) or requires anyone who lusts to gouge out an eye (Matt. 5:27–29). When we turn to the Gospel of Matthew, we see that Jesus qualifies his condemnation by allowing divorce in the case of *porneia*, "sexual immorality" (5:31–32; 19:9).

How do we explain this addition in Matthew? Perhaps Jesus mentioned the allowance for sexual immorality in a conversation where the phrase ʿ*erwat dābār*, "nakedness of a thing," in Deuteronomy 24:1 was explicitly discussed, and this was the basis for Matthew's addition.[83] The exception clause that appears in Matthew shows that the absolute prohibitions in Mark and Luke express Jesus's core teaching on divorce—namely, that God intends marriage to last for life—but these absolute prohibitions were not meant to be comprehensive legal rulings.

In fact, Jesus's position on divorce is based not really on his legal interpretation of Deuteronomy 24:1–4 but on his theological understanding of marriage as rooted in creation. In Matthew 5:31–32, the requirement to write a document of separation according to Deuteronomy 24 is introduced by "it was said," whereas Jesus's warning against divorce is prefaced with "but I say to you." Jesus sets his own teaching against Deuteronomy 24, at least as it was being applied in his context.

The Old Testament basis for Jesus's view is explained in Matthew 19:4–6: Since the beginning of creation, God has made people male and female (Gen. 1:27). For this reason, a man will leave his father and mother and be joined to his wife, and the two will become one flesh (Gen. 2:24). Therefore, because God has joined the couple together, making them one flesh, people should not seek to separate them through divorce. Even if the exception for sexual immorality derives ultimately from Deuteronomy 24:1, the key verses for Jesus are Genesis 1:27 and 2:24.

The problem was not simply that Jesus's opponents were interpreting Deuteronomy 24:1 incorrectly. Rather, they were attempting to address the topic of divorce based solely on a legal restriction, without reference to God's design for marriage in creation. Of course, the law served a useful function— namely, to provide some measure of protection for the woman in a situation caused by hardness of heart (Matt. 19:8; Mark 10:5). The teaching point of Deuteronomy 24:1–4 as Christian Scripture can be sought in this function.

---

83. According to Keener, *And Marries Another*, 112, the exception for sexual immorality may not have been part of this particular conversation but was added by the Gospel of Matthew in keeping with Jesus's teaching as an act of "translating" the message for a specific audience. On the other hand, Instone-Brewer, *Divorce and Remarriage*, 134–36, argues that the reference to ʿ*erwat dābār* / *porneia* was part of the original conversation underlying Mark 10 *and* Matt. 19 and that Mark omitted this reference when he abbreviated the conversation.

For Jesus, however, the theological reality of marriage as depicted in Genesis 1–2 should guide our thinking about divorce.

In 1 Corinthians 7, Paul follows the teaching of Jesus on divorce, but he also appeals to core biblical values to address a new situation specific to his context. First of all, when Paul says that he is speaking to "those who have married" (v. 10), he seems to mean "those among you who are Christians married to other Christians." To this group, he passes on what he learned by tradition about Jesus's teaching ("not I, but the Lord," v. 10).[84] Paul's admonition based on what Jesus said is that the wife should not depart from her husband, and the husband should not forsake his wife (vv. 10–11).

After this, Paul turns to address a new situation, one that would not have arisen among Jesus's Jewish audience in quite the same way as it did among the new converts in Corinth. What if a member of the church at Corinth is married to someone who is not a Christian? Paul does not seem to have a tradition from Jesus to answer this question ("I, not the Lord," v. 12). Yet Paul is able to draw on Jesus's core teaching on marriage—namely, that God intends marriage to last for life—to advise the Corinthians that they should remain in their marriages with unbelievers, provided that the unbelieving spouse is willing to stay (vv. 12–14). But what should a Christian do if the unbelieving spouse leaves? Again, Paul has no direct tradition from Jesus on this topic, but he does have resources to use. The first is a principle: "God has called you in peace" (v. 15). God's gift of peace is a major theme in the Old Testament and in the teaching of Jesus.[85] The second resource is a practical, pastoral consideration: If one felt the need to win back the deserting spouse so as to bear Christian witness to him or her, there is no need because we cannot know whether the believer would have a saving influence (v. 16). In light of these considerations, Paul says that the deserted believer is "not bound" (or, "not enslaved") in this circumstance. In other words, the believer is free

84. Although Paul did not know Jesus during his earthly ministry and 1 Corinthians was probably written before any of the canonical Gospels were composed, Paul knows what Jesus taught about divorce through oral or written traditions handed down in the churches or perhaps through direct revelation from the risen Jesus.

85. On God's bestowal of peace on Israel and the nations in the Old Testament, see (for example) Num. 6:26; Pss. 29:11; 37:11; 85:8; Isa. 9:6–7; 26:3, 12; 52:7; 53:5; 54:10, 13; 55:12; 57:19; 66:12; Jer. 29:11; 33:6, 9; Ezek. 34:25; 37:26; Zech. 9:9–10. On peace in the sayings of Jesus, see especially Matt. 5:9; Luke 7:50; 8:48; 24:36; John 14:27; 20:19, 21, 26. As evidence that Paul highly valued this dimension of Old Testament theology, he typically opened his letters with wishes of "grace and peace." See Rom. 1:7; 1 Cor. 1:3; 2 Cor. 1:2; Gal. 1:3; Eph. 1:2; Phil. 1:2; Col. 1:2; 1 Thess. 1:1; 2 Thess. 1:2; Titus 1:4; Philem. 3. On the theme of peace in Paul, see also Rom. 5:1; 15:33; Phil. 4:9; 1 Thess. 5:23; 2 Cor. 13:11; Gal. 6:16; Eph. 2:13–18; 6:15; Col. 1:20; 3:15; 2 Thess. 3:16.

from the marriage and presumably able to remarry "in the Lord" (v. 39).[86] In this passage, Paul follows the core teaching of Jesus and applies it to a new situation with pastoral sensibility in light of God's calling in peace.

Much more could be said about marriage in the Bible. I have chosen to discuss the purpose of marriage, the practice of polygamy, and divorce because these topics offer complementary perspectives on the broader subject of marriage, and because they furnish useful examples of inner-biblical interpretation. In looking for insights to guide our theological reflection and interpretation of specific passages, we should recognize two foundational concepts: first, that marriage is part of God's good creation, and second, that God's ultimate plan for human beings does not include marriage.

I have identified seven central insights from the passages treated above: (1) Marriage is a covenant relationship designed by God to last for life. (2) Faithfulness to God is the first priority in all matters related to marriage. (3) Marriage provides a unique occasion for ministry in the life of another person. (4) The marital relationship should be characterized by Christian love. (5) Personal qualities suitable to Christian marriage are purity, modesty, and restraint. (6) There are limited situations where divorce is permitted due to hardness of heart and concern for human well-being. (7) Celibacy is an ideal for which some are gifted.

Putting the Pieces Together

A coherent theological picture of marriage can be developed out of these inner-biblical insights. The ultimate goal of marriage, as with all human relationships, is closeness to God. Married people should promote the holiness of their spouses and encourage godliness in their children. As a picture of God's faithfulness and for the sake of human flourishing, God has designed marriage to last for life. This provides the best context for lifelong sanctification, and it also offers long-term opportunities for people to care for one another. Alongside closeness to God, human well-being in our present condition is marriage's second great goal. Marriage is a benevolent gift that God has granted to humanity to provide for our welfare. In the next age, God will perfect our holiness and meet every human need so that marriage will no longer be necessary. Until then, Christians should promote closeness to

---

86. For a different view on remarriage after divorce, see Wenham, *Jesus, Divorce, and Remarriage*, 99–102. According to Wenham, in saying that the believer is "not bound," Paul means simply that the believer is free to let the unbelieving spouse depart but that this does not allow the abandoned spouse to remarry.

God through marriage and care for the needs of their spouses and families. Some who are gifted by God will live without marriage in this life, for the sake of unencumbered ministry and in witness to our future life. It is not good that marriage should end except by death, but divorce is allowable in certain circumstances when the primary goals of marriage are severely threatened.

Our theological understanding of marriage should be informed by Scripture's core teaching as embodied in Jesus. An obvious focal point can be found in Jesus's statement on the two greatest commandments: love of God and love of neighbor. The first commandment, love of God, is the ultimate goal of marriage. For the second commandment, love of neighbor, marriage provides a special context for fulfillment. Even though the specific type of neighborly love that is expressed through marriage will cease to exist at the resurrection, love of neighbor will never disappear. This reminds us that even if marriage does not exist in the afterlife, the love that married people have for each other will not be lost but will be perfected, even as it changes. Furthermore, because marriage affects not only individuals but also entire families and societies, Scripture's core ethical values should inform our understanding of marriage. For example, as Jesus humbled himself and took on the form of a servant, Christians who marry should humbly serve within and through their marriages. Passages such as the Ten Commandments and the Sermon on the Mount teach us to restrain our evil desires and to practice respect and love. These values should guide our behavior in marriage, or else in our calling not to marry. Lastly, our application of Scripture's teaching on marriage should be shaped by the principle of doing for others what we would want done for ourselves.

Many books have been written on the practical application of biblical teaching to various aspects of marriage. The issues can be complex, and the details of specific situations matter. I will not attempt to set forth any definitive statements on the topics addressed in this chapter. Several helpful books are available on divorce and remarriage from a biblical perspective.[87] Biblical texts that address the purpose of marriage raise questions about singleness and celibacy.[88] Polygamy is not a major concern for Christians in the Western world, but there are cultures where pastoral wisdom is needed in applying the biblical ideal of monogamy to the complicated realities of people's lives.[89]

---

87. E.g., Strauss, *Remarriage after Divorce*; Keener, *And Marries Another*, 104–10; Instone-Brewer, *Divorce and Remarriage*, 268–314; and Roberts, *Not under Bondage*.

88. Singleness and celibacy have been discussed from many angles. Recent studies include Hitchcock, *Significance of Singleness*; Danylak, *Redeeming Singleness*; Zurlo, *Single for a Greater Purpose*; and Yarhouse and Zaporozhets, *Costly Obedience*.

89. See Ntagali and Hodgetts, *More Than One Wife*; Hillman, *Polygamy Reconsidered*.

Although I cannot provide detailed guidance on these issues, I will conclude this chapter with a few general suggestions on how we might interpret different types of passages as part of a coherent theological framework.

The creation of woman from man in Genesis 2:18–25 is the most theologically fruitful account of marriage in the Old Testament. Malachi 2:15 alludes to Genesis 2:24 in its argument that God made the Judean men "one" with their wives for the sake of godly offspring. Jesus cites Genesis 2:24 along with Genesis 1:27 to show that husband and wife are joined by God and should not be separated (Matt. 19:4–6). For Paul, Genesis 2:24 teaches that a man should love his wife as he loves his own body, because the two are one flesh (Eph. 5:31). By interpreting Genesis 2:18–25 thoughtfully in light of the rest of Scripture and our contemporary context, even more theological insights could be explored. For example, the fact that the woman was created as a helper who uniquely corresponds to the man can serve as the basis for a deeper theology of companionship and friendship in marriage. The New Testament is not altogether lacking in this area; for example, husbands are commanded to love their wives as themselves (Eph. 5:25–33) and to honor them as fellow heirs of the grace of life (1 Pet. 3:7). Practical themes that could be developed include a husband and wife sharing joys and sorrows, speaking kindly to each other and about each other, participating in each other's interests and pursuits, listening well, giving truthful advice, not insisting on their own way, joining together in daily tasks, sympathizing with each other's hopes and concerns, spending time with one another, and showing hospitality to each other's family and friends.[90]

New Testament passages that identify celibacy as a gift should be given their proper place, without condemning marriage. First, those who possess this gift will best be able to recognize their giftedness if the biblical concept of celibacy for the kingdom of God is openly discussed. Second, these passages can help all Christians remember that our human relationships are ultimately defined by our relationship to God. Marriage is created by God, serves a proper function for the present, and remains part of human experience for many people, but it does not define us and is not fundamentally necessary for human flourishing. As for 1 Corinthians 7, Paul's advice to abstain from marriage should find a listening audience in the church. In particular, his observation

90. Despite many objectionable passages, Plutarch's *Advice to Bride and Groom* contains useful snippets of practical advice on the relational dimension of marriage. See *Advice to Bride and Groom* 14, 20, 22, 27, 34, 48 (Babbitt, *Plutarch*, 307–9, 311–15, 319, 323–25, 337–43). Companionship in marriage can be enriched through basic principles of friendship, such as those discussed in Cicero's *Laelius: On Friendship*. This work was influential on Latin Christian authors, such as Augustine; see van Bavel, "Influence of Cicero's Ideal," 59–72. See also Augustine's *Against the Academics* 3.6.13.

that unmarried people are free to show undivided concern for the things of God (1 Cor. 7:32–35) deserves careful reflection. At the same time, in terms of application, Paul's perspective on marriage was shaped by his concern for the "present distress" that faced the Corinthians (1 Cor. 7:26) and by his conviction that "the time is short" (1 Cor. 7:29). It is not fully clear whether the same arguments in favor of remaining single apply to Christians in all times.

The presence of the Song of Songs in Scripture attests to the positive view of sexual desire that is possible within a Christian framework. As a balance to the negative view of sexual desire that sometimes appears in the New Testament (e.g., 1 Cor. 7:9; 1 Tim. 5:11), the Song of Songs in its literal sense provides a biblical anchor point for affirming human sexual expression within marriage. Sex is a potential source of physical delight, but more importantly, it is a way to show care and demonstrate companionship. In light of the Bible as a whole, however, it is important not to overemphasize the importance of sex, even within marriage. Moreover, I think there is value in the traditional figurative reading of the Song of Songs. To be sure, attempting to assign allegorical meanings to individual details in the Song is not helpful.[91] Nonetheless, theological truths about divine love may be found in the book's major ideas about human marital love (cf. Eph. 5:31–32). For example, there is great joy when the lovers are together, there is great sadness when they are apart, love is as strong as death, and love is worth more than all of one's possessions (Song 8:6–7). Such lessons about love in general speak powerfully to the reality of God's love. For early readers who knew the metaphor of God and Israel as husband and wife, but only as depicting a broken relationship (e.g., Hosea 1–2), reading the Song of Songs as a metaphor for divine and human love offered an encouraging alternative.

Certain societal dimensions of marriage in the Old Testament do not apply today as they did in ancient Israel, but the biblical texts that treat these dimensions remain instructive. Thus, the earth is no longer so sparsely populated that people need to multiply and fill it, and the church is not a literal family into which people are physically born. Still, giving birth remains a blessing from God that is necessary to preserve the human race (cf. Luke 20:36), and families with children still play an important role in building the church. Perhaps evangelism is a good application of God's promise to Abraham to

---

91. In most traditional interpretations of the Song, the woman is read as a detailed representation of God's people. For example, the woman's two breasts in Song 4:5 are taken to be Moses and Aaron in the midrash Song of Songs Rabbah 4.5.1 (Simon, *Midrash Rabbah*, 9:198), and they are springs of teaching that offer milk or solid food as appropriate (cf. 1 Cor. 3:2; Heb. 5:12) according to Theodoret of Cyrus (Hill, *Theodoret of Cyrus*, 79). Figural interpretation of the Song at this level of detail is so inventive as not to be genuinely useful for instruction.

multiply his descendants (cf. Gal. 3:29). As for the Old Testament's regulation of the communal and economic dimensions of marriage (inheritance, levirate marriage, etc.), the spiritual identity of the church and the differences between modern and ancient cultures render these passages inapplicable as societal norms. Nevertheless, these biblical texts can yield useful insights for Christians today. For example, good marriages can provide financial and social stability, and rules should protect those who are vulnerable within families.

In view of the Old Testament's subtle critique of polygamy and the New Testament's consistent orientation toward monogamy, passages in the Old Testament that reference or allow polygamy should be understood as examples of God's willingness to work through flawed people and customs (cf. Judg. 14:4). In addition, the topic of polygamy can serve as a reminder of human sinfulness and the need to restrain our evil passions.[92] The custom of polygamy in ancient Israel gave men the opportunity to pursue their desires for sexual gratification, wealth, and status. By contrast, Christians are called to practice self-control.[93]

How we apply the instructions for husbands and wives in New Testament household codes depends largely on which elements we think represent Christian ideals for relationships and which elements we think express Christian ideals in a specific cultural context.[94] The counsel of Scripture as a whole, however, plays some part in discerning how particular passages should be applied. For example, Paul urges older women to teach younger women to be "workers at home" (Titus 2:5). This resembles Plutarch's recommendation that wives should stay at home all day and not interact with others.[95] But if we apply Titus 2:5 along the lines of Plutarch's view, it would run counter to what we would otherwise conclude about women's roles based on Deborah (Judg. 4–5), Huldah (2 Kings 22:14–20), and the model wife of Proverbs 31 (vv. 14–16, 20, 24, 31), as well as women with whom Jesus interacted.[96] Our application of New Testament household codes depends partly on what role we think culture played in these passages and partly on how we understand Scripture's theology of gender.

Old Testament passages in which divorce was allowed (Deut. 24:1–4) or required (Ezra 10) must be interpreted in light of the New Testament. As noted above, Deuteronomy 24:1–4 does not command divorce; rather, it regulates a

92. E.g., Rom. 1:26; Col. 3:5; 1 Thess. 4:5.

93. E.g., Acts 24:25; Gal. 5:23; 2 Pet. 1:6.

94. The literature on this subject is extensive. The following books are a selection of those worth reading: France, *Women in the Church's Ministry*; Stackhouse, *Partners in Christ*; Köstenberger and Köstenberger, *God's Design for Man and Woman*; and Lee-Barnewall, *Neither Complementarian nor Egalitarian*.

95. See Plutarch, *Advice to Bride and Groom* 9, 30–32 (Babbitt, *Plutarch*, 305, 321–23).

96. E.g., John 4:4–42; Mark 14:3–9; Luke 10:38–42.

particular scenario that assumes divorce. Given this scenario, the biblical text discourages divorce, seeks to prevent sexual immorality, and above all protects the woman's right to remarry, which safeguards her future well-being. These are the themes we should highlight when interpreting this text. As for Ezra 10, because of our New Testament perspective on culture and the people of God (see chap. 3), we would not require a Christian to divorce a non-Christian spouse, especially in view of what Paul says in 1 Corinthians 7:12–14. Still, this biblical text conveys an important message—namely, that faithfulness to God should be at the center of marriage.

The church's teaching on divorce should follow the trajectory established by Jesus and the New Testament. The basic principle is that God designed marriage to last for life. The church, therefore, should generally take a restrictive view on divorce. This means that careful consideration should be made before Christians marry in the first place. Ideally, Christian marriages should endure with such regularity that they serve as a testimony to God's faithfulness. It is debatable whether the specific exceptions that allow for divorce in the New Testament were meant to be exhaustive. For one, no single passage captures the entire picture. Thus, divorce is forbidden without qualification in Mark 10:11–12 and Luke 16:18, whereas an exception is made for sexual immorality in Matthew 5:31–32 and 19:9. And allowance is made for divorce in the case of abandonment by an unbelieving spouse in 1 Corinthians 7:15. Because the contexts and specific details of the situations seem to matter, could some other situation warrant divorce when a major purpose of marriage has been violated? On the one hand, the church should not seek to make divorce common, because God is the one who joined husband and wife together. On the other hand, if it is possible for a person to break the marriage bond (against God's will) by doing harm to a spouse, as if destroying their own body (cf. Eph. 5:28–33), the church should not use biblical rules to enable harm. If it is true that the Sabbath was made for people, not people for the Sabbath (Mark 2:27), and it is lawful to do good on the Sabbath (Matt. 12:12), perhaps the same valuation of people over rules should apply to divorce when there is genuine need to do good (e.g., protecting the vulnerable).

All the topics addressed in this chapter deserve careful thought, earnest prayer, and the cooperative guidance of one's church. The biblical texts must be studied in their historical contexts and as part of the whole Bible, with the transition from Old Testament to New Testament taken into account, and cultural differences between antiquity and today in mind. Broader theological perspectives on topics such as gender and the afterlife also come into play. In the end, we should seek to put the biblical pieces together so that each text makes its distinctive point but the result is a coherent message.

5

Sacrificial Offerings

Devoting Our Lives Fully to God,
Receiving the Greater Gift

T he subject of this chapter is the practice of offering animals, grains, veg-
etables, and liquids as part of rituals that facilitate people's relationship
to God. Common Old Testament terms for sacrificial offerings include *zebaḥ*,
"ritually slaughtered animal"; *ʿōlâ*, "burnt offering"; *minḥâ*, "gift, grain offering"; *qorbān*, "offering"; and *ʾiššeh*, "offering by fire."[1] The Old Testament assumes from its earliest narratives that people should make sacrificial
offerings to God, and the core ideas related to sacrifice in the Old Testament
are essential for the theology of the New Testament. Nevertheless, the Bible
exhibits some diversity and historical development in how it handles the concept of sacrifice. We will see below how the various biblical perspectives fit
together and culminate in Jesus.

Biblical Perspectives

Biblical texts often presuppose ideas about sacrificial offerings that were common in the ancient world. The ritual sacrifice of animals and other food items

---

1. On sacrificial offerings in the Old Testament, see Averbeck, "Sacrifices and Offerings,"
706–33; Anderson, "Sacrifice and Sacrificial Offerings," 5:870–86; and Beckwith and Selman,
Sacrifice in the Bible, 1–87.

is known from sources in Mesopotamia and Egypt from early times. Sacrifices were offered throughout the Old Testament period in these regions and elsewhere, including Asia Minor, Syria, and Greece.[2] A major purpose of sacrifice in many ancient cultures was to feed the gods. This point serves as the background for several Old Testament passages. Some features of Mesopotamian practice that remind us of the Old Testament are daily offerings in temples, the ritual burning of fat portions, and the requirement that sacrificial animals be cultically pure.[3] At the same time, Old Testament concepts of sacrifice often differ considerably from what we know about sacrifice in neighboring cultures. For example, whereas the Sumerian king Shulgi (ca. 2000 BC) reformed the sacrificial system to promote his own power, Old Testament narratives insist that the king exists for the sake of proper worship, not vice versa, and the goal of sacrifice is to maintain the relationship between God and the people, not God and the king.[4] It will be useful in this survey to keep this general ancient context in mind.

Sacrificial offerings are foundational for Israel's worship in early Old Testament narratives, priestly sources, and mainstream Old Testament tradition. Certain prophetic passages and psalms criticize Israel's practice of sacrificial worship, but these books also contain affirmations of ritual sacrifice. Both the affirmations and the criticisms anticipate fresh theological developments that take place in the New Testament. The following overview of biblical perspectives will include (1) general depictions of sacrifice in the Old Testament, (2) sacrificial offerings in priestly texts, (3) Old Testament reflections on sacrifice, and (4) the New Testament's trajectory on sacrifice.

General Depictions of Sacrifice in the Old Testament

Old Testament narratives depict sacrifice as a proper human response to God, using a general set of terms to describe the sacrificial offerings that were made. This is already evident in the book of Genesis. Cain and Abel each bring a "gift" (*minḥâ*) to the LORD (Gen. 4:3–5). Abel's gift of the firstborn of his flock and their fat portions is accepted by the LORD, but Cain's gift of some of the fruit of the land is not accepted. This probably reflects the value found elsewhere in the Old Testament of offering one's best to God. After the flood,

---

2. For an overview, see Becker et al., "Sacrifice," 832–56. Although many ancient peoples made sacrificial offerings, there is no global theory of sacrifice that explains what this practice signified for everyone. On theories of sacrifice as applied to the Hebrew Bible, see Klawans, *Purity, Sacrifice, and the Temple*, 21–46.

3. Renger, "Sacrifice II A," 838–39.

4. Janzen, *Social Meanings of Sacrifice*, 250–53.

Noah builds an altar and sacrifices "ritually clean" cattle and birds as burnt offerings (ʿōlōt) to the LORD (Gen. 8:20–21). This likewise presupposes ideas known from elsewhere in the Old Testament, in this case regarding ritually clean and unclean animals (e.g., Lev. 11).

Both Abraham and Isaac build altars to the LORD and "call on the name of the LORD."[5] Jacob makes a sacrificial offering (zebaḥ) that is accompanied by a meal (Gen. 31:54; cf. Gen. 46:1). The most important sacrificial narrative in Genesis is Abraham's near sacrifice of Isaac as a burnt offering (ʿōlâ), where Abraham is told not to sacrifice his son but instead is provided a ram to sacrifice as a burnt offering in place of his son (Gen. 22:2–8, 13). This illustrates the substitutionary aspect of sacrifice in the Old Testament.

Other Old Testament narratives continue these patterns and add further details. The Israelites in Egypt are instructed to ask Pharaoh to let them go in order to make sacrifices (zbḥ) to the LORD,[6] which include zəbāḥîm and ʿōlōt (Exod. 10:25). The ritual slaughter of the Passover lamb is called the LORD's zebaḥ-pesaḥ, the ongoing remembrance of which includes sacrificing (zbḥ) firstborn male animals but "redeeming" the firstborn of Israel.[7] Later, Moses's father-in-law, Jethro, offers to God zəbāḥîm and ʿōlōt and shares a meal with Moses, Aaron, and the elders of Israel (Exod. 18:12) in a manner reminiscent of Jacob in Genesis 31:54 and also the peace/fellowship offering of Leviticus. In Exodus 20:24–26, Israel is instructed to erect altars in every place where God causes his name to be remembered, where they will sacrifice burnt offerings (ʿōlōt) and peace/fellowship offerings (šəlāmîm). The combination of burnt and peace/fellowship offerings is found elsewhere,[8] as is the presence of solitary altars in the land of Israel.[9]

The atoning function of sacrifice is shown in Job's making burnt offerings in case his children sin (Job 1:5; cf. 42:8). Similarly, in the judgment against Eli it is stated that the iniquity of Eli's house will never be "atoned for" (kpr) by zebaḥ or minḥâ (1 Sam. 3:14); in other words, they will not bring atonement as one would expect.

The idea that an offering is supposed to represent a genuine giving up of something valuable to oneself (i.e., "sacrifice" in the modern sense) is expressed in the story of David insisting that he purchase the oxen of Araunah the Jebusite on the grounds that "I will not offer to the LORD my God burnt

5. Gen. 12:7–8; 13:4; 26:25.
6. Exod. 3:18; 5:3, 8, 17; 8:8, 25–29.
7. Exod. 13:13–15; cf. Exod. 30:12; Num. 3:12, 40–51; 18:14–16.
8. E.g., Judg. 20:26; 21:4; 2 Sam. 24:25. The burnt offering is mentioned alone in Judg. 6:26.
9. E.g., Deut. 27:5–7; Josh. 8:30–35; Judg. 6:24–27; 1 Sam. 7:17; 9:12; 2 Sam. 24:18, 25 (1 Chron. 21:26); 1 Kings 18:30–35; 19:10, 14.

offerings at no cost to me" (2 Sam. 24:24; cf. 1 Chron. 21:24). A major idea
that underlies many sacrificial texts in the Old Testament is the connection
between sacrifice and covenant.[10] For the most part, Old Testament narratives
use general terms such as *zebaḥ*, "ritually slaughtered animal"; *ʿōlâ*, "burnt
offering"; *šəlāmîm*, "peace/fellowship offering"; and *minḥâ*, "gift, grain offering," to describe sacrificial offerings. Words such as *qorbān*, "offering";
ḥaṭṭāʾt, "sin offering"; and *ʾāšām*, "guilt offering," occur primarily in passages
that present technical information relevant for the duties of priests.[11]

Sacrificial Offerings in Priestly Texts

The book of Leviticus and some texts in Exodus and Numbers contain
passages that present more complete descriptions of the Old Testament sacrificial system using technical priestly terminology. I will summarize below
main points about the five major sacrifices mentioned in Leviticus 1–7, the
Passover sacrifice, and the Day of Atonement.

The first offering listed in Leviticus is the burnt offering (*ʿōlâ*).[12] The burnt
offering is the sacrifice of a male animal without defect, on which the worshiper places a hand before it is killed. The placing of the hand probably symbolizes identification, and the animal's lack of defect makes it fit to serve as a
substitute and makes it a worthy gift. The ritual involving the animal's carcass,
which includes burning the fat and other portions and sprinkling blood on the
altar, speaks of purification through the blood and the intent to seek God's
favor. The burnt offering is said to produce "an aroma pleasing to the LORD"
(Lev. 1:9, 13, 17)—that is, an aroma that serves to soothe or appease (*nîḥôaḥ*).
The result is that the offering atones for (*kpr*) the worshiper by appeasing
God (Lev. 1:4), just as Jacob sought to appease (*kpr*) Esau with gifts (Gen.
32:19–21). The burnt offering was typically made together with grain and
drink offerings, and it was the standard offering for expressing commitment
or devotion to God as part of the daily offering at the tabernacle or temple.[13]

The next offering listed in Leviticus is the grain offering.[14] This consisted of
flour or grain baked in a prescribed fashion with oil and incense. In imitation
of the Passover festival, the grain offering was prepared without yeast (Lev.
2:11; 6:17). It was seasoned with "salt of the covenant" (Lev. 2:13; cf. Num.

10. E.g., Gen. 8:20–9:17; 15:1–21; 31:44–54; Exod. 24:1–8.
11. As exceptions to this general rule, the guilt offering is mentioned in 1 Sam. 6:3–17, and
both guilt and sin offerings are referenced in 2 Kings 12:16. For examples of priestly terminology in poetry, the sin offering appears in Ps. 40:6 and the guilt offering is found in Isa. 53:10.
12. Lev. 1:3–17; 6:8–13; cf. Num. 15:1–12.
13. Exod. 29:38–42; Num. 28:3–8; cf. Ezek. 46:13–15.
14. Lev. 2:1–16; 6:14–23; cf. Num. 15:1–21.

18:19), which may have signified the enduring quality of the covenant in view of salt's usefulness as a preservative. Reference is made to the grain offering as "firstfruits" (Lev. 2:12, 14) to indicate that God receives the best portion. Part of the grain offering is consumed by the priest, and the other part is burned as a "memorial" offering to the LORD (Lev. 2:2, 9, 16). This may suggest that God is reminded of the worshiper's devotion, since the burnt part produces an aroma pleasing to the LORD.[15] Grain and drink offerings accompanied the daily burnt offerings (Num. 28:3–8). On some level, this represents a complete meal and could imply that Israel is feeding God with their offerings.

After the burnt and grain offerings in Leviticus comes the *zebaḥ šəlāmîm*, "the peace/fellowship sacrifice" (Lev. 3:1–17; 7:11–34). The word *šəlāmîm* is derived from *šālôm*, "peace, well-being," so this sacrifice is sometimes called the "peace" offering. It may indeed signify well-being between God and the people. If so, this is especially communicated through the meal that is shared among the priest, the worshiper, and anyone who is ritually clean (Lev. 7:19). Due to this communal aspect, the *šəlāmîm* is also called the "fellowship" offering. As with the burnt offering, the animal must be without blemish, a hand is placed on the animal, the fat is burned, and blood is sprinkled on the altar. The peace/fellowship offering can express thanksgiving, accompany a vow, or act as a freewill offering (Lev. 7:12–18; cf. 22:17–30). The burning of the portion offered by fire produces an aroma pleasing to the LORD (Lev. 3:5, 16). The peace/fellowship offering uniquely illustrates how God gives the people well-being and fellowship with one another through their devotion to him.

The fourth offering is typically called the "sin" offering, because the word for "sin" (*ḥaṭṭā't*) is also used for the "sin offering" (Lev. 4:1–5:13; Num. 15:22–31). The *ḥaṭṭā't* functions to remove "sin," in the sense of ritual impurity. It is therefore best understood as a purification offering. A sin/purification offering can be made for a priest, the whole congregation, a leader, or a regular individual. For this offering, the animal must be without defect, a hand is laid on the animal, and the fat is burned. The purpose of this offering is to effect purification for violations that were made by mistake (*šəgāgâ*; Lev. 4:2, 22, 27) against the LORD's commands. Examples of such violations include failing to speak up as a witness, touching something unclean, and making a thoughtless oath (Lev. 5:1–4). The individual involved must confess the sin and bring a sin offering, and then the priest will make atonement for him (Lev. 5:5–6). Conditions of ritual impurity that require a sin offering do not necessarily arise from wicked behavior. For example, although having children is a great blessing in the Pentateuch, the act of giving birth puts a woman into a state

15. Lev. 2:2, 9; 6:15, 21.

of ritual impurity that requires a sin/purification offering (Lev. 12). With this offering, the woman becomes ritually "clean" (*ṭāher*), and the meaning of *kpr* (Lev. 12:7) is not "atone for" but "purge, wipe away"—that is, "purify" that which is ritually impure.[16]

The key to the sin/purification offering is the system of rituals by which the blood was used to purify the sanctuary. Blood was sprinkled in the holy place for priests and the whole congregation, but only on the altar for leaders and common individuals because the goal was to decontaminate the sanctuary from ritual impurity in places where the people involved were permitted to go. The sin offering was seen as effecting forgiveness.[17] The cleansing of ritual impurity was needed to make the sanctuary fit for God's presence so that he might dwell among the people.

The fifth and final major offering in Leviticus 1–7 is the guilt offering.[18] Like the sin offering, the guilt offering can deal with holy things and violations done by mistake (Lev. 5:15). A distinguishing feature of the guilt offering is that it requires making restitution (5:16). This involves paying compensation for the violation and adding an additional fifth.[19] Many details for the performance of this offering are similar to previous sacrifices. Through the guilt offering, the priest makes atonement and the violator is forgiven.[20] In Leviticus 6:1–7, we see how wrongdoing that directly harms other people is addressed. If one person wrongs another by robbery, oppression, deception, or false swearing, the wrongdoer must restore what he stole, lied about, or extorted and then add one fifth on top of this. Only after full reparation is made can the wrongdoer bring a guilt offering so that the priest can make atonement. In other words, where restitution is possible, there is no mechanism for forgiveness apart from making right the wrong that was done.

The order in which these five sacrifices are presented in Leviticus 1–7 is not the order in which they always appear in the Pentateuch. According to Anson Rainey, Leviticus 1–7 gives a *didactic* order, which groups sacrifices together

16. See Averbeck, "Reading the Ritual Law," 141–42. Otherwise, the verb *kpr* is often best translated "make atonement," although its precise meaning is difficult to pinpoint. Some connect *kpr* to the Arabic word *kafara*, "to cover," so that making atonement involves covering over sin. Others think that *kpr* is related to the Hebrew word *kōper*, "ransom" (e.g., Exod. 21:30; 30:12; Num. 35:31–32), so that making atonement involves redemption by paying the sacrificial offering as a ransom. As is evident from its usage in Leviticus, *kpr* can be employed for a range of related ideas, including appeasement, purification, and forgiveness.

17. Lev. 4:20, 26, 31, 35; 5:10, 13.

18. Lev. 5:14–6:7; 7:1–7; cf. Num. 5:5–10.

19. Lev. 5:16; 6:5; Num. 5:7.

20. Lev. 5:16, 18; 6:7.

according to conceptual associations for the purpose of training priests.[21] In passages that show the *procedural* order (e.g., Lev. 9:15–22; Num. 6:16–17), we see that the first sacrifices performed were sin and guilt offerings. After this came burnt offerings with their accompanying grain and drink offerings. Finally, worshipers offered burnt and peace/fellowship offerings as the climax of their worship. This procedural order communicated important theological lessons for Israel. If sin or guilt existed, it needed to be addressed first. Next, burnt offerings expressed the full commitment to God necessary for atonement. Finally, the peace/fellowship offerings showed that communion with God was restored, providing opportunity for thanksgiving and freewill offerings. Both the individual sacrifices on their own and the sequence of sacrifices together possessed deep religious significance.

Of the many appointed days in ancient Israel's ritual year, I will focus on two that hold special theological significance: Passover and the Day of Atonement.

The Passover sacrifice is introduced in the book of Exodus as part of the narrative of Israel's deliverance from Egypt.[22] The Passover lamb should be a one-year-old male without defect and is selected on the tenth of the month from among the sheep or the goats (Exod. 12:3–5). On the fourteenth day of the month, the Passover lamb is slaughtered at twilight (12:6), and its blood is put on the doorposts and lintel (12:7). The blood is described as a sign for the people, but God is the one who will see the sign and protect the household from the destructive plague (12:13). The verb often translated "pass over" is *psḥ*.[23] This verb resembles a word that means "to be lame, limp" and perhaps "to leap,"[24] and consequently it has been taken to mean that God "leaped over" or "passed over" the Israelite houses. In fact, *psḥ* in Exodus 12 probably means "to spare," as it does in Isaiah 31:5. In other words, when God sees the blood, he spares those inside the house. The Israelites eat the Passover lamb as a people who are prepared to depart Egypt, confident in God's deliverance: the animal cannot be boiled in water (as if the family is settled enough to cook with a pot and utensils) but must be roasted over a fire (as if the family is ready to break camp and go), and the celebrants eat wearing their belts and sandals, with staff in hand ready to leave in haste (Exod. 12:9–11). Along with eating the Passover lamb, the Israelites eat bitter herbs and bread without yeast (12:8). The sacrificial animal is eaten inside the house (12:46). The Passover sacrifice is described as an abiding statute for generations to come

21. On this paragraph, see Rainey, "Order of Sacrifices," 485–98.
22. Exod. 12:1–13, 21–28, 43–49.
23. Exod. 12:13, 23, 27.
24. 2 Sam. 4:4; 1 Kings 18:21, 26.

(12:14, 24). Focal points of the memorial celebration are God's deliverance and protection, and also Israelite identity (12:43–49).

The most solemn sacrificial ritual in the Pentateuch is the Day of Atonement (Lev. 16; 23:26–32). On this day, the high priest makes atonement for the people in the presence of the LORD, who appears in a cloud above the atonement cover of the ark (16:2). To atone for his own sin and that of his household, the high priest must present a bull as a sin offering, sprinkling some of the blood on the atonement cover before the LORD (16:6, 11–14). The high priest also selects two goats. The first is offered as a sin offering for the people, and the second is sent away from the people as a scapegoat (16:7–10). Blood from the first goat is sprinkled on the atonement cover, the tent of meeting, and the altar to purify these sacred items and make atonement for them because of Israel's uncleanness, transgressions, and sins (16:15–19). With the second goat, the high priest places both hands (not just one hand) on its head, indicating close identification, and he confesses all the iniquities, transgressions, and sins of the people, thereby placing these on the goat's head. This second goat is then sent into the wilderness so that it carries away the people's iniquities (16:20–22). The result of this ritual is atonement for the most holy place, the tent of meeting, the altar, the priests, and all Israel.[25] The Day of Atonement was a Sabbath of solemn rest (16:31; 23:28), and on this day Israelites were to "afflict" themselves, perhaps by abstaining from food and bodily care.[26] As an annual ritual, the Day of Atonement addressed guilt and uncleanness that accumulated throughout the year. It also exemplified the general concept of atonement that lay at the heart of Israel's entire sacrificial system.

Old Testament priestly texts give special insight into the theology of Israel's sacrificial offerings. The covenantal context of this system is made clear by the promises of blessing and warnings of punishment in Leviticus 26. Numerous ideas are communicated through these offerings, such as the nature of God's holiness, the problem of sin, the connection between death and atonement, the possibility of substitution, the efficacy of confession and restitution, and the need for full devotion to God. Profound lessons could be found in the rituals accompanying Israel's sacrifices by anyone who paid careful attention to them.

The straightforward sense of these texts is that sacrificial offerings "work"; that is, they actually accomplish atonement, ritual cleansing, and forgiveness. The precise nature of their efficacy is subject to interpretation. For example,

25. Lev. 16:30, 33; 23:28.
26. Lev. 16:29, 31; 23:27, 29, 32; cf. 2 Sam. 12:16–23.

it is frequently stated that an offering produces "an aroma pleasing to the LORD."[27] The apparent effectiveness of such offerings can be illustrated from Noah's burnt offering. The text states that the LORD smelled the pleasing aroma and then said in his heart that he would never again curse the ground because of humanity or destroy all living creatures (Gen. 8:20–22). This leads directly to God's covenant with Noah (Gen. 9:1–17). One could conclude that God's promises and covenant came in response to the pleasing aroma that soothed him. Otherwise, it could be argued that God was pleased with Noah's righteousness (Gen. 6:9), obedience in building the ark (Gen. 6:22), and commitment to God as expressed in the burnt offering (Gen. 8:20). As another example, certain passages could imply that God received nourishment from sacrificial offerings (e.g., Lev. 9:24).[28] Then again, Israel did not have a cultic statue of God that the people fed with offerings, as other ancient Near Eastern peoples did. These issues receive clarification in the prophets and Psalms.

Old Testament Reflections on Sacrifice

The topic of sacrificial offerings is subject to further reflection in other parts of the Old Testament. The book of Deuteronomy addresses how Israel should perform sacrifices once they enter the promised land. The psalms show how sacrifices function within the broader context of worship and piety. Prophetic books deal with sacrifice as part of their oracles of judgment and restoration. The Old Testament's last reflections on sacrificial offerings are found in books written after the return from exile. I will touch on each of these sources now and return to them in greater detail under "Inner-Biblical Insights" below.

The centerpiece of Deuteronomy's legislation on sacrificial offerings is the expectation that all such offerings should be brought to a central location of the LORD's choosing. This idea is set forth clearly in Deuteronomy 12. When Israel enters the land, they must not worship the LORD in the same manner as the previous nations worshiped their gods, but they must destroy the altars and images of the previous nations wherever they are found (vv. 1–4). As for Israel, they should bring their burnt offerings, sacrifices, tithes, and other offerings to a central place that God will choose. In that place they will eat, rejoice, and experience God's blessing (vv. 5–7). In the future, Israel should not do as they previously did, with everyone making sacrifices locally as they saw fit. Instead, once they enter the land and find secure rest from their enemies, they should bring all their sacrificial offerings to

---

27. E.g., Exod. 29:18, 25, 41; Lev. 1:9, 13, 17; 2:2, 9, 12; 3:5, 16; 4:31; 6:15, 21; 8:21, 28.

28. See also "the food of your God" in Lev. 3:11, 16; 21:6, 8, 17, 21–22; 22:25; cf. Num. 28:2, 24.

the place the LORD chooses, which is the only place they may worship (vv. 8–14). If the Israelites wish to eat meat in the places where they live (outside the central location), they are permitted to slaughter and eat animals in a nonsacred manner, provided that they do not consume the blood. In other words, all sacred slaughtering for the purpose of sacrifice must be brought to the central place of God's choosing, but "secular" slaughtering is permitted anywhere (vv. 15–27). Israel must be careful to obey these commands, so that they are not tempted to serve other gods or worship the LORD as the other nations worship their gods. These other nations even burn their sons and daughters in fire as sacrifices to their gods. Israel must not do this (vv. 28–32). Deuteronomy's law of centralization aims to keep Israel's worship distinct from that of the surrounding peoples.

The book of Psalms presents a full picture of what we experience in our relationship with God, from gratitude and joy to frustration and distress. In life with God in the Old Testament, sacrificial worship in the temple played an important role. I will give just a few examples. In Psalm 54:6, the psalmist declares that he will praise God's name with the sacrifice of a freewill offering. In Psalm 96:7–9, a gift offering is employed to ascribe glory, majesty, and strength to God in his sanctuary. When the psalmist is in trouble, he cries out to God for help and asks that his gifts and burnt offerings be remembered (20:2–4). In a time of uncertainty, the psalmist urges others to make proper sacrifices and trust in the LORD (4:5). After the psalmist has experienced deliverance, he shows his gratitude by fulfilling his vows, calling on God's name, and sacrificing a thanksgiving offering in the temple (116:12–19). Elsewhere, the psalmist proclaims God's deeds and makes a thanksgiving sacrifice with a loud cry (107:21–22) or performs his sacrifice with a joyous shout and singing (27:6). The general expectation in the book of Psalms is that those who trust in the LORD will express their devotion and gratitude in the temple through sacrificial offerings.

The prophetic books criticize Israel's sacrifices as part of their oracles of judgment, but they also contain promises that suggest the restoration of sacrificial offerings. This can be illustrated from the book of Micah. The worship that takes place in Samaria is condemned because the people make use of idols and images (1:7). Israel is reproached for various acts of injustice, and part of the problem is that the priests instruct people for pay (3:8–12). On several occasions Micah catalogs Israel's acts of dishonesty, greed, and violence (e.g., 6:10–11; 7:2–3). In Micah 6:6–8, the prophet challenges the idea that God requires any kind of animal or produce offering, declaring that God truly desires justice, steadfast love, and humility. Nevertheless, the book of Micah also depicts a glorious future when the Temple Mount will be lifted up above all mountains, and nations will stream to it (4:1). If the exaltation of the temple is imagined, sacrificial offerings are likely also in view. The prophetic criticism and future restoration of sacrificial worship will receive further attention below.

The proper restoration of sacrificial offerings is a major concern for postexilic literature. For example, the rebuilding of the temple in Jerusalem takes center stage in Ezra 1–8. The priests and all the people offer many animal sacrifices, including sin offerings, at the dedication of the temple (6:16–17). After this, all the people celebrate the Passover, with the Levites slaughtering the Passover lambs on behalf of everyone else (6:19–22). The Persian king charges Ezra to provide the temple with "bulls, rams, and lambs, and their grain offerings and their drink offerings" so that these may be offered as sacrifices (7:17, 21–23). It is soon reported that the people offered burnt offerings and sin offerings to the LORD (8:35). In Nehemiah 10:32–33, those obedient to God's law agree to maintain various offerings, including burnt and grain offerings, festival offerings, and sin offerings, to make atonement for the people. Far from ignoring sacrificial worship, the books of Ezra and Nehemiah show an interest in sacrificial offerings similar to what we see in priestly sources.

The New Testament's Trajectory on Sacrifice

As for the New Testament, both the Gospels and the book of Acts presume that sacrifices are being offered in the temple, but the overall trajectory of the New Testament is that Jesus's death serves as the ultimate sacrifice that transforms how sacrificial concepts are understood.

Jesus and his family were observant Jews, so it would be natural to find them involved in temple worship. When Joseph and Mary brought Jesus to the temple to present him before the Lord, they offered a sacrifice in accordance with what is written in the law of the Lord (Luke 2:24; cf. Lev. 5:7). Jesus's teaching on being reconciled to one's neighbor assumes that people are going to the altar to offer sacrificial gifts (Matt. 5:23–24). After healing a man with leprosy, Jesus tells him to show himself to the priest and offer the gift that Moses commanded, "as a testimony to them" (Matt. 8:4; Mark 1:44). In the Gospel of John, we learn of several occasions when Jesus went to Jerusalem for a festival day.[29] Although sacrificial worship is not a prominent theme in the Gospels, Jesus seems to have embraced Jewish worship as part of his religious identity.

29. John 2:13, 23; 5:1; 7:10–14; 10:22–23; 12:1, 12, 20; 13:1.

Even after Jesus's death and resurrection, Christians regarded the temple as a sacred place. In the book of Acts, the early church met in the temple courts (2:46) and visited the temple at times of prayer (3:1). Even the apostle Paul underwent ritual purification at the temple, together with men for whom offerings were made, to demonstrate his respect for Mosaic customs out of concern for the Jews (21:17–26).[30] Paul also says that he worshiped in Jerusalem and presented offerings (24:11, 17–18). This may partly reflect Paul's commitment to practice as a Jew under the law in order to win the Jews for Christ (1 Cor. 9:20–21). Despite the new perspective on sacrifice that emerged after Jesus's resurrection, temple worship remained important for Christian ministry.

At the same time, it is evident already in the Gospels that Jesus's death would satisfy the need for sacrificial offerings and change how Christians relate to sacrificial worship. On two occasions Jesus quotes Hosea 6:6 to say that God desires mercy, not sacrifice (Matt. 9:13; 12:7). Elsewhere, Jesus commends a teacher of the law for saying that love of God and neighbor is more important than all burnt offerings and sacrifices (Mark 12:33). Jesus came into the world to save people from sin, and he himself has the authority to forgive sins (Matt. 1:21; Mark 2:5–12). In the Gospel of John we learn that Jesus takes away the sin of the world (John 1:29) and that he lays down his life "on behalf of" others.[31] If Jesus came to forgive sin and remove its effects, then temple sacrifices will no longer be necessary. In fact, Jesus anticipates a time when the temple will be no more (Mark 13:1–2) and worship will no longer be centered on Jerusalem (John 4:19–24). The clearest statement on Jesus's sacrificial death appears in his comment on servanthood: "For even the Son of Man did not come to be served, but to serve, and to give his life as a ransom for many" (Mark 10:45; Matt. 20:28).

In the preaching of the early church, forgiveness of sins is obtained through repentance and commitment to Jesus rather than through sacrificial offerings.[32] Paul refers to the church as those whom the Lord acquired for himself "with his own blood" (Acts 20:28). In Romans 8:3, Paul says that God sent his own Son in the likeness of sinful flesh and *peri hamartias* (concerning sin), thereby condemning sin in the flesh. The phrase *peri hamartias* is frequently used as a translation for the Hebrew *ləḥaṭṭā't*, "as a sin offering."[33] It is likely that Paul

30. Acts 18:18 may refer to Paul taking a Nazirite vow. But the syntax of this verse is not fully clear, and the passage may be talking about Aquila.

31. John 6:51; 10:11, 15; 11:50–52; 15:13; 18:14.

32. Acts 2:38; 3:19; 5:31; 10:43; 13:38; 22:16; 26:18.

33. E.g., in the LXX, see Lev. 5:6–7, 11; 7:37; 9:2–3; 12:6, 8. In the New Testament, see Heb. 10:6, 8 (cf. Ps. 40:6) and Heb. 13:11 (cf. Lev. 16:15).

means that Jesus was sent in human form (in the "likeness" of sinful flesh, but without sin) to be a sin offering for humanity and thus to condemn sin. Similarly, in 2 Corinthians 5:21, Paul says that "God made him who had no sin [Jesus] to be sin [or a sin offering] on our behalf, so that in him we might become the righteousness of God." As 1 John 3:5 says, Jesus was revealed so that he might take away sins, and (like a blameless offering) there is no sin in him.

The theological categories established in the Old Testament through sacrificial offerings remain essential for New Testament teaching. In the New Testament, however, the reality of sacrifice is fulfilled in Jesus, whereas Old Testament practices are seen as instructional shadows that show what the contour of the reality looks like (Heb. 10:1–4; Col. 2:16–17). The application of sacrificial ideas to Christian life will be addressed in the next section.

Inner-Biblical Insights

Sacrificial offerings appear in early Old Testament narratives and feature prominently in the Pentateuch. Some ideas and details about sacrifice in these sources are presupposed in other Old Testament texts, which may be seen as responding to earlier traditions. Of course, the practice of offering sacrifices in the priestly manner stretches from Sinai to the postexilic period, so not all texts that respond to Israel's earliest traditions are later than all priestly sacrificial texts. Nevertheless, it is possible to see the phenomenon of inner-biblical interpretation in several places. First, the book of Deuteronomy re-applies earlier sacrificial practices to the new context of inhabiting the land. Second, Psalms, Proverbs, and certain prophetic texts presuppose a sacrificial system that could be construed mechanically, and their critique of this system constitutes a corrective interpretation of the tradition. Third, prophetic and postexilic texts that affirm temple sacrifice represent a constructive interpretive trajectory. Finally, the New Testament offers a fresh interpretation of Old Testament sacrifices in light of the death and resurrection of Jesus.

The Reapplication of Sacrificial Practices

Deuteronomy's expectation that all offerings in the promised land should be brought to a central location (Deut. 12) requires numerous legal adjustments.[34] The Passover celebration illustrates how the book of Deuteronomy

---

34. Looking at Deuteronomy, one might expect local altars (cf. Exod. 20:24–26) to have become taboo once Israel entered the land. It is therefore unclear why such altars continued to be

transforms sacrificial ritual. Exodus 12 describes the Passover as a festival that takes place in individual homes (v. 3), with the sacrificial lamb eaten inside each person's house (v. 46). In Deuteronomy, however, the Passover sacrifice cannot be eaten in local towns; instead it must be slaughtered and eaten at the place the LORD chooses (Deut. 16:5–7). Although the Passover ritual in Exodus is described as an "abiding statute for your generations" (Exod. 12:14, 24), Deuteronomy updates the manner in which it is celebrated. In fact, the centralization of the Passover in Deuteronomy deepens a motif already present in Exodus—namely, that the Passover festival should distinguish Israel from those around them.[35] The change fits the new historical context by reapplying a core theological idea.

The Passover festival receives further elaboration in several other passages in the Old Testament. In Numbers 9:1–14, Israel celebrates the Passover in the wilderness of Sinai in the year following their deliverance from Egypt. In light of the purity laws given at Sinai, this passage explains how Israelites are to celebrate if they are ritually unclean or traveling away from home. Major Passover celebrations are reported in the days of Hezekiah (2 Chron. 30) and Josiah (2 Kings 23:21–23; 2 Chron. 35:1–19). Josiah's Passover is described as unlike any such celebration since the period of the judges, with the full participation of the priests, Levites, and all the people (2 Kings 23:22; 2 Chron. 35:18). One particular detail in the account of Josiah's Passover stands out. According to Exodus 12:9, the Passover lamb should not be eaten raw or boiled in water but must be roasted in fire. Yet Deuteronomy 16:7 states that Israelites should "boil and eat" the Passover lamb. Consequently, in 2 Chronicles 35:13, "they boiled the Passover offering in fire according to the regulation, and they boiled the holy offerings in pots, pans, and bowls." In keeping with Deuteronomy 16:7, the Passover lamb is boiled, but as prescribed in Exodus 12:9, the Passover lamb is also cooked "in fire." Second Chronicles 35:13 affirms both versions of the Passover festival by harmonizing them.

The practice of tithing offers another example of how Deuteronomy elaborates on received biblical tradition. A yearly tithe of grain, fruit, and cattle is

---

constructed after the time of Deuteronomy by figures such as Joshua, Gideon, Samuel, David, and Elijah (Josh. 8:30–35; Judg. 6:24–27; 1 Sam. 7:17; 9:12; 2 Sam. 24:18, 25; 1 Kings 18:30, 38). Part of the answer may be that specific circumstances required local altars; for example, direct conflict with pagan shrines called for special altars to the one true God (e.g., Judg. 6:24–27; 1 Kings 18:30, 38). Part of the answer may be that Deuteronomy's centralization was meant to take effect after Israel found "rest" in the land (Deut. 12:8–10), and this rest for God's sanctuary was not fully achieved until Solomon built the temple in Jerusalem (1 Kings 7–8; cf. Josh. 21:44). On this latter point, and on the discussion of this issue in modern scholarship, see Averbeck, "Cult in Deuteronomy," 241–56.

35. See Deut. 12:4–6, 31–32; cf. Exod. 12:43–49.

described in Leviticus 27:30–33. This tithing law receives further specification in Numbers 18:21–32, which says that the Levites receive the tithes collected from the other tribes as payment for their work because they did not receive an inheritance of land. The Levites, in turn, give the best tenth of what they receive as an offering to the LORD. The practice of tithing is described somewhat differently in Deuteronomy. According to Deuteronomy 14:22–26, Israelites bring their tithes of produce and cattle to the central place of the LORD's choosing, where they themselves eat their own tithes. The Levites, however, are not forgotten. The people are told not to neglect the Levites who live in their towns, since the Levites have no land of their own (Deut. 14:27). Moreover, at the end of every third year, Israelites are to use their tithes to provide for local Levites, sojourners, orphans, and widows (Deut. 14:28–29). In conjunction with this third-year tithe, the people are instructed to profess before the LORD that they have provided for the Levite, the sojourner, the orphan, and the widow and that they have treated the sacred portions properly (Deut. 26:12–14). It is on the basis of performing these obligations that they are to ask for God's blessing (Deut. 26:15). Without neglecting the Levites, Deuteronomy expands the list of those who benefit from tithing to include sojourners, orphans, and widows. It also creates a liturgy that reminds Israel of the connection between God's blessing, proper care for the LORD's portion, and provision for those in need.

Psalms, Proverbs, and Prophetic Texts Offer a Corrective Interpretation

By the eighth century, many in Israel were making sacrificial offerings while also practicing idolatry and injustice. These Israelites apparently believed that they could gain the LORD's favor through sacrifices even if they also worshiped other deities or violated the Torah's ethical standards. The prophets criticize sacrificial worship understood in this way. Similar criticisms are found in Psalms and Proverbs. Key questions include, Are these sacrificial offerings necessary? Do they please God apart from obedience in other areas? Does God even want sacrifices at all?

Before looking at the key prophetic texts, I will briefly review how sacrificial offerings are challenged or explained in Psalms and Proverbs. Psalm 50:7–15 makes clear that God does not eat or drink Israel's sacrifices (v. 13) since he owns "the cattle on a thousand hills" (v. 10). The LORD is depicted as saying, "If I were hungry, I would not tell you, because the world and its fullness are mine" (v. 12). Even so, the psalmist approves of making thanksgiving sacrifices to God, as well as keeping vows and calling on God (vv.

14–15). It is not that sacrifices are worthless; it is simply that God does not need them for food. Ritual worship should be an expression of devotion and trust. Similarly, in Psalm 141:2, the psalmist asks that his prayers be accepted as incense and that the petitionary lifting up of his hands be accepted as an evening sacrifice. Psalm 69:30–31 presses the point further, saying that praising God in song and giving thanks are better than animal sacrifice. In two passages, in fact, the psalmist seems to say that God does not want sacrificial worship at all. First, according to Psalm 40:6, "You do not delight in sacrifices and offerings. . . . You did not ask for burnt offerings and sin offerings." Second, in a context of deep repentance, Psalm 51:15–17 says that God accepts praise and a contrite spirit and does not delight in sacrifices or burnt offerings. These two texts probably express poetic exaggeration, as is suggested by Psalm 51:19, where animal sacrifices are acceptable to God, provided that they are "sacrifices of righteousness." Sentiments similar to these are found in the book of Proverbs. The LORD prefers righteousness and justice to sacrifice (Prov. 21:3). When the wicked sacrifice, it is an abomination, but the prayers of the upright please God (15:8; cf. 21:27). Without rejecting sacrificial worship, Psalms and Proverbs emphasize that God does not need sacrificial offerings and that right actions and attitudes are the keys to proper worship.

The idea that sacrifices on their own please God is challenged with even greater force in prophetic literature. A paradigmatic passage on this topic is Samuel's rebuke of Saul, who justified keeping some of the Amalekites' cattle in disobedience to God's command by claiming that he planned to sacrifice these animals to the LORD. Samuel says to Saul, "Does the LORD delight in burnt offerings and sacrifices as much as he does in obedience to the LORD's voice? To obey is better than to sacrifice, and to pay attention is better than the fat of rams" (1 Sam. 15:22). In the same vein as Samuel, prophets who criticize a mechanical view of sacrifice provide an interpretation of earlier scriptural traditions that aims to realign sacrificial worship with general obedience to God.

The book of Hosea frequently criticizes Israel's idolatry and their worship of foreign deities.[36] Crimes of injustice such as murder, stealing, and lying likewise receive rebuke (e.g., Hosea 4:2; 7:1). What is more surprising, Hosea also condemns Israelite worship practices, such as new moons, Sabbaths, and sin offerings.[37] The key text on Israel's sacrificial worship appears in Hosea 6:6: "For I desire steadfast love, not sacrifice; I desire knowledge of God more

36. E.g., Hosea 2:8; 3:1; 4:12–13, 17; 8:4–6; 10:1–2, 5–6; 11:1–2; 13:1–2; 14:3, 8.
37. Hosea 2:11; 4:7; 8:11–13; 12:11.

than burnt offerings." This could mean that Hosea categorically rejects all sacrifice, but two arguments suggest that this is not the case. First, because the prophet so strongly rejects idolatry, we may assume that he favors exclusive worship of the LORD. Second, Hosea threatens Israel with the cessation of sacrificial worship (Hosea 3:4; 9:4–5), as if sacrifices were otherwise desirable. At the very least, the book of Hosea strongly asserts that sacrifices are worthless apart from justice and loyalty to God.

A passage that rejects sacrificial worship in favor of social ethics figures prominently near the beginning of the book of Isaiah (Isa. 1:11–17). This word of the LORD is introduced as God's Torah (v. 10). The text is quoted at length below:

> What to me is the multitude of your sacrifices?
>   says the LORD.
> I have had enough of burnt offerings of rams
>   and the fat of fed cattle.
> I do not delight in the blood of bulls,
>   lambs, and goats.
>
> When you come to appear before me,
>   who required this from your hand,
>   trampling on my courts?
> Bring me no more vain offerings;
>   incense is an abomination to me.
> new moon, Sabbath, and the calling of convocations—
>   I cannot bear iniquity and assembly.
> My soul hates your new moons and appointed feasts;
> they are a burden to me
>   that I am tired of bearing.
> When you spread out your hands,
>   I will hide my face from you.
> When you multiply your prayers,
>   I will not listen.
>   Your hands are full of blood.
> Wash! Be cleansed!
>   Remove your evil deeds
>   from before my eyes!
> Stop doing evil!
>   Learn to do what is good!
> Pursue justice!
>   Correct oppression!
> Make judgments on behalf of the orphan!
>   Plead for the widow! (Isa. 1:11–17)

This oracle places the whole burden of Israel's responsibility before God in the area of social ethics. The rhetorical question, "Who required this from your hand?" (v. 12), implies that God never asked them to bring sacrifices in the first place. But if sacrificial worship were being rejected categorically, the same would be true of prayer (v. 15). It seems unlikely that the prophet is categorically rejecting prayer and seeking God's face. The force of this passage might be that just as prayers can be effective when one's hands are not full of blood, sacrificial worship can be acceptable when one's actions reflect God's justice. Still, there is no denying that Isaiah 1:11–17 elevates ethics to a position of such importance that sacrifices and offerings are virtually irrelevant in comparison. This constitutes a clear theological commentary on Israel's tradition of sacrificial worship.

Other prophetic passages that criticize ritual sacrifice are Micah 6:6–8, Jeremiah 7:1–15, and Amos 5:21–24. A series of rhetorical questions in Micah 6:6–8 asserts that no sacrifice can please God because God requires nothing more than for his people to do justice, practice steadfast love, and walk humbly with him. Jeremiah's "temple sermon" insists that the temple and its sacrifices are worthless as long as the people are worshiping idols, oppressing the helpless, and violating basic ethical standards (Jer. 7:1–15; cf. 14:12). A sharp condemnation of sacrificial offerings is found at Amos 5:21–24, which concludes with the famous words, "Let justice roll down like waters, and righteousness like an ever-flowing stream" (v. 24). Not only does Amos express God's rejection of their sacrifices in severe terms (e.g., "I hate, I reject your feasts," v. 21), but there is nothing in the book of Amos to suggest that this prophet has any concern for ritual worship whatsoever (cf. Amos 4:4–5).

A peculiar historical tradition appears in a few prophetic books related to the origins of sacrificial worship. We have already seen Isaiah's question: "When you come to appear before me, who required this from your hand, trampling on my courts?" (Isa. 1:12). This implies that God did not instruct them to bring sacrificial offerings. Amos asks a question with similar force about the wilderness wandering period: "Did you bring me sacrifices and offerings in the desert for forty years, O House of Israel?" (Amos 5:25). Jeremiah articulates this tradition most clearly: "For I did not speak with your fathers, and I did not command them on the day when I brought them up from the land of Egypt, concerning matters of burnt offering and sacrifice" (Jer. 7:22). From this perspective, the whole practice of making sacrificial offerings was Israel's idea, not God's. This appears to be at odds with the Pentateuch. Perhaps these passages reflect rhetorical exaggeration.

Isaiah 66:1–4 offers a remarkable statement on the ineffectiveness of sacrificial offerings. Since heaven is God's throne, how could anyone build a house (a temple) for God? (Isa. 66:1; cf. 1 Kings 8:27). In other words, closeness to God is not about physical proximity to a building. In reality, the LORD favors those who are lowly, contrite in spirit, and reverent before his word (Isa. 66:2). According to this prophetic critique, slaughtering a bull is no more effective than killing a person, sacrificing a lamb is no different from breaking a dog's neck, presenting a grain offering is like offering pig's blood, and burning incense is equal to blessing an idol (v. 3). The actions cited for comparison in this passage are either meaningless or harmful. It is a person's inner disposition that counts with God (v. 2), whereas sacrificial worship is worthless or even detrimental.

In sum, the prophetic perspective discussed in this section interprets Israel's sacrificial heritage by focusing on social justice, the prohibition against idolatry, and inner devotion. Any notion that sacrifices appease God on their own is thoroughly rejected.

Prophetic and Postexilic Texts Offer a Constructive Interpretive Trajectory

Alongside criticisms of sacrificial offerings, certain prophetic books also contain passages that promise the restoration of sacrificial worship. As noted above, postexilic historical books likewise take seriously the restoration of temple sacrifices. These biblical sources offer a constructive interpretive response to Israel's earliest traditions on sacrifices and offerings.

Some of the prophetic books that offer strong condemnations of sacrificial offerings also depict an ideal future that includes them. I have already mentioned the vision in Micah 4:1–2 and Isaiah 2:2–3 in which the Temple Mount is lifted up and the nations stream to it, presumably to make sacrifices. Isaiah presents a stunning prophecy, according to which Egypt will have an altar to the LORD where sacrifices and offerings are made, and they will worship alongside Israel and Assyria.[38] Despite Jeremiah's opposition to the temple worship of his day, the book of Jeremiah contains several promises of restored temple sacrifices (e.g., Jer. 17:26; 31:14), including a declaration that God will never break his covenant with the Levites who minister before him (Jer. 33:19–22). Such prophecies show that prophetic criticism of sacrifice did not necessarily lead to an absolute rejection of sacrificial offerings.

The book of Ezekiel has more to say about sacrificial worship than any other prophetic book. Ezekiel is identified as a priest (Ezek. 1:1–3). Jeremiah was also a priest, but Ezekiel's priestly identity has a more profound impact on his message. Like other prophets, Ezekiel recognizes that God is not pleased

---

38. Isa. 19:19–25; cf. Zeph. 2:11; 3:10.

with the people's worship. In an extended vision (chaps. 8–11), Ezekiel sees the glory of the LORD depart from the temple because of sins such as idolatry (8:10), violence (8:17), injustice (9:9), and failure to observe God's statutes (11:12). Ezekiel 22 offers a list of Judah's sins that resembles the charges made by other prophets (e.g., idolatry, bloodshed, robbery, slander, adultery), although Ezekiel also condemns the failure to distinguish between clean and unclean and between holy and common (v. 26). Moreover, he considers all these sins to be "abominations." For Ezekiel the priest, eating animals with blood defiles the land as Leviticus suggests (e.g., Lev. 17:10–14), and idolatry and shedding blood also cause defilement.[39] In other words, Ezekiel pays particular attention to ritual violations that reflect priestly concerns, but he also employs priestly vocabulary to condemn a wider range of sins. At the conclusion of the book, Ezekiel reports a vision of the restored temple (chaps. 40–48). This vision clearly imagines sacrificial worship, including burnt, sin, and guilt offerings.[40] Ezekiel offers an interpretation of ritual sacrifice that both embraces priestly categories and also extends these categories to address idolatry and injustice.

The postexilic prophets and historical books understand temple sacrifices to be an enduring part of Israel's worship. The prophets Haggai and Zechariah encourage the Jews to rebuild the temple. Malachi rebukes the people for making unworthy sacrifices (Mal. 1:6–10), but he clearly expects that they should bring worthy offerings (1:12–14). Furthermore, Malachi anticipates a day when people will bring offerings in righteousness (3:3–4) and when many nations will present pure offerings to the LORD (1:11). The focus on temple and sacrifice in the book of Ezra was noted above. This same point can be illustrated by comparing the accounts of Hezekiah's reign as reported in 2 Kings and 2 Chronicles. The account of Hezekiah's reform in 2 Kings 18:1–4, which reflects preexilic and exilic interests, gives little attention to temple worship. But 2 Chronicles 29, which shows what postexilic writers saw as important, devotes considerable attention to Hezekiah's cleansing the temple, including a detailed description of the sin offerings that were made (29:21–24). These late Old Testament books did not reject ritual sacrifice but instead saw themselves as heirs to the priestly tradition of sacrificial worship as described in the Pentateuch.

The New Testament Offers a Fresh Interpretation

In the New Testament, Jesus fulfills the various human needs that Old Testament sacrifices were meant to address, such as atonement, forgiveness, and

39. E.g., Ezek. 33:25–26; 36:17–18.
40. E.g., Ezek. 40:39; 42:13; 43:19–25; 44:27–29; 45:17–25; 46:20.

purification. The language of sacrifice remains meaningful for New Testament writers, but it functions primarily as background for explaining the work of Jesus and as a metaphorical way to describe the Christian life.

Jesus's death as a sacrifice for sin sets the stage for the New Testament's reception of sacrificial imagery. In the letters of the New Testament, we learn that Jesus became a sin offering (Rom. 8:3), a propitiation for sins,[41] and an offering and sacrifice that gives a pleasing aroma (Eph. 5:2). Like a sin offering, Jesus's blood purifies people from all sin (1 John 1:7). Of course, not every concept connected to sacrifice is given equal attention in the New Testament, and sometimes ideas are combined in new ways. For example, Jesus died at the time of the Passover,[42] and the point is made that none of his bones were broken (John 19:36), as if to present his death as a Passover sacrifice (cf. Exod. 12:46). This is likely the intent when John the Baptist says, "Behold, the Lamb of God who takes away the sin of the world" (John 1:29, 36). Paul explicitly calls Jesus "our Passover offering" (1 Cor. 5:7). This identification probably underlies the reference to Christ as a lamb without blemish in 1 Peter 1:19 (cf. Exod. 12:5) and also the picture of Jesus as a slain Lamb in the book of Revelation.[43] In the Old Testament, the Passover lamb was not a sacrifice to atone for sin, although it did protect the Israelites from destruction (Exod. 12:13), and lambs were used in other contexts as guilt offerings (e.g., Lev. 14:12). The New Testament combines the protecting motif from the Passover sacrifice with atonement and forgiveness motifs from other Old Testament passages. The result is a composite theology of Jesus as the definitive sacrifice that fulfills all the requirements of the sacrificial system.

The book of Hebrews explains how Jesus served as the perfect sacrifice and now functions as the eternal high priest to obtain the ultimate forgiveness of sins. Jesus is a high priest who is able to sympathize with human weakness, so he can minister on our behalf. But he is also without sin, so unlike a normal priest, he does not need to make atonement for himself. Jesus was appointed a priest forever, so he never needs to be replaced. Whereas a regular priest ministers at an earthly sanctuary that merely represents God's presence, Jesus mediates for humanity before the heavenly throne of divine majesty. Jesus administers a superior covenant that is inaugurated by his own blood, which truly cleanses the conscience and provides forgiveness of sins. The priesthood of Jesus is superior to Levitical priesthood in its effectiveness, permanence,

41. 1 John 2:2; 4:10; cf. Rom. 3:25.
42. John 13:1; 18:28, 39; 19:14, 31, 42.
43. E.g., Rev. 5:6, 9, 12; 7:14; 12:11.

and divine authenticity.[44] As a sacrifice, Jesus identified with humanity so that he might taste death on behalf of all and free us from death (Heb. 2:9, 14–15). Just as the sin offering on the Day of Atonement was burned outside the camp (Lev. 16:27), Jesus suffered outside the city gate in order to sanctify people through his blood (Heb. 13:10–13). Without the shedding of blood, there is no forgiveness of sins (Heb. 9:22). But the blood of bulls and goats cannot truly take away sins (Heb. 10:4), so Jesus's death was necessary to provide forgiveness once and for all (Heb. 9:28; 10:12). Hebrews 10:5–10 explains Psalm 40:6–8 as Christ speaking about his crucifixion as the means by which God set aside the old covenant of Levitical sacrifices to establish the new covenant as foretold in Jeremiah 31:31–34 (cf. Heb. 8:7–13). The atoning death of Jesus functions as the interpretive key for understanding what the New Testament as a whole does with the theology of sacrificial offerings.

In the wake of Jesus's death and resurrection, New Testament writers employ sacrificial language to describe the various ways that Christians offer their lives in service to God. The application of sacrificial imagery begins with Jesus and encompasses both the church and individual believers. Evangelism, good works, suffering, and worship all constitute forms of nonliteral sacrifice.

Within the New Testament's network of related sacrificial images, the temple plays a foundational role. Jesus identified his body as the sanctuary of God that would be destroyed and raised in three days (John 2:18–22). Just as the Old Testament temple was meant to represent the epicenter of God's presence on earth, so also Jesus's body constituted the incarnation of the divine presence on earth. Jesus could also be likened to a rejected stone that became the temple's chief cornerstone (Mark 12:10–11; Ps. 118:22–23). With Jesus as the living cornerstone, the people of God are built up to become a spiritual house and a holy temple in the Lord (Eph. 2:19–22; 1 Pet. 2:5–6). Jesus said that when he went to the Father, he would ask the Father on behalf of those who love him, and the Father would send the Spirit in Jesus's name.[45] In Paul's writings, the church as a community is the temple of God because the Spirit dwells among them (1 Cor. 3:16–17; 2 Cor. 6:16), and the bodies of individual Christians are temples of the Holy Spirit (1 Cor. 6:19). Through Jesus and the Holy Spirit, Christians receive the spiritual identity of God's temple.

The image of firstfruits was used by New Testament writers as a metaphor to describe how God receives people into his favor. Israelites were commanded

44. On the priesthood of Jesus in Hebrews, see Heb. 4:14–16; 5:5–10; 6:19–20; 7:23–27; 8:1–6; 9:11–15, 23–28; 10:1–8.
45. John 7:39; 14:16–17, 25–26; 15:26; 16:13; 20:22; Acts 1:4–8.

to bring the firstfruits of their produce to the LORD.[46] When God the Father vindicated Jesus by raising him from the dead, Jesus became the firstfruits of those who are raised: first, Jesus was raised, and later, those who have died in the Lord will be raised (1 Cor. 15:20–23). Among people whom the Lord gathered to himself, the people of Israel are identified as God's firstfruits, and the gentiles who believe in Jesus come later (Rom. 11:13–16). The first person to accept the gospel in Asia was a man named Epenetus, so he is "the firstfruits of Asia for Christ" (Rom. 16:5). The first group of converts in Achaea was the household of Stephanas, so they are "the firstfruits of Achaea" (1 Cor. 16:15). From the perspective of Old Testament offerings, everything belongs to God, but the firstfruits are devoted to God's special purpose as representative of the whole and as symbols to show that God's portion should be the best. It is a remarkable honor for these New Testament Christians to be called the firstfruits of their region. The metaphor suggests that everyone in the region belongs to God, and after the firstfruits many more people will be received into God's household through Christ.

A life of obedient devotion to God can be construed theologically as a kind of sacrificial offering. In 1 Peter 2:5, Christians are being built into a "holy priesthood" so that they may offer "spiritual sacrifices that are pleasing to God through Jesus Christ." The whole of 1 Peter, which includes Christian doctrinal teaching and practical life instruction for a Roman context (1 Pet. 2:13–17), provides a picture of what it meant for the recipients of this letter to present "offerings" that please God. Paul urges the Christians in Rome (Rom. 12:1) to "present their bodies as living sacrifices that are holy and pleasing to God," as an act of "rational worship" (*logikē latreia*). The adjective *logikos* means either "pertaining to speech" or "pertaining to reason." In this passage, it can be translated as "rational," but not in the sense of "intellectual" instead of "emotional." For many ancient Greek thinkers *logos*, "reason," is the perfect, rational ordering principle that holds everything together and guides all right thought and action. This *logos* is grasped conceptually—that is, immaterially. In the Greek Old Testament, the "word" (*logos*) of the Lord instructed the prophets, and in the Gospel of John, the divine Word (*logos*) became flesh. Paul is saying that Christians should present their bodies not as literal, material sacrifices that are slain on an altar but as living sacrifices that please God through obedience to the divine *logos*.[47]

Several passages in the New Testament show how sacrificial imagery could be applied to specific activities. Paul's preaching of the gospel to the gentiles

46. E.g., Exod. 23:19; Lev. 23:9–14; Num. 18:12–13; Deut. 26:1–4.

47. See also 1 Pet. 2:2: "As newborn babies, long for pure rational (*logikon*) milk." Or as the KJV puts it, "The sincere milk of the word."

is described as "administering as priestly service" (*hierourgounta*) the gospel of God, which he did "so that the offering of the gentiles might become well-pleasing, sanctified by the Holy Spirit" (Rom. 15:16). The gifts of support that Paul received from the church at Philippi are "a fragrant aroma, an acceptable offering, pleasing to God" (Phil. 4:18). Christians can offer "the sacrifice of praise" to God as "the fruit of lips that give recognition to his name" (Heb. 13:15–16; cf. Hosea 14:2). In the book of Revelation, the prayers of the saints are like incense burned on the altar (Rev. 5:8; 8:3–4). In Paul's trials and imprisonment for the sake of the gospel, he can say that he is being "poured out like a drink offering on the altar" (Phil. 2:17; cf. 2 Tim. 4:6). Paul uses sacrificial imagery to address Christian ethics in 1 Corinthians 5:6–8. In correcting the church's boasting, Paul warns them that even a little sin causes much harm, just as a little yeast leavens a whole lump of dough. This reminds him of the Festival of Unleavened Bread, which continues for seven days after Passover (Exod. 12:14–20). Because Christ, "our Passover offering," has been sacrificed, the Corinthians should "celebrate the festival, not with old leaven, the leaven of malice and evil, but with the unleavened bread of sincerity and truth." In other words, Christians no longer celebrate this festival literally because Christ fulfilled the sacrificial system—but they should live out a festival of sincerity and truth in their lives.

Four streams of inner-biblical interpretation were identified in this chapter: Deuteronomy's transformation of earlier sacrificial practices, the prophetic critique of sacrificial worship, the affirmation of temple sacrifices found in some prophetic and postexilic texts, and the New Testament's theology of sacrifice in light of the death and resurrection of Jesus. Right moral action and proper intentionality are common themes in these sources. Both Deuteronomy and Ezekiel update earlier biblical traditions and expand the ethical implications of sacrifice. Certain prophetic texts, supported by select psalms and proverbs, suggest that sacrificial worship may be unnecessary. This move seems to prefigure the New Testament's nonliteral application of sacrificial imagery to Christian life. Still, some prophetic texts and postexilic books affirm the enduring value of temple worship and thus testify to the need for literal sacrifice.

These four streams of inner-biblical interpretation yield the following insights: (1) The practice of a ritual can change in different contexts while still maintaining continuity with the ritual's core ideas. (2) The devotion to God symbolized in Old Testament sacrificial worship is more important than the physical performance of the sacrifices. (3) Ethical behavior toward others is more important than sacrificial offerings. (4) Sacrifice, atonement, cleansing, and forgiveness are abiding needs for human beings. (5) Jesus fulfilled the requirements of the Old Testament sacrificial system by his death, and he now serves as an eternal high priest and mediator of a new covenant. (6) Because of Jesus's death, Christians no longer make literal offerings of animals or produce, but they fulfill the core ideas that were symbolized through these offerings by devoting their lives to God.

Putting the Pieces Together

Jesus's death and resurrection are key to understanding how the various biblical perspectives on sacrificial offerings fit together. Numerous important concepts are expressed through ritual sacrifice in the Old Testament, but already in the prophets we learn that genuine love of God (no idolatry) and practical love of neighbor (social justice), rather than worship through sacrifices and festivals, are the essential characteristics of a life rightly lived. This insight prepares the way for Jesus's sacrificial death, which eliminates the need for Christians to offer literal animal sacrifices and opens the door to nonliteral "sacrifices" and "offerings." When interpreting any biblical text that deals with sacrificial offerings, the most important context is the salvation-historical one—namely, where in Scripture the passage occurs in relation to Jesus's death and resurrection.

The practice of ritual sacrifice was common throughout the ancient world. Sacrifices in the Old Testament served in part as an accommodation to the surrounding cultures. In other words, the God of Israel accepted and adapted a form of worship that was culturally familiar. In the end, the core ideas were essential, not the actual offerings. God did not need the food, and the blood of bulls and goats cannot take away sins (Heb. 10:4). Still, Israel's sacrifices and festivals were like "shadows" (Heb. 10:1; Col. 2:16–17) that positively revealed the outlines of true realities. Therefore, the outward forms of sacrificial worship served as reminders of sin (Heb. 10:3) and as symbols for theological truths that Israel could learn if they paid attention to the rituals they performed.

In terms of putting biblical passages together into a coherent picture, we can generally interpret New Testament texts either as explanations of Jesus's ministry or as lessons for Christian living that apply today with only occasional cultural updating. Likewise, prophetic texts and passages in Psalms and Proverbs that emphasize ethics and inner devotion rather than sacrifice can be applied today in relatively straightforward ways. Many Old Testament texts, however, seem less relevant for Christians, who no longer practice the detailed sacrificial rituals that are described. I suggest that the metaphorical application of sacrificial imagery as found in the New Testament should serve as a model for the contemporary application of Old Testament sacrificial texts. The first task is to ascertain what core ideas the Old Testament passage communicated in its original context. Then, these core ideas can be applied metaphorically to Christian life as guided by the rest of the New Testament.

I will give three examples: (1) Numerous details in sacrificial law, such as the need for an unblemished animal and the practice of burning the fat portion to God, express that we should give our best to God (cf. Col. 3:23; 1 Cor. 9:24–27). (2) The law of centralization in Deuteronomy 12 that seeks to prevent Israel from worshiping other deities teaches that we should not give to anything else the devotion that belongs to God alone (cf. Luke 4:8; Acts 5:29). (3) The fact that guilt offerings in Leviticus cannot be made unless the guilty party first makes restitution to the person wronged shows that genuine repentance must be accompanied by action (cf. Matt. 3:8; Luke 19:8–10). Practical theological insights like these are found throughout the Old Testament sacrificial system. Anyone who studies these texts carefully will be rewarded with insights that are relevant for contemporary Christian life.

In the Old Testament, Israelites gave their sacrificial offerings to God, but they received the greater gifts—namely, atonement, cleansing, and forgiveness. In the New Testament, Christians offer themselves as living sacrifices to God, but in return they receive much more, including eternal life (cf. Mark 10:29–31). The basic principle is that when we offer what we have to God, however little it may be, we are blessed with the greater gift of God's presence.

6

The Afterlife

Old Testament Hopes Become Reality in Jesus

The Old Testament does not say as much about the afterlife as we might expect. The God of Israel is strongly associated with life, not death. The primary focus of the Old Testament is God's work in this world. Still, indications of thought about the afterlife are not totally absent.[1] Certain practices and expressions that appear in the Old Testament point to belief in existence after death. A few passages can be found that address the hereafter directly, although whether the biblical writer is speaking literally or metaphorically is often difficult to tell. What we encounter frequently in the Old Testament are theological themes relevant to the afterlife, such as God's justice, goodness, and power over life and death. These elements eventually serve as jumping-off points for the promise of everlasting life in Daniel 12 and the New Testament's fully developed theology of resurrection.

Two major issues that confront us as we attempt to understand how different parts of Scripture deal with the afterlife are the role of culture and the question of theological development. First, basic assumptions about death and the netherworld that were common in the ancient Near East play a significant role in shaping how Old Testament texts address this topic. Even what the New Testament says about the afterlife can be situated within a current of Jewish thought that came to full force in the Greco-Roman world. We need to

---

1. Valuable studies on the afterlife and the Old Testament include Johnston, *Shades of Sheol*; Spronk, *Beatific Afterlife*; and Tromp, *Primitive Conceptions of Death*.

consider how best to interpret these texts as Scripture in light of their various cultural contexts. Second, the subject of this chapter offers a prime example of theological development within Scripture. Our survey of biblical perspectives will show that the Old Testament devotes much less attention to the afterlife than the New Testament does, and yet the New Testament builds its theology of life after death out of the Old. We will need to ask one key question: Now that we have New Testament teaching, how do we interpret Old Testament afterlife passages theologically as Christian Scripture?

Biblical Perspectives

The following survey of biblical perspectives on the afterlife begins with a discussion of the Old Testament's cultural context. After this are subsections that address the range of viewpoints and relevant theological ideas that one finds in the Old Testament. The final subsection offers a brief overview of major New Testament concepts. The individual subsections cover the following: (1) the afterlife in ancient Near Eastern thought, (2) death as the end of earthly life in the Old Testament, (3) the afterlife concepts underlying the Old Testament, (4) the Old Testament building blocks for afterlife theology, and (5) the afterlife in the New Testament.

The Afterlife in Ancient Near Eastern Thought

Because our knowledge of what Old Testament writers thought about the afterlife depends so heavily on assumptions behind the texts and allusions that are not fully explained, we do well to inquire into the beliefs and practices of Israel's neighbors to get some idea of the Old Testament's broader cultural context. An important observation is that the cultures surrounding ancient Israel generally gave more attention to the afterlife than the writers of the Old Testament did. Of course, no common theology of the hereafter was shared by all ancient peoples, and our sources for most regions are quite limited. But a general sense of the Old Testament's conceptual environment can be achieved by summing up a few major ideas about life after death in the cultures around Israel.

Ancient Egypt provides our clearest evidence for afterlife beliefs and practices. This evidence includes burial texts from royal tombs, afterlife instructions written on coffins, and books about the netherworld that explain how the soul or spirit of the deceased can arrive safely in the next world.[2] Bodies

2. Lesko, "Death and the Afterlife," 3:1763–74.

were preserved, and provisions of food and other items were supplied for the dead, which shows that a general sense of continuity was felt between this life and the next. Conceptions of the afterlife could be positive—for example, sailing across the sky with the sun god or traveling to the Field of Offerings, which came to be viewed as a kind of Paradise.[3] Nevertheless, the journey to the netherworld could be perilous. The deceased needed to know the proper spells and the names of underworld beings and objects to reach their final destination. Certain texts, such as the Instruction of Merikare and the Book of the Dead, suggest that one's moral deeds on earth help determine one's fate in the afterlife.[4] Egyptian beliefs about death and the hereafter obviously were not uniform everywhere or in every period, but these basic concepts remained current in Egypt throughout the Old Testament era.

Belief in the survival of the soul after the body's death is well attested in Mesopotamian sources.[5] Provisions were placed in graves to nourish the deceased for their journey to the netherworld. Regular offerings were required to sustain the souls of the departed, since food does not grow in the region of the dead.[6] In general, the netherworld was seen as a dark, gloomy place below the earth's surface where people eat dust and clay and where a road leads in but there is no way out.[7] Proper burial and mourning rites, along with regular offerings, needed to be performed by the living on behalf of the dead to improve their condition. Thus, according to one mythological text, the deceased person who receives no food offerings from surviving relatives must eat scraps, whereas the person who is survived by six sons rejoices, and the one who has seven sons sits among the lesser gods.[8] With proper care from the living, souls in the netherworld become part of the family's ancestral

3. Lesko, "Death and the Afterlife," 3:1768.

4. See Lichtheim, "Instructions," 1:63, 65; and Faulkner et al., *Egyptian Book of the Dead*, plates 3A–4B, 15A–15B, 30A–32A (pp. 117, 129–30). In the picture of the deceased person's arrival at the Hall of Justice in the Book of the Dead (plates 3A–3B), the individual's heart is weighed against the feather of *ma'at* (justice). A deceased person who is deemed unworthy is devoured by a monster, Amamet. Afterlife punishments vary in different texts. According to the Book of Caverns, for example, those consigned to the Place of Destruction are decapitated and lose their souls. See Darnell and Darnell, *Ancient Egyptian Netherworld Books*, 352–53.

5. Scurlock, "Death and the Afterlife," 3:1883–93. See also Haas, "Death and the Afterlife," 3:2021–30.

6. On making provisions for the dead in Mesopotamian practice, see Katz, *Image of the Netherworld*, 197–98, 235–37.

7. Dalley, "Descent of Ishtar," 1:381; and Dalley, "Nergal and Ereshkigal," 1:386. In "The Netherworld Vision of an Assyrian Crown Prince," Prince Kumaya enters the netherworld in a dream and sees fifteen ghastly demons. See Foster, *Before the Muses*, 832–39.

8. See the early Sumerian version in Gadotti, *"Gilgamesh, Enkidu, and the Netherworld,"* 159–60; and the later version of this narrative in tablet 12 of the Epic of Gilgamesh, in Dalley, *Myths from Mesopotamia*, 123–25.

spirits, until eventually the remnant of a person's soul is recycled in a newly born human.[9]

The presentation of offerings to the dead was beneficial not only for the deceased but also for the living. Departed spirits who did not receive proper attention, as well as those who died wretched deaths (e.g., burning in fire), could cause harm to the living. One reason to treat the dead properly was to protect the living against such malevolent spirits. The well-being of society as a whole depended in part on the worship of deceased royal and noble ancestors.[10] Icons representing the spirit of the deceased often played a role in venerating them. Those who were harassed by restless spirits or wanted to communicate with the dead performed rituals that involved incantations to invoke the deceased. Attending to the dead was more than an act of kindness or duty. It was essential for the well-being of the living.

According to many Mesopotamian sources, the netherworld is ruled by gods (e.g., Ereshkigal and Nergal) who render judgments in matters pertaining to their realm. Some sources mention a court composed of deities, the "court of the Anunnaki," who assign the newly departed to their places in the netherworld and otherwise issue decrees to settle matters among the gods.[11] Other texts speak of a mortal (e.g., Gilgamesh) who is appointed to determine justice among the deceased in the next life.[12] There is no clear evidence, however, that the dead were judged in the netherworld on the basis of their moral deeds in this life.

Belief in the soul's existence after death is also clearly attested in ancient Canaan.[13] Archaeological discoveries across the region indicate that people provided ongoing nourishment for the departed. Textual sources from Ugarit and Ebla in Syria confirm the practice of making offerings to the dead. Children were responsible to see that proper burial and mourning rites were performed and that appropriate offerings were made for their parents. Therefore, it was a tragedy for anyone to die childless.[14] Deceased royalty and heroes were worshiped at both Ugarit and Ebla. In certain sacrificial rituals known

9. Scurlock, "Death and the Afterlife," 1892.

10. See Haas, "Death and the Afterlife," 2028–29; Scurlock, "Death and the Afterlife," 1888.

11. See Scurlock, "Death and the Afterlife," 1887–88. For an example of the court of the Anunnaki pronouncing judgment before Ereshkigal, see Inanna's Descent to the Netherworld in Pritchard, *Ancient Near Eastern Texts*, 55. On the Anunnaki rendering judgments for mortals, see the Epic of Gilgamesh in Dalley, *Myths from Mesopotamia*, 109.

12. See the Sumerian work, the Death of Gilgamesh, in Katz, *Image of the Netherworld*, 187–88.

13. Xella, "Death and the Afterlife," 3:2059–70; Spronk, *Beatific Afterlife in Ancient Israel*, 139–236; and Lewis, *Cults of the Dead*.

14. E.g., in the Epic of Aqhat one important duty of a son toward his father is "to rescue his smoke from the Underworld, to protect his steps from the dust." See Parker, "Aqhat," 53.

from Ugarit, the spirits of deceased nobles are summoned to participate. A distinction can be made between general provision of food for the dead and the veneration of royal ancestors. Although food offerings were provided for the deceased at various levels of society, ancestors across the social spectrum were not necessarily worshiped. Nevertheless, if deceased rulers were worshiped as divine beings who could bestow benefits on the living, it is possible that lesser deceased persons, such as family heads, might also have been venerated and petitioned for assistance.[15]

Literary compositions from Ugarit give special attention to death and the restoration of life. Unlike Egyptian sources, however, Ugaritic texts contain no images of potential bliss in the hereafter, nor do any Ugaritic works speak of afterlife judgment. Death is primarily an unpleasant reality that all must face. Thus, in the Epic of Aqhat, when the goddess Anat offers immortality to the human Aqhat in return for his bow, he scoffs at the offer as if it were impossible, saying, "The death of all I shall die, I too shall die and be dead."[16] In Ugaritic mythology Mot (death) is a personified deity who devours the dead. Those who die, whether mortal or divine, are depicted as descending down Mot's throat into the subterranean realm.[17] Not much is said about conditions in the underworld, but people continue to exist there, albeit in a highly undesirable state.

Spirits known as Rapiuma (shades) appear in several Ugaritic texts. The Rapiuma are deceased kings and nobles who normally inhabit the underworld but are summoned by the living at certain festivals. Their precise nature is difficult to determine, but they appear to receive sacrificial offerings and seem able to benefit the living.[18] One text that extols Shapsh (the sun goddess) says, "Shapsh rules the *Rephaim* [Rapiuma], Shapsh rules the Gods. Your company are the divinities, See, the dead are your companions."[19] This shows the connection between the Rapiuma, the dead, and the gods. Moreover, the Rapiuma are associated specifically with Baal. Just as Baal triumphed over Mot, the Rapiuma emerge from the netherworld as part of

15. Xella, "Death and the Afterlife," 2066.

16. Parker, "Aqhat," 61–62.

17. E.g., Smith, "Baal Cycle," 141. In this passage, the image of being devoured by Mot appears in a speech directed at the god Baal.

18. See Johnston, *Shades of Sheol*, 134–40; and Spronk, *Beatific Afterlife in Ancient Israel*, 161–96. According to Spronk, the Rapiuma are deified ancestors who are called up from the netherworld to take part in the celebration of Baal's return to life, and they possess healing powers (195). According to Xella, the Rapiuma were the spirits of deceased rulers and warriors who were venerated by the people as saviors, "healing their diseases, providing oracular responses, protecting them on a personal and community level, and fostering fertility" ("Death and the Afterlife," 2065).

19. Smith, "Baal Cycle," 164.

Baal's army: "There the 'shades' [*rpu*] of Baal, Warriors of Baal, Warriors of Anat."[20] Apparently not everyone who died became part of the Rapiuma; rather, this group of spirits was composed strictly of deceased rulers. Yet the cognate word *rp'm* (shades) occurs in at least two Phoenician inscriptions, where it refers to a desirable afterlife condition that anyone could potentially attain.[21]

In view of the preceding discussion, it is surprising that the Old Testament does not say more about the afterlife. There is nothing in the Old Testament to match Egyptian texts. Even compared to Mesopotamian sources, the Old Testament is reticent about the hereafter. This does not mean, however, that Old Testament writers revealed nothing of their beliefs. Our brief survey of ancient Near Eastern perspectives will help us identify what assumptions were operative in ancient Israel. In the end, though, it is worth asking why the Old Testament says so little about what follows death. One reason might be that Israel's neighbors worshiped the dead and sought guidance from deceased spirits. These behaviors were seen as incompatible with singular devotion to the LORD.[22] In addition, two other explanations may be considered: (1) Israel's God was strongly associated with life, so it was deemed inappropriate to present him as Lord of the dead—that is, an underworld deity. (2) Israel's mission was so exclusively focused on the present world that attention to the world to come was considered unnecessary or even distracting.

Death as the End of Earthly Life in the Old Testament

When Old Testament writers talk about dying, their immediate focus is usually the end of our present existence. This is often expressed poetically in describing the harsh reality of death. For example, Job sums up one of his speeches by saying, "For now I will lie down in the dust, and you will seek me, but I will not be" (Job 7:21; cf. Ps. 39:13). At death, people return to dust (Gen. 3:19), or they are like water poured out that remains ungathered (2 Sam.

20. Lewis, "Rapiuma," 203.
21. See Johnston, *Shades of Sheol*, 141. One text, which is a curse meant to dissuade tomb robbers, states, "May they have no resting place with the *rp'm*, nor be buried in a grave, nor have a son or seed in their place." It seems that would-be tomb robbers might be able to find rest with the *rp'm*, provided that they refrain from robbing tombs.
22. Consulting the dead is forbidden or condemned in Lev. 19:31; 20:6, 27; Deut. 18:11; 26:14; 1 Sam. 28:7–10 (1 Chron. 10:13); 2 Kings 21:6 (2 Chron. 33:6); 2 Kings 23:24; Isa. 8:19–22; 19:3 (Egypt's necromancy is condemned); 29:4 (futility of consulting the dead is employed metaphorically). Worshiping the dead is condemned in Ps. 106:28 (cf. Num. 25:2, where *'ĕlōhîm* may be taken in Ps. 106:28 as referring to spirits of the dead, as in 1 Sam. 28:13).

14:14). From this perspective, death is a place from which there is no return (e.g., Job 7:9–10; 10:21–22). Likewise, there is no remembrance of God, no giving thanks to God, and no declaring God's faithfulness.[23] The dead know nothing, and memory of them disappears (Eccles. 9:5). Even God no longer remembers the deceased, for they are cut off from his hand (Pss. 88:3–5; 146:4). According to one passage in Ecclesiastes, people die and return to dust just as animals do, and we do not know what comes next (Eccles. 3:18–22; cf. 9:2–4). These passages express the basic viewpoint on death that is found in much of the Old Testament—namely, that death is the termination of life and the negation of earthly experience.

The Hebrew word for the netherworld is *šə'ôl* (Sheol).[24] Its etymology is uncertain, and it can be used metaphorically in various ways. For now, I will highlight uses of the word "Sheol" that correspond to death as the end of earthly life. For example, "Sheol" can refer to a physical grave in which people are buried (e.g., Isa. 14:11). Sometimes "Sheol" is a poetic equivalent for death, as in Psalm 89:48: "What man is there who can live and not see death, who can rescue his life from the hand of Sheol?" (cf. Isa. 28:15, 18). When "Sheol" stands for the cessation of life, there is no work, knowledge, or wisdom there (Eccles. 9:10). According to one image, the deceased are swallowed by Sheol (Prov. 1:12; cf. Ps. 69:15). Just as people on earth continue to die, Sheol and destruction are never satisfied (Prov. 27:20; 30:15–16). A few texts speak of saving someone from the brink of death as rescuing them out of Sheol, as in Psalm 30:3: "O Lord, You brought up my life from Sheol, You preserved me alive from going down to the pit."[25] Also, wisdom that helps a person avoid untimely death can deliver that person from Sheol (e.g., Prov. 15:24; 23:14). As we will see below, the word "Sheol" can refer to the netherworld as a place of afterlife existence. But it also frequently occurs as a metaphor for death, where emphasis falls on Sheol as the conclusion of life, not the beginning of some future state.

Given the Old Testament's basic concern for the present world, a common way to think about life after death is that people "live on" through their descendants. This is a major reason why progeny is so important. One sees this clearly when characters express fear over their lack of progeny. For example, Saul asks David to swear not to cut off Saul's descendants, so that his name is not destroyed from his father's house (1 Sam. 24:21). Likewise, Absalom builds a monument for himself because he thinks, "I have no son to keep my

---

23. Pss. 6:5; 30:9; 88:11–12; Isa. 38:18–19.
24. See Johnston, *Shades of Sheol*, 70–75.
25. Cf. Pss. 18:5–6, 16–19; 86:13; 116:3–4; Jon. 2:2.

name in remembrance" (2 Sam. 18:18). We often see a connection between having children and preserving one's name.[26] Whoever has many offspring to keep his name alive can die "in good old age" (e.g., Gen. 25:1–8; cf. Job 5:25–26).[27] Surviving beyond death through one's descendants and through the memory of the living is considered a legitimate form of "afterlife" in the Old Testament.

Afterlife Concepts Underlying the Old Testament

A few basic concepts about the afterlife in the Old Testament reflect assumptions that were shared between ancient Israel and its Near Eastern neighbors. This is especially the case with regard to three topics: (1) Sheol as an inhabited netherworld, (2) spirits of the dead, and (3) burial customs.

First, several Old Testament passages depict Sheol as an actual netherworld that is populated by the conscious dead. In Numbers 16:30–33, the LORD causes the ground to open its mouth so that those involved in Korah's rebellion might be "swallowed" by the earth and "go down alive into Sheol." They did not simply fall into a pit and die. Rather, they were taken to a place under the earth designated for the dead, and the ironic twist is that they entered while still living. A similar picture is given by Psalm 55:15: "Let death come upon them, let them go down alive to Sheol."[28] Two texts in particular give especially lucid descriptions of Sheol. First, Isaiah 14:3–21 foretells the doom that will befall the king of Babylon and his miserable fate in the afterlife. The departed spirits of the underworld (shades), who are the kings of other nations, rise up to greet him when he enters Sheol, informing him that he has become weak like them and that his body will be covered with worms (vv. 9–11). Second, Ezekiel 32:17–32 contains laments for the armies of various foreign nations. Specific burial customs are described (e.g., vv. 26–27), and reference is made to people descending to the "lower parts of the earth" (vv. 18, 24) or "the pit" (e.g., vv. 23–25). A clear indication of the conscious existence of the dead occurs in verse 21, where deceased warriors in Sheol speak to Egypt and its allies about their condition in the netherworld. Although the actual experience of dwelling in Sheol is seldom depicted in the Old Testament, these texts portray an unhappy yet conscious state for foreign enemies who go there.

26. E.g., Ps. 109:13; Deut. 25:6; Ruth 4:5, 10; Job 18:16–17.
27. See Alexander, "Old Testament View," 41–42.
28. Other passages frequently discussed include Deut. 32:22, which describes a fire that burns "as far as Sheol below" and consumes the earth, and David's comment about his deceased son: "I will go to him, but he will not return to me" (2 Sam. 12:23). See also "the land of forgetfulness" in Ps. 88:12.

Second, a few Old Testament texts refer to sentient spirits of the dead. A key term for such spirits is *rəpā'îm*, "shades," as in Isaiah 14:9 mentioned above.[29] This is closely related to the Ugaritic Rapiuma and the Phoenician *rp'm*. As an example, Job 26:5–6 says, "The shades tremble beneath the waters, and those who inhabit them [the waters]. Sheol is naked before him [God], and destruction has no protection." In Proverbs 9:18, the shades are said to be in the depths of Sheol. Proverbs 21:16 warns that whoever wanders from the path of understanding will find rest among the shades. The most startling picture of afterlife existence in the Old Testament is the summoning of Samuel's ghost in 1 Samuel 28:3–25. Saul decides to seek advice from the deceased Samuel, so he goes to a woman of Endor who practices mediumship to request that she bring up Samuel from the dead (vv. 8–11). When the woman sees Samuel, she describes him by saying, "I see a god [*'ĕlōhîm*] coming up out of the earth" (v. 13), and later adds, "an old man is coming up, wrapped in a cloak" (v. 14). Despite Saul's reverent attitude, Samuel scolds him, asking, "Why did you disturb me, bringing me up?" (v. 15), and he issues Saul a stern rebuke (vv. 16–19). Three significant details in this passage should not be missed: First, the medium of Endor calls Samuel a "god" (*'ĕlōhîm*), but it seems that this word can mean "undead spirit" (cf. Isa. 8:19).[30] Second, Samuel is recognizable as an old man wearing a cloak; he is not simply a rotted corpse. Third, Samuel speaks to Saul out of the knowledge and personality he had when he was alive. The account of Samuel's ghost shows that belief in the continuing existence of the dead in an underworld was not outside the purview of some Old Testament writers.

Third, Old Testament burial customs indicate some expectation that life continues beyond death. Reports of burial for major and minor figures appear regularly with varying degrees of detail.[31] To take one example, Joseph's request that his bones be returned to the promised land (Gen. 50:25; cf. Exod. 13:19) suggests that what happens to his remains after death affects his well-being in the netherworld.[32] Alongside burial, evidence exists for formal mourning rituals, such as Joseph's seven-day mourning for his father (Gen.

29. Other Old Testament texts that mention *rəpā'îm* are Job 26:5; Ps. 88:10; Prov. 2:18; 9:18; 21:16; Isa. 26:14, 19.

30. See Day, "Development of Belief," 233.

31. E.g., Sarah (Gen. 23:19), Abraham (Gen. 25:8–10), Rachel (Gen. 35:19–20), Isaac (Gen. 35:29), Joshua (Josh. 24:29–30), Eleazar (Josh. 24:33), Asahel (2 Sam. 2:32), Gideon (Judg. 8:32), Samson (Judg. 16:31), Samuel (1 Sam. 25:1), Ahithophel (2 Sam. 17:23), Saul and Jonathan (2 Sam. 21:14), and Joab (1 Kings 2:34).

32. Other significant discussions of burial include Abraham's efforts to properly acquire a burial place for Sarah in the promised land (Gen. 23:4–20) and Ruth's declaration to Naomi: "Where you die, I will die, and there I will be buried" (Ruth 1:17).

50:10–11) and the thirty-day periods of mourning for Aaron and Moses (Num.
20:29; Deut. 34:8).[33] As one might expect, to be denied burial or mourning
is a miserable fate (e.g., Jer. 16:4–7; Eccles. 6:3).[34] By contrast, it is highly
beneficial to be buried in the tomb of one's father.[35] One expression used
in the Old Testament in connection with death and burial is that someone
"slept with his fathers." Typically this implies a peaceful death. For example,
David, who died peacefully, "slept with his fathers," but Joab, who perished
violently, simply "died" (1 Kings 11:21).[36] A related idiom that occurs strictly
in the Pentateuch is that a deceased person "was gathered to his people."[37]
That this is not simply an equivalent for "he was buried" is shown by the fact
that Jacob "expired and was gathered to his people" (Gen. 49:33) and only
later was buried by his family (Gen. 50:13). The underlying concept appears
to be that the departed join the company of their ancestors in the afterlife.[38]
All of these ideas, however, are merely implicit in the Old Testament. On the
one hand, most Old Testament figures probably accepted some notion of
an afterlife. On the other hand, the rituals typically associated with burial
in their cultural context were religiously unacceptable (e.g., worshiping the
dead). Apparently, they buried their dead with a sense of trust in God but
downplayed ceremonial elements that smacked of idolatry.

Many Old Testament texts that mention Sheol, spirits of the dead, and
burial reflect an underlying belief in an afterlife. Yet with few exceptions (e.g.,
1 Sam. 28), life after death was not at the forefront of what these texts were
talking about. What we have in these passages is not a fully formed theology

33. Cf. Gen. 23:2 (Abraham mourns for Sarah); Gen. 37:34–35 (Jacob mourns for Joseph);
Deut. 21:13 (a captive woman is permitted one month to mourn for her father and mother);
2 Sam. 1:11–12 (David and his men mourn, weep, and fast for Saul, Jonathan, the people of the
Lord, and the house of Israel); 2 Chron. 35:25 (Jeremiah laments over Josiah).

34. According to Deut. 21:23 even someone who has been executed and hung on a tree should
be buried. In 2 Sam. 21:10–14, it is clearly important that the bones of Saul and Jonathan are
not left exposed but are properly buried.

35. See the burial reports for Asahel (2 Sam. 2:32), Gideon (Judg. 8:32), Samson (Judg. 16:31),
Ahithophel (2 Sam. 17:23), and Saul and Jonathan (2 Sam. 21:14). The elderly Barzillai says
that he wants to die near the tomb of his father and mother (2 Sam. 19:37). In 1 Kings 13, the
man of God from Judah is told that he will not be buried in the tomb of his fathers because he
disobeyed God (vv. 20–22). Nevertheless, the old man from Bethel buries him in his own city
and mourns for him (vv. 29–30), and he asks his sons to bury him next to the man of God from
Judah with their bones next to each other, in recognition that the man of God's prophecy will
come true (vv. 31–32).

36. Tromp, *Primitive Conceptions of Death*, 169–71. The expression "he slept with his
fathers" is applied most frequently to kings of Israel and Judah.

37. Gen. 25:8, 17; 35:29; 49:29, 33; Num. 20:24, 26; 27:13; 31:2; Deut. 32:50.

38. See Johnston, *Shades of Sheol*, 33–34. See also Gen. 25:8 (Abraham gathered to his
people) and Gen. 25:9 (Abraham is buried). One also finds variations on this idiom, such as
"to gather to one's fathers" (e.g., Judg. 2:10; 2 Kings 22:20; 2 Chron. 34:28).

of the afterlife but a vague assumption that people continue to exist in some way after they die. This assumption, however, encourages us to take careful note of other passages where Old Testament writers address theological ideas that have implications for life after death.

Old Testament Building Blocks for Afterlife Theology

Several recurring themes in the Old Testament could be taken as conceptual building blocks for constructing a theology of the afterlife. A few passages may even address life after death directly. For many of these texts, whether the language was intended entirely as metaphor or with some measure of concreteness is uncertain. In places where the afterlife may be in view, a distinction can be made between settled doctrine and the writer's hopes and aspirations. If we interpret these texts against the backdrop of the Old Testament's general assumption that people somehow exist after death, the idea that they speak about the afterlife seems more plausible.

God's Power over Life and Death in the Old Testament

God's power over life and death is an important theme in the Old Testament. A penetrating statement on this topic appears at 1 Samuel 2:6: "The LORD causes death and makes alive; he brings down to Sheol and he raises up" (cf. Deut. 32:39; Ps. 33:19). God can both send people down to the netherworld and also bring them up again. If the medium of Endor can bring up Samuel (1 Sam. 28:8, 11, 13), there is no reason why the LORD is not able to do the same and more. God's power over death is remarkably evident in the narratives of Elijah and Elisha, where the dead are restored to life.[39] Other texts affirm that God's presence extends to Sheol (Ps. 139:8), that God can fetch people out of Sheol (Amos 9:2), that Sheol is naked before God (Job 26:6; cf. Prov. 15:11), and that even those who go down to the dust bow before God (Ps. 22:29).[40] In a poetic affirmation of complete trust in God's protection, the psalmist says,

> I set the LORD before me always;
>   because you are at my right hand, I will not be moved.
>
> Therefore my heart is glad, my glory rejoices,
>   and my flesh dwells secure.

39. 1 Kings 17:17–24; 2 Kings 4:18–37; 13:20–21.
40. As Ben Ollenburger comments on this passage, "If God reigns, then death's kingdom is invaded." See Ollenburger, "If Mortals Die," 35.

> For you will not forsake my life to Sheol;
>   you will not allow your pious one to see corruption.
>
> You lead me in the path of life;
>   satisfied with the joys of your presence,
>   delights are at your right hand always. (Ps. 16:8–11)

This may be taken as an artistic expression of confidence in God's enduring care in this life. Even if the psalmist believed that God would rescue him from an untimely death, presumably he expected that he would eventually die. At the same time, if the delights of God's presence abide "always," perhaps God's power to keep the pious from Sheol has implications for the afterlife.

Images related to life after death are found in several prophetic passages that deal with national restoration. In the book of Hosea, following an admonition to return to the LORD, the prophet assures, "He will revive us in two days, on the third day he will raise us up, and we will live before him" (6:2). Ezekiel's famous prophecy about the valley of dry bones applies the imagery of personal resurrection to the promise of national renewal (Ezek. 37:1–14). The bones come together (v. 7), receive new flesh (v. 8), and are revived with breath (v. 10). The return of the Israelites to their land is described as bringing them out of their graves (vv. 12–13).[41] Two passages in the book of Isaiah employ afterlife imagery to depict Israel's future blessing. In Isaiah 25:7–8, the prophet says that God will remove the shroud that covers all nations, and he will "swallow death forever," "wipe away the tears from all faces," and "remove the disgrace of his people from all the earth." The context shows clearly that he is speaking of the nation (25:1–8), but the text nevertheless affirms God's power to swallow death permanently. In Isaiah 26:1–21, the restoration of Judah is celebrated in song. As part of this celebration, foreign powers who ruled God's people will fall. As it says, "Dead, they will not live. Shades [rəpā'îm], they will not rise. . . . You will destroy every remembrance of them" (v. 14). But as for Judah, "Your dead will live. Your corpses will arise.[42] Awake and shout for joy, you who dwell in the dust. For your dew is a dew of light, and the earth will bring forth its

41. Descriptions of national death in Ezekiel that invoke underworld imagery are found in the oracles against Tyre (26:19–21) and Egypt (31:14–18; 32:17–32).

42. The preserved Hebrew text (the Masoretic Text and the Qumran Isaiah scroll, 1QIsaᵃ) has nblty, "my corpses" (nəbēlâ, "corpse," is a collective noun—thus, "my corpse" or "my corpses"). The LXX translates without the "my" suffix: "those who are in tombs." The text is difficult. Some suggest "your corpses" or "their corpses" (= Syriac Peshitta). I have translated "your corpses" for the sake of clarity, but I regard this reading as uncertain.

shades [rəpā'îm]" (v. 19). The overall tenor of the passage is the redemption
of Judah as a group, but the text presupposes (or even suggests) the idea of
personal resurrection.

The Expectation of God's Presence in the Old Testament

The hope or expectation· of being with God forever also contributes to
the Old Testament's vision for life after death. In the story of the garden of
Eden, humanity inhabits a garden in which God "walks about" (Gen. 3:8),
but Adam and Eve lose this close fellowship with God when they are expelled
(Gen. 3:22–24). This shows how people long for unending nearness to God,
even though it seems far removed from our present experience (cf. Eccles.
3:9–14). Other passages, however, suggest that eternal life with God is not
beyond hope. Genesis 5:24 contains the enigmatic report that "Enoch walked
about with God, and he was not, because God took him." For other characters in this chapter, the text simply says, "And he died." Evidently, because
Enoch "walked about" with God in this life, God "took" him in some special
way into the next. We are left wondering if others who walk with God might
experience the same afterlife blessing. Hope for God's presence that was lost
in Genesis 3 is perhaps restored in Genesis 5:24.

Numerous psalms express hope in God's future presence. In Psalm 17:15,
the psalmist concludes an appeal for deliverance by declaring to God, "I will
see your face at my vindication, I will be satisfied with your likeness when I
awake." The immediate subject matter is earthly distress, but the idea of seeing
God's likeness when he "awakes" creates an inspiring afterlife image. Another
psalm ends by contrasting the dead who do not praise the LORD with God's
people, who "will bless the LORD, now and forevermore" (115:18). This text
does not promise life after death, but the contrast between the dead who do
not praise God and those who bless him "forevermore" is suggestive. Psalm
73 reflects on the apparent prosperity of the wicked as the psalmist cries out
to God for vindication. Eventually the psalmist confesses, "But I am with you
continuously; I have grasped your right hand. By your counsel you guide me;
and afterward, you will take me in glory" (vv. 23–24). The psalm makes sense
as a yearning for closeness to God now (v. 28) and a declaration of confidence
that the LORD will restore the psalmist's honor in this life. But the reference
to "afterward" hints at a restoration to God's presence that might take place
in the future. The word for "take" (lqḥ) in Psalm 73:24 is the same one used
for Enoch in Genesis 5:24.[43]

---

43. Cf. Ps. 49:15: "But he will redeem my life from the hand of Sheol, because he will take
[lqḥ] me."

On the subject of being with God, it is appropriate to say something about the imagery of "the heavens" in the Old Testament. In Hebrew, the word "heavens" (*šāmayim*) refers to the sky.[44] Geographically, this is the opposite of Sheol, which is below the earth.[45] Whereas Sheol is considered an unhappy place,[46] the psalmist says of the sky, "Our God is in the heavens; he does whatever he pleases" (115:3).[47] In other words, the "heavens" could be understood as the place where God dwells. His throne is established in the heavens, high above the earth (e.g., Ps. 103:11, 19). When Elijah is taken to be with God, the text says that the LORD has brought him up to the heavens (2 Kings 2:1, 11). It is not surprising, therefore, that later readers imagined entering God's presence as going to heaven. However, this way of speaking is not found in the Old Testament.

God's Role as Judge in the Old Testament

The idea that God judges all our deeds is another building block for a theology of the afterlife. Frequently in the Old Testament, divine judgment and reward are meted out during the lifetime of the person or persons responsible for the action. This is expressed in Proverbs 10:27: "The fear of the LORD prolongs days, but the years of the wicked are shortened."[48] In some cases, however, God rewards or punishes people in the future through their descendants (see chap. 2 of this book). In Psalm 37:37–38, for example, the upright man of peace will have a "latter end" (*'aḥărît*), whereas the "latter end" (*'aḥărît*) of the wicked will be cut off. In all likelihood, the word

44. The noun *šāmayim*, "heavens," appears to be dual or plural and thus can be translated "heavens." In many ancient and modern translations, the word is rendered in the singular as "heaven."

45. See Job 11:8; Ps. 139:8; Amos 9:2; cf. Isa. 7:11.

46. E.g., both Jacob (Gen. 37:35; 42:38; 44:29, 31) and Hezekiah (Isa. 38:10, 17–18) lament that they are going down to Sheol when faced with the prospect of dying under miserable circumstances.

47. On a different note, Solomon says, "The heavens and the highest heavens cannot contain you; how much less this house that I have built" (1 Kings 8:27).

48. Two verses from Proverbs (12:28; 14:32) that are sometimes cited as evidence for afterlife thinking should be addressed. First, the Masoretic Text of Prov. 12:28 could be translated as, "In the path of righteousness is life, but the way of pathway [*ntybh*] is not [*'al*] death." However, the phrase "way of pathway" does not make good sense. I think it is more likely that a word such as *mšwbh*, "backsliding," was present in the original text instead of *ntybh*, "pathway" (cf. Prov. 1:32), and that the original text intended *'el*, "unto" (as in the Septuagint), instead of *'al*, "not." The translation should be, "In the path of righteousness is life, but the way of backsliding leads unto death." Second, Prov. 14:32 probably does not say that the righteous person has refuge (*ḥsh*) in the midst of his death (*b-mwt-w*), since the idiom *ḥsh + b-* means "to take refuge in something," not "to take refuge in the midst of something." Therefore, a more likely reading for this verse is, "The wicked will be thrust down in his evil, but the righteous takes refuge in his integrity [*b-twm-w*]." Therefore, both of these verses refer to punishment and reward in this life, not the next.

'aḥărît refers to "posterity"—that is, physical descendants. The upright will be blessed with many descendants, but the wicked will suffer the loss of their offspring. This passage may not address personal afterlife directly, but it does highlight the fact that God rewards the righteous and punishes the wicked after they are gone.

Another passage that deals with future recompense through offspring is the final prophecy of Isaiah (Isa. 66:22–24). God already announced his plan to create new heavens and a new earth (65:17). Just as these will endure forever, the name and descendants ("seed") of God's people will endure (66:22). All people will come to worship before the LORD (v. 23), and when they see the corpses of the wicked, something loathsome (dērā'ôn) will meet their eyes: their worm will not die, and their fire will not be quenched (v. 24). In other words, the elements that consume dead bodies (worms, fire) will always be available to consume the bodies of the wicked. Because the future blessing of God's people involves their posterity (v. 22), the point of verse 24 may be that death will insatiably devour the posterity of the wicked. But the enduring quality of the heavens and the earth, combined with the picture of undying worms and unquenchable fire, hints at a divine judgment whose effects are never-ending.

In a few cases, the fact that God will judge our deeds is stated with such finality that summative afterlife judgment is easy to infer. A well-known example is Psalm 1:5–6, which says, "The wicked will not stand [arise] in the judgment, nor sinners among the assembly of the righteous, because the LORD knows the way of the righteous, but the way of the wicked will perish." The judgment in question could involve a human court. Yet the decision seems conclusive and is based on divine knowledge. Another key text is Ecclesiastes 12:13–14, which sums up the book as follows: "Fear God, and keep his commandments, for this applies to all people; because God will bring every deed into judgment, even hidden deeds, whether they are good or evil." Similar thoughts are expressed earlier in the book (e.g., 3:17; 11:9), along with other sentiments that run in the opposite direction (e.g., 2:12–16). The unity of Ecclesiastes is a notoriously difficult problem, and the material in the conclusion (12:9–14) does not necessarily represent every idea stated in the book when read in isolation. But in attempting to apply the book's various teachings to his audience, the final editor describes a divine judgment that covers everything in life and extends to what is hidden from human knowledge.

Lastly, afterlife judgment is suggested by references to divine scrolls that record the names of the righteous. Psalm 69:28 mentions such a book: "Let them be blotted out from the scroll of the living, and let them not be recorded with the righteous." This resembles Exodus 32:32–33, where Moses asks God to blot him out from God's scroll if Israel cannot be forgiven, and God replies that he will blot out from his book only those who sin against him. There are a few other passages that allude to the same idea (e.g., Isa. 4:3; Mal. 3:16). The scrolls of Daniel 7:10 and 12:1 will be discussed below. Although texts such as Psalm 69:28 and Exodus 32:32–33 do not mention afterlife judgment, if God keeps a "scroll of the living" inscribed with the names of the righteous, it would make sense for God to use this scroll as the basis for final judgment in the next life.

The Need to Vindicate God's Justice in the Old Testament

The final Old Testament afterlife theme is trust in God's justice despite this world's apparent injustice. I will mention two passages: Job 19:25–27 and Isaiah 52:13–53:12.

In Job 19:25–27, Job expresses confidence that he will eventually meet God, perhaps even after death. The book of Job is not lacking in passages that envision death as the end of human experience (e.g., Job 3:16–19). There are also several places where Job wishes for arbitration with God to present his case and find resolution.[49] Among such passages, Job 19:25–27 presents a rare moment of absolute trust in God. The Hebrew text of this passage is difficult to interpret. I offer here my attempt at a brief summary. The text begins, "I know that my redeemer lives, and that he will stand [arise] as the last upon the earth [over the dust]" (v. 25). The redeemer is God, who arises or stands (perhaps in judgment) when nothing else remains because all has returned to dust. The next verse says, "And after my skin has been destroyed, then from my flesh I will see God" (v. 26). The phrase "from my flesh" might mean "apart from my flesh"; that is, Job will see God as a bodiless shade. Or it might mean "from the vantage point of my flesh"; that is, Job will get new flesh after his skin has been destroyed. The last verse concludes, "Whom I will see for myself; and my eyes will behold, and not a stranger. My feelings [kidneys] are consumed inside of me" (v. 27). It is God whom Job expects to see. If the "eyes" are literal, then verse 26 means that Job will see God from the vantage point of his restored flesh. In any case, Job clearly believes that he will see God after his flesh has been destroyed. He has experienced extreme suffering, such as one might associate with divine punishment, even though he has committed no sin grave enough to merit this. A gap exists between what Job believes about God's justice and what he perceives as injustice. Ideally, Job wishes for an opportunity to present his case before God in this life. If that does not happen, however, Job 19:25–27 shows that he expects to see God after he dies.

Isaiah 52:13–53:12 describes God's servant, who will "act wisely" (52:13). He will be highly exalted (52:13), but many will be appalled at his marred

49. E.g., Job 9:33–35; 14:13–15; 16:19–21.

appearance (52:14). The servant is despised and suffers greatly (53:3). He carries the iniquity of the people and takes their punishment on himself (53:4–6). Although he does no wrong, the servant is oppressed, cut off from the land of the living, and given a grave with the wicked (53:7–9). The ill treatment of the servant seems to be out of step with God's justice. If God punishes the guilty and rewards the righteous, why does the servant suffer and die a miserable death? This problem is resolved in Isaiah 53:10, which says that the servant will see his descendants ("seed"), prolong his days, and cause God's will to prosper. The final two verses confirm that although the servant carries the people's sins, he also receives spoils of victory with the strong and mighty (53:11–12). Many details in this passage could be explored to uncover what precisely it says about the relationship between the servant and the people, or the nature of the servant's suffering on behalf of others.[50] For the present, however, the main point is that the servant is depicted as suffering a wretched death (53:7–9) but also prospering after his affliction (53:10–12). God's justice is vindicated when the servant is blessed after he dies. This implies some form of afterlife for the servant.

I am not suggesting that the passages discussed in this section were intended to convey a doctrine of the afterlife. A few of them evidently express some belief in life after death. If most ancient Israelites thought that people continue to exist after death as shades, it is not unrealistic to suppose that certain writers developed this idea a bit further. More important than any single text, however, are the four theological themes: God's power over life and death, the desire or expectation of God's presence forever, God's role as judge of human deeds, and the need to vindicate God's justice in light of this world's injustice. When we come to the New Testament, we will see that core ideas expressed in specific Old Testament texts serve as the scriptural building blocks for developing a Christian theology of the afterlife.

The Afterlife in the New Testament

By the second century BC, belief in a conscious afterlife was widely accepted among Jewish writers. Many texts envision bodily resurrection, while others speak of the immortality of the soul.[51] Differences exist between sources on specific details—for example, regarding who will take part in a future

---

50. Earlier in Isa. 40–55, the servant is identified as the nation of Israel (41:8–9; 42:19–20; 44:1–2, 21; 45:4; 48:20), but in 49:5–6 and 53:2–12 the servant is distinguished from the people as a whole. On the figure and mission of the servant in Isaiah, see Abernethy, *Book of Isaiah*, 137–60.

51. For a clear affirmation of resurrection, see 2 Macc. 7 (e.g., vv. 14, 36). On the immortality of the soul, see Philo, *The Sacrifices of Abel and Cain* II–III (5–10). A vivid picture of afterlife judgment can be found in 1 En. 22 (perhaps third century BC).

resurrection. But the general expectation that humans will experience life after death is well attested in Jewish writings of this era.[52]

The development of Jewish beliefs about the afterlife between 300 BC and AD 100 has often been attributed to Persian or Greek influence. This is plausible to some extent. However, three other factors should be kept in mind. First, we should not rule out the possibility that Egyptian or Mesopotamian sources contributed to Jewish thinking. Second, much of what we see in Jewish literature of this period can be explained as a natural development based on the trajectory within the Old Testament. Third, Jewish writers adapted whatever ideas they borrowed to their own categories so naturally that the new elements no doubt seemed to them as if they had always been present.

In light of Jesus's death and resurrection, the doctrines of eternal life with God and bodily resurrection became essential tenets of Christian faith. I obviously cannot survey everything the New Testament says about the afterlife or address every point of ambiguity (e.g., what happens between death and the final resurrection). Instead, I will highlight a few basic beliefs about life after death that are affirmed in one way or another in the New Testament, merely to set the stage for the following discussion of inner-biblical interpretation.

God grants eternal life to those who die in Christ.[53] Paul says that when he dies, he will be "absent from the body" but "at home with the Lord" (2 Cor. 5:8) and also "with Christ" (Phil. 1:23). At the second coming, those who died in Christ will rise first. Then those who are alive will be snatched together with them to meet the Lord in the air, and thus all Christians will be with the Lord always (1 Thess. 4:16–17).

There will be a resurrection of the dead. This is grounded in Jesus's resurrection, which is the climax of all four Gospels.[54] In his earthly ministry,[55] and even by his death (Matt. 27:52–53), Jesus brought people back from the dead. The resurrection of Jesus serves as the initial installment of the ultimate resurrection of all Christians to eternal life.[56] Through his resurrection Jesus achieved our justification with God (Rom. 4:25) and defeated death so that God may be all in all (1 Cor. 15:24–28). Without Jesus's resurrection, Christian

---

52. On the afterlife in early Jewish sources, see Elledge, *Resurrection of the Dead*; Sigvartsen, *Afterlife and Resurrection Beliefs in the Apocrypha*; and Sigvartsen, *Afterlife and Resurrection Beliefs in the Pseudepigrapha*.

53. E.g., Rom. 5:21; 6:22–23; Gal. 6:8; 1 Tim. 1:16; 6:12; Titus 1:2; 3:7. Other phrases are used to express this same idea, e.g., "life and immortality" (2 Tim. 1:10).

54. Matt. 28:1–20; Mark 16:1–7; Luke 24:1–52; John 20:1–21:25. See also 1 Cor. 15:4–8.

55. Luke 7:11–17; Mark 5:21–24, 35–43 (Luke 8:40–42, 49–56; Matt. 9:18–26); John 11:1–44.

56. Acts 26:23; 1 Cor. 15:20; Col. 1:18; Rev. 1:5.

faith is meaningless (1 Cor. 15:12–23). But thanks to Jesus, Christians will be resurrected with incorruptible spiritual bodies (1 Cor. 15:35–49), which will be conformed to the body of Jesus's glory (Phil. 3:10–11, 20–21).

There will be a final judgment that determines what people experience in the afterlife. The story of the rich man and Lazarus illustrates afterlife judgment that is meted out immediately after death. The rich man suffers torment in Hades, while the poor man, Lazarus, is carried by angels to Abraham's side (Luke 16:19–31). People are appointed to die once; then comes judgment (Heb. 9:27). All must appear before the judgment seat of Christ (2 Cor. 5:10).[57] At the return of Jesus there will be a resurrection of the just and unjust (Acts 24:15, 25) and a general judgment of all humanity, both the living and the dead.[58] When the Son of Man comes in his glory, he will separate people based on their treatment of the least of his brothers, with the wicked going to eternal punishment and the righteous to eternal life (Matt. 25:31–46). Those who believe in Jesus will come out of their tombs to a resurrection of life, but those who do not believe will go to a resurrection of punishment.[59] The book of Revelation envisions a general resurrection and a final judgment scene where books are opened and people are judged based on what they did in life (Rev. 20:4–6, 11–15).

Those who receive a negative final judgment will experience punishment in the afterlife. This can be described as the coming of God's wrath (e.g., 1 Thess. 1:10; Rom. 2:5). The day of final judgment will result in the destruction of the ungodly, with the heavens and earth suffering dissolution by fire (2 Pet. 3:7–13). In the Gospels, Jesus speaks of afterlife punishment as outer darkness or as a fiery furnace where there is weeping and gnashing of teeth.[60] Jesus also warns of afterlife punishment in Gehenna (e.g., Matt. 10:28; Luke 12:5),[61] a valley in Jerusalem that came to symbolize destruction because of atrocities committed there.[62] Sometimes punishment in the afterlife involves dramatic reversal. For example, there will be weeping and gnashing of teeth when certain people who expect to enter the kingdom of God are thrown out but see outsiders coming from around the world to feast in the kingdom (Luke 13:22–30). According to the parable of the tenants, the kingdom of

57. Cf. Rom. 14:10; 1 Cor. 4:5.

58. Acts 10:42; 2 Tim. 4:1; 1 Pet. 4:5. Cf. Heb. 6:2, where the resurrection of the dead and eternal judgment are identified as basic Christian teachings. See also Rom. 2:6–11.

59. John 5:28–29; cf. Acts 24:15; 2 Thess. 1:5–10.

60. Matt. 8:10–12; 13:36–43, 49–50.

61. Cf. Mark 9:43–48, where "Gehenna" is used alongside "unquenchable fire" and is described as a place where "their worm does not die and the fire is not quenched." See also Matt. 5:22: "Gehenna of fire."

62. See 2 Chron. 28:3; 33:6; 2 Kings 23:10; Jer. 7:31; 19:1–6; 32:35.

God will be taken away from the wicked and given to those who produce the fruit of the kingdom (Matt. 21:43–44). Jesus speaks of afterlife punishment being more bearable for some than others, depending on the opportunities each had to repent (Luke 10:13–15; 11:31–32). Cataclysmic punishments are described in the book of Revelation, including a lake of burning sulfur[63] and a lake of fire.[64]

Those who receive a positive final judgment will be rewarded in the afterlife. When the Son of Man comes in clouds, he will send his angels and gather his elect (Mark 13:24–27; Matt. 24:27–31). Jesus prepares a place for his disciples in his Father's house, where he will take them when he comes again (John 14:2–3). Those who believe in Jesus receive eternal life and will be raised up on the last day (John 6:39–40, 54). Recompense will be given for good deeds. For example, if someone provides a luncheon for those who cannot repay, God will repay that person at the resurrection of the righteous (Luke 14:1, 12–14). Jesus encourages his disciples to store up treasures in heaven, not on earth (Matt. 6:19–21). When Christ appears, he will bring salvation and redemption from the effects of sin.[65] Those who persist in Christ obtain an eternal inheritance (Heb. 9:15) and a crown of life (James 1:12; cf. 2 Tim. 4:8). They will be glorified together with Christ (Rom. 8:17) and will rule together with him (2 Tim. 2:12). Christians who die because of their faith will be vindicated in the afterlife.[66] The return of Jesus will bring about a "restoration of all things" (Acts 3:21). The blessed future can be depicted as a "new heaven and new earth" (Rev. 21:1), a heavenly Jerusalem coming down to earth (Rev. 21:2–22:5), and a restored garden of Eden (Rev. 22:1–5).

Christian belief in the afterlife stems from Jesus's teaching and from his resurrection and ascension. As we will see, this belief is also justified and explained in the New Testament by recourse to themes and specific passages from the Old Testament.

Inner-Biblical Insights

It may be surprising to see how many different Old Testament passages were employed by later biblical writers to comment on the afterlife. This shows the extent to which new experiences can inspire readers to find fresh insights

---

63. Rev. 19:20; 20:10; 21:8.

64. Rev. 20:14–15. Cf. 6:12–17; 9:13–21; 11:15–19; 14:14–20; 16:1–21; 18:18–24; 19:11–21; 20:7–10; 21:8.

65. Heb. 9:28; Eph. 4:30; Titus 2:11–14.

66. Rev. 6:9–11; 7:13–14; 20:4.

in old texts. By paying careful attention to the themes in these texts, we can recognize the Old Testament basis for the New Testament's theology of resurrection and eternal life.

Old Testament Afterlife Themes in Daniel 12

The clearest picture of personal revival from the dead in the Old Testament is found in Daniel 12. This passage resolves a theological problem in the history of God's people by presenting a vision of the afterlife that draws on earlier Old Testament concepts.

The first six chapters of the book of Daniel contain narratives about Daniel and his companions at the royal courts of Babylon and Persia. Chapters 7–12 report four visions that deal with the future of the Jewish people. The historical referents for many details in these visions are uncertain, but one subject that is clearly addressed is the persecution of the Jews by the Seleucid king Antiochus IV (ca. 167–164 BC), as recounted in the books of Maccabees. In chapter 8, the goat's "great horn" (Alexander the Great) is killed and his empire is divided into four kingdoms (vv. 8, 21). Out of one of these kingdoms (the Seleucid kingdom) comes a boastful "little horn" who acts arrogantly against God, magnifies himself against the "beautiful" land (Judea), violates God's sanctuary (the temple), and tramples on God's people (vv. 9–14, 22–25). This little horn is Antiochus IV. Daniel 11 likewise opens with an allusion to Alexander the Great (the "great king" of Greece) and the division of his empire (vv. 2–4). Verses 5–20 describe major events in the conflict between the Seleucid kingdom in Syria (the kings of the north) and the Ptolemaic kingdom of Egypt (the kings of the south). In verses 21–35, the wicked deeds of Antiochus IV are cryptically portrayed, including his desecration of the temple (v. 31) and his success in tricking some Jews into apostasy (v. 32). Other Jews, however, offer resistance. The wise among the people give understanding to many, even though they will suffer by the sword, fire, and plunder (v. 33). The wicked deeds of Antiochus IV are summarized (vv. 36–39), and an account is given of his death (vv. 40–45).[67] This is the context for the afterlife vision in Daniel 12.

67. For a summary of the historical background of Dan. 11, see Lucas, *Daniel*, 273–93. Many scholars date this material to ca. 165 BC, after the events described in such great detail in vv. 2–35 but before the account of Antiochus IV's death in vv. 40–45, which is typically considered inaccurate. In fact, we do not have reliable historical information about the death of Antiochus IV. It is notable, however, that the historical-review segment of this vision report is much longer than what we find in chaps. 7, 8, or 9. In the end, there is reason to think that this vision report did not reach its final form until the second century BC (see Lucas, *Daniel*, 306–16). As Philip Johnston points out, the clear picture of afterlife revival in Dan. 12 was not appropriated by

In response to Antiochus IV's persecution, Daniel 12 promises that the dead will return to life. Just as Daniel 7 juxtaposes a visionary account of historical persecution (vv. 2–8, 23–25) with a picture of final judgment (vv. 9–14, 26–27), Daniel 11–12 juxtaposes its account of the Seleucid persecution (chap. 11) with a picture of the dead being raised (chap. 12). According to this pattern, God will bring an end to Antiochus IV and Seleucid rule in Judea (through the Maccabean revolt), and God will eventually raise the dead (at the final judgment). These two events are placed next to each other as a literary-prophetic device to encourage those who must suffer. This is similar to what we see in the book of Revelation, which juxtaposes historical judgment against Rome (e.g., Rev. 17:9, the "City of Seven Hills") with the final return of Jesus (Rev. 19).

The raising of the dead in Daniel 12 recalls several earlier Old Testament passages, especially from the book of Isaiah.[68] In Daniel 12:1, it is stated that "all who are found written in the scroll" will be delivered. This hearkens back not only to Daniel 7:10 ("scrolls were opened") but also to passages dealing with God's scrolls of judgment (e.g., Isa. 4:3).[69] Daniel 12:2 says that "many of those who sleep in the ground of the dust will awake," adapting language from the resurrection image of Isaiah 26:19: "Awake . . . you who dwell in the dust."[70] Moreover, while some in Daniel 12 are designated for "everlasting life," others are designated for "everlasting loathing [*dērā'ôn*]." This alludes to the only other passage that uses this word ("loathsome"), Isaiah 66:24, where the worm does not die and the fire is not quenched in consuming the corpses of transgressors. Finally, the faithful Jews who endure persecution in Daniel 11–12 are identified with the suffering servant of Isaiah 52:13–53:12. In Isaiah 52:13 the servant "will act wisely [*yaśkîl*]," and in Isaiah 53:11 the servant "will cause righteousness [*yaṣdîq*] for many [*lārabbîm*]." In Daniel the "wise" (*maśkîlîm*) stand firm against persecution (Dan. 11:33–35), and they "cause the righteousness of many" (*maṣdîqê hārabbîm*, Dan. 12:3); that is, they instruct others to remain faithful (cf. Dan. 11:33; 12:10). These allusions to Isaiah serve as the background for Daniel's picture of the afterlife. Just as the "wise" servant in Isaiah 52:13–53:12 is raised up and vindicated (e.g., Isa. 52:13; 53:12), the "wise" who stay faithful to God and yet die during the persecution of Antiochus IV will be raised to everlasting life.

---

other Old Testament writers, either because it was deemed theologically marginal or because it was chronologically marginal (Johnston, *Shades of Sheol*, 227).

68. See Elledge, *Resurrection of the Dead*, 21–23, 68–71; and Fishbane, *Biblical Interpretation in Ancient Israel*, 493.

69. See also Ps. 69:28; Exod. 32:32–33; Mal. 3:16.

70. In other Old Testament passages, when people are said to "sleep" in death, it is assumed that they cannot awake (Job 14:12; Jer. 51:39, 57).

What Daniel 12 says about the afterlife stems from ideas already present in previous scriptural texts, but it also reflects fresh thinking in response to specific historical circumstances. The idea of scrolls that record people's standing with God contributed to the general idea of final judgment. The eternal punishment of the wicked was inspired by Isaiah 66:24, and God's power to revive his people was drawn from Isaiah 26:19. Most important, the figure of a righteous sufferer who obtains vindication from God after death was found in Isaiah 52:13–53:12. All of this was combined in the book of Daniel to address a troubling theological problem: If God rewards the righteous, why do faithful Jews die during persecution? The answer is that God will reward them after he wakes them up from the dead.

Old Testament Afterlife Themes in the New Testament

The New Testament clearly affirms life after death. In fact, eternal life with God, final judgment, and the resurrection of the body are central New Testament doctrines. Ultimately, these flow from the teaching and resurrection of Jesus. But they are also justified and explained on the basis of Old Testament texts. Some of these texts are obviously relevant, whereas others might not seem applicable at first sight. Below I discuss how Old Testament passages are employed in the New Testament to address life after death. These are organized around the four major themes treated above as building blocks for an afterlife theology.

God's Power over Life and Death in the New Testament

Old Testament texts that show God's power over life and death made important contributions to the New Testament's understanding of the afterlife. This was especially the case where the resurrection of Jesus was in view.

Psalm 16:8–11 expresses confidence in God's power (see "God's Power over Life and Death in the Old Testament"). In its original context, the statement "You will not forsake my life to Sheol; you will not allow your pious one to see corruption" (v. 10) naturally refers to God's deliverance from mortal peril in this life. At the same time, the next line, "You lead me in the path of life," together with the hope of enjoying God's presence always (v. 11), opens the door to a theological interpretation whereby God's power to rescue from Sheol is matched by his power to give the psalmist life without end. In Peter's sermon at Pentecost, a reference to the resurrection of Jesus (Acts 2:24) is followed by a scriptural proof showing that it was not possible for death to contain him (Acts 2:24–36). The key passage quoted is Psalm 16:8–11, and the interpretation given is that David cannot be speaking about himself, because he died and remained dead (his soul was left in Sheol/Hades).[71] Instead, David spoke prophetically about the resurrection of Christ, who was not forsaken in Hades and whose flesh did not see corruption (Acts 2:31).[72] In other words, if Psalm 16:10 is interpreted as promising permanent deliverance from death, the details of this verse do not fit David; yet Christ fulfills them concretely by his resurrection. Much more could be said about this passage, but the sum of the matter is that God's power to rescue people from death as stated in Psalm 16:8–11 finds fulfillment in Jesus's resurrection from the dead.[73]

God's military might in Psalm 68 provides imagery that Paul uses to explain the benefits of Christ's resurrection and ascension. Psalm 68:1–18 celebrates God's victories over his enemies and his powerful march from Mount Sinai to Mount Zion (e.g., vv. 16–17). Verse 18 says, "You ascended to the height; you took captivity captive; you received gifts among human beings." In its original context, God's ascension "to the height" (or "on high") probably refers to his ascent to his sanctuary on Mount Zion. Paul quotes this passage in Ephesians 4:8 to show the connection between Christ's victory over all things and his distribution of gifts to the church. As Paul explains, grace was given to each Christian according to the measure of Christ's gift (Eph. 4:7), which is why he says, "Having ascended on high, he took captivity captive; he gave gifts to people" (Eph. 4:8). As for the reference to "gifts," Paul explains that Christ gave some to be apostles, some prophets, some evangelists, and some pastors and teachers (Eph. 4:11). Of course, whereas the triumphant LORD in Psalm 68 received gifts among people, Christ distributes the spoils of his spiritual victory to the church. This is why Paul changes the verb in Psalm 68:18 from "receives" to "gives" (Eph. 4:8).[74] On the topic of the afterlife, however, Paul's most significant comment comes in verses 9–10. After quoting Psalm 68:18, he offers the following interpretation: "What does it mean that 'he ascended,' except that he also descended into the lower parts of the earth? He that descended is the same one who also ascended above all the

71. The Hebrew *šəʾōl* (Sheol; Ps. 16:10) was translated into Greek as *hadēs* (Hades; Acts 2:27).

72. The Hebrew text labels Ps. 16 a "Miktam of/for David." The Septuagint calls this an "Inscription for/by David." This explains why Peter takes David to be the speaker.

73. Cf. Acts 13:32–37, where Paul quotes Ps. 2:7 to establish Jesus's messianic identity and then quotes Isa. 55:3 and Ps. 16:10 to substantiate Jesus's resurrection, with an interpretation of Ps. 16:10 similar to what we see in Acts 2:24–36.

74. This change has been much discussed by commentators. For example, Theodore of Mopsuestia (ca. 350–428) explains in his *Commentary on the Psalms*, "Now, the apostle cited this text, not as a prophecy about Christ, but as one applicable to Christ in that while we were captives of the Devil, he was victorious in battle with him and carried us off for himself. Hence, since the phrase 'you received gifts' did not apply, in our normal practice in using it in ecclesiastical usage he replaced 'you received' with 'he gave,' this being more applicable to Christ, who did not receive but gave the gifts of the Spirit after the ascension into heaven." See Hill, *Theodore of Mopsuestia*, 879.

heavens, in order that he might fill all things" (Eph. 4:9–10). In other words, Paul takes the verb "ascend" in Psalm 68:18 to refer to Christ's ascension, and this ascension implies that Christ previously descended to the "lower parts" of the earth, which probably refers to Christ's descent into the underworld (cf. 1 Pet. 3:19; 4:6).[75] The Old Testament image of God conquering in battle and ascending to his sanctuary serves as a paradigm that Jesus fulfills by rising from the dead and ascending above the heavens.

Several Old Testament texts dealing with God's power over life and death contribute to Paul's discussion of resurrection in 1 Corinthians 15. In verses 12–23, Paul explains that Christ rose from the dead and that Christians will rise when Christ returns. This leads to "the end," when Christ will abolish every authority, rule, and power and hand the kingdom over to the One who is God and Father (v. 24). Paul justifies this statement by saying, "For he must rule until he puts all his enemies under his feet" (v. 25), which is an allusion to Psalm 110:1. The connection between Christ's incremental subjection of all enemies and the final resurrection is then made clear: "The last enemy to be abolished is death" (v. 26). Paul supports this by quoting Psalm 8:6: "For he subjected all things under his feet."[76] The context of Psalm 8 is God's crowning "man" (= "the son of man") with glory and honor (vv. 4–5). Hebrews 2:5–9 reads Psalm 8 as if it were speaking about Jesus, just as we find in 1 Corinthians 15. Paul's logic is as follows: If God is in the process of putting "all things" under Jesus's feet, death must be included among "all things."[77] Therefore, death will also be subjected to Jesus. When this happens, the time for the final resurrection will have arrived. In Psalm 8, God brings all creation under the authority of humanity. Paul's interpretation assumes that Jesus is the human for whom this statement is most true and that death is among those created things that are brought under Jesus's power.

Later in this chapter (1 Cor. 15:50–57), Paul combines two prophetic texts to affirm God's power over the grave. The main point of this passage is that God grants victory over sin and death through Christ. Because Jesus was raised from the dead, we can be confident that we also will be raised. The first text

---

75. On this concept and its development in Christian history, see Kelly, *Early Christian Creeds*, 378–83.

76. The original text of Ps. 8:6 uses the second person in addressing God directly: "You placed all things under his feet." Paul uses the third person to adapt the quotation to its new syntactic context.

77. Paul adds one qualification: "When it says that all things are subjected, it is clear that this excludes the One who subjected all things to him" (1 Cor. 15:27). In other words, the One who is God and Father will not subject himself to Jesus. Paul concludes this argument: "And when all things are subjected to him [Jesus], the Son himself will be subjected to the One who subjected all things to him, so that God may be all in all."

that Paul cites to demonstrate this point is Isaiah 25:8, an oracle of restoration that uses afterlife imagery (see "God's Power over Life and Death in the Old Testament"). Although the Hebrew text of Isaiah 25:8 says, "He swallows death forever," Paul quotes it as, "Death was swallowed in victory" (1 Cor. 15:54). The Greek word *nikos*, "victory," sometimes occurs in the Septuagint for the Hebrew word *nēṣaḥ* (*lāneṣaḥ*, "forever"), and it was probably the reading found in Paul's Greek text of Isaiah 25:8.[78] Paul picks up this word again in verse 57 when he speaks of God "who gives us the victory" (*nikos*). Paul's use of this passage is simple: Isaiah depicts Israel's redemption as God swallowing death, which implies that God has power over death. This is the power by which Jesus has been raised from the dead.[79] The second text that Paul cites is Hosea 13:14, which is part of an oracle of judgment. In Hosea's context it seems that the first two statements should be taken as rhetorical questions, and the following two exclamations should be understood as laments. If so, the sense would be, "Shall I ransom them from Sheol? [No!] Shall I redeem them from death? [No!] Alas, O death, your plagues! Alas, O Sheol, your sting! Compassion is hidden from my eyes." In 1 Corinthians 15:55, Paul uses the two exclamations to mock death: "Where, O death, is your victory? Where, O death, is your sting?"[80] In sum, Paul employs Isaiah 25:8 to assert that God is able to swallow death, and then he jeers at death using the language of Hosea 13:14.

Lastly, Jesus invokes God's power when he likens his death and resurrection to the sign of Jonah. In the first chapter of Jonah, once the wayward prophet has been thrown overboard, God appoints a great fish to swallow Jonah, and he remains in the fish for "three days and three nights" (Jon. 1:17). In Jonah's prayer of thanksgiving, he recalls the terrors of the sea, using imagery of death and resurrection, such as "From the belly of Sheol, I cried out" (2:2) and "You brought up my life from the pit" (2:6). Right after this ordeal, Jonah proclaims a message of doom to Nineveh (3:3–4), and the Ninevites repent (3:5–10). Jesus recalls this story when people ask him for a sign (Matt. 12:38–42; Luke

78. For *nēṣaḥ* as *nikos* in the Septuagint, see LXX 2 Sam. 2:26; Job 36:7; Amos 1:11; 8:7; Jer. 3:5; Lam. 3:18; and the later Jewish Greek versions of Aquila and Theodotion at Isa. 25:8. In Aramaic, there is a verb *nṣḥ* that means "to be victorious." For preserved LXX manuscripts at Isa. 25:8, the translator renders the Hebrew *nṣḥ* as a verb that means "to prevail."

79. The promise in Isa. 25:8 that the LORD "will wipe away the tears from all faces" is applied to afterlife blessing in Rev. 7:17; 21:4.

80. The meaning of the Hebrew word *'ĕhî*, which I translated "Alas!" is not certain. Both the LXX and Paul render this word as *pou*, "Where?" For what the Masoretic Text represents as "plagues" (*deber*), the LXX has "penalty" (*dikē*) and Paul gives "victory" (*nikos*). The original reading for this word is not clear, and Paul may have simply followed what was in his manuscript. It is also possible that Paul adapted his text to match the theme of "victory" as found in his copy of Isa. 25:8.

11:29–32). Their request earns a rebuke from Jesus, who says that no sign will be given except the sign of Jonah (Matt. 12:38–39). "For just as Jonah was in the belly of the large fish for three days and three nights, thus the Son of Man will be in the heart of the earth for three days and three nights" (Matt. 12:40). As a final point, Jesus states that the men of Nineveh will condemn his generation at the final judgment, because Nineveh repented at Jonah's preaching, but Jesus's generation will refuse to repent despite seeing a greater sign (Matt. 12:41). This passage seems to assume the following interpretation: Jonah figuratively died in Sheol, and his life was brought up from the "pit." This represents death and resurrection. Jonah spent three days and nights in the great fish, just as Jesus will spend (at least some part of) three days in the grave. Moreover, the Ninevites heard of Jonah's remarkable experience in the fish, and this "sign" encouraged them to repent (cf. Luke 11:30). Jesus's death and resurrection will be a "sign" like this for his generation, but it will be greater. Of course, the story of Jonah does not claim that the prophet literally died and came back to life. But God's display of power through Jonah functioned as a literary prefiguration of God's victory over death through Jesus.

The Expectation of God's Presence in the New Testament

In several Old Testament texts, people express their desire to live forever in God's presence (see "The Expectation of God's Presence in the Old Testament"). In the New Testament, God acts through Jesus to grant people eternal life. As a result, while some emphasis remains on the life-giving power of God's commandments and people's yearning for life with God, special attention is given to God's actions to give life to people.

According to Jesus, the commandments of God can lead to eternal life. In one narrative, Jesus is asked by an expert in God's law, "What must I do to inherit eternal life?" Jesus sends him back to the Torah: "What is written in the law? How do you read it?" (Luke 10:25–26). When the man quotes Deuteronomy 6:5 ("Love the Lord your God") and Leviticus 19:18 ("Love your neighbor as yourself"), Jesus says, "You answered correctly. Do this, and you will live" (Luke 10:27–28). Yet the expert seeks to justify himself by raising the question of who counts as his neighbor. In reply, Jesus explains that we should act like a neighbor toward others (10:36). As Jesus reads the law, the commandments provide a pathway to eternal life, provided that one embraces their core values and relational implications (cf. Matt. 5:17–47). A similar point is made in the narrative about the rich young ruler (Luke 18:18–30).[81] When the ruler asks, "What must I do to inherit eternal life?" Jesus tells him to observe the Ten

---

81. Cf. Matt. 19:16–30; Mark 10:17–31.

Commandments, in particular those dealing with human relationships (18:20).[82]
It is hard to tell whether the young man's response, "I have observed all these
things from my youth," is boastful or sincere. In any case, Jesus tells him to
embrace the Torah's core values and put them into action. For the rich young
ruler, this means selling his possessions, giving to the poor, and following Jesus
(18:22). Again, the commandments in their essence lead to eternal life, and they
lead to Jesus. At the end of the narrative, Jesus takes up the question of whether
any person can truly live out the commandments in this way: "Things that are
impossible for people," he says, "are possible for God" (18:27).

In Romans 10, the fact that God made his commandments accessible to
Israel serves as a paradigm for justification by faith. Paul distinguishes between
two approaches to receiving God's righteousness, one approach through law
and another through faith (10:5–8). He illustrates righteousness through the
law by quoting Leviticus 18:5: "The one who does these things will live by
them" (Rom. 10:5). As Paul argues elsewhere, because no one is able to do
the commandments perfectly,[83] it is impossible to receive God's righteousness
through the law. Paul explains righteousness through faith, however, by quoting from Deuteronomy 30:11–14.[84] In its context, Deuteronomy says that
God's commandment is not too difficult for Israel (v. 11). It is not in the
heavens, so that someone would need to ascend there to bring it down, and
it is not across the sea, so that someone would need to go there to bring it
back (vv. 12–13). Rather, the word is very near to Israel, so that they can do it
(v. 14). In other words, God put his commandment of laws and statutes within
human reach, so that Israel could follow them.[85] On display in this passage is
God's compassionate consideration for Israel's limitations.

Paul applies this theme to God's gracious accommodation to human weakness in the gift of righteousness through faith in Christ. As the apostle interprets the text, the phrase "who will ascend into heaven" (Deut. 30:12) refers

---

82. The Gospel of Luke lists these commandments in the following order: "Do not commit
adultery," "Do not murder," "Do not steal," "Do not bear false witness," and "Honor your
father and mother." Both Matthew and Mark give the commandments from "Do not murder" to
"Do not bear false witness" in the order in which they appear in Exod. 20:13–16, with "Honor
your father and mother" (Exod. 20:12) at the end. Mark also adds, "Do not defraud" after "Do
not bear false witness" (10:19), and Matthew adds, "Love your neighbor as yourself" at the
end (19:19), perhaps to emphasize that these commandments represent the full responsibility
of one person toward another.

83. E.g., Rom. 2:25; Gal. 3:10–11; 5:3; cf. James 2:10.

84. As with Lev. 18:5, the context of this passage speaks of God's desire that Israel should
live: "I have set before you today life and good, death and evil" (Deut. 30:15).

85. This might be taken as contrary to Paul's argument that people cannot keep the law,
although the accessibility of the law combined with the observation of universal human sin
supports the idea that people (rather than God) are guilty for their failures (cf. Rom. 3:9–20).

to ascending to heaven to bring Christ down to earth (Rom. 10:6); and the phrase "who will descend into the abyss" (Deut. 30:13, rendered freely) refers to raising Christ from the dead (Rom. 10:7). God did not expect humans to do any of this. On the contrary, he accomplished these things in Christ so that the message of faith would be accessible. Paul concludes, "What does it say? 'The word is near you, in your mouth and in your heart' [Deut. 30:14], that is: the word of faith which we preach" (Rom. 10:8). In short, Paul interprets Deuteronomy 30:11–14 as a proclamation of Jesus's descent to the abyss and resurrection from the dead, which provides an accessible path to eternal life by means of a righteousness that comes through faith.

In a dispute between Jesus and the Sadducees, Jesus uses the reality of God's abiding relationship to the patriarchs to provide evidence for the afterlife.[86] The Old Testament text to which Jesus refers is Exodus 3:6. Near the beginning of the book of Exodus, God remembers his covenant with Abraham, Isaac, and Jacob (2:24–25). God appears to Moses at the burning bush (3:2) and summons him to bring Israel out of Egypt (3:10). In this encounter with Moses, God introduces himself by saying, "I am the God of your father, the God of Abraham, the God of Isaac, and the God of Jacob" (3:6). When Jesus quotes this passage, he is debating with the Sadducees about marriage and the afterlife. Part of Jesus's argument is that marriage will no longer exist at the resurrection.[87] But he also argues that resurrection is taught in Scripture. As he explains, "That the dead are raised Moses also showed at the bush [Exod. 3], when he calls the Lord 'the God of Abraham, the God of Isaac, and the God of Jacob.' So he is not the God of the dead, but of the living; for all are alive to him" (Luke 20:37–38). When the LORD says that he is "the God of Abraham" in the book of Exodus, this might be taken to mean simply that God remembers his covenant with Abraham, or perhaps that Abraham continues to live through his offspring. Jesus, however, interprets this type of afterlife more concretely. The fact that God continues to identify himself with the dead shows that he regards them as still alive. According to Jesus, God plans to raise the dead to new life through resurrection.

God's Role as Judge in the New Testament

The Old Testament presents God as the ultimate judge of human deeds. In the New Testament this theme develops into an affirmation that God will render righteous judgments in the afterlife. For example, references to heavenly

---

86. See Luke 20:27–40; Mark 12:18–27; Matt. 22:23–33. I will focus on the version in Luke because it gives the clearest account of how Jesus understands the Old Testament text.
87. See "The Purpose of Marriage" under "Inner-Biblical Insights" in chap. 4.

scrolls in the Old Testament suggest that God keeps records of what people do so that their actions can be recompensed in the future (cf. Esther 2:23; 6:1–3). Psalm 69:28 mentions a "scroll of the living" that records the names of the righteous, and Daniel 12:1 promises deliverance for those whose names are written in a scroll (see "God's Role as Judge in the Old Testament"). The final and eternal aspects of this idea become more concrete in the New Testament. In the book of Revelation, those who enjoy afterlife blessing are recorded in a "scroll of life."[88] Similarly, Jesus tells the seventy-two disciples to rejoice because their names are written in heaven (Luke 10:20; cf. Heb. 12:23).

As another example, the final chapters of Isaiah envision future blessing for Israel and punishment for transgressors. The restored people of God will be rewarded with "new heavens and a new earth" (Isa. 65:17; 66:22). The corpses of the wicked will be consumed by worms that do not die and fires that are not quenched (Isa. 66:24). In the New Testament, the eternal home of the righteous is likewise described as "new heavens and a new earth" (2 Pet. 3:13; Rev. 21:1). As for negative judgment, Jesus also warns of afterlife punishment where "their worm does not die and the fire is not quenched" (Mark 9:47–48). Imagery for depicting divine judgment was already present in the Old Testament, and the New Testament adapted this imagery to its more clearly defined picture of the afterlife.

The Need to Vindicate God's Justice in the New Testament

The justice of God can be difficult to reconcile with the fact that the wicked sometimes prosper while the righteous suffer. One solution to this problem is that God will punish the wicked and reward the righteous in the afterlife. This solution was introduced in the Old Testament (see "The Need to Vindicate God's Justice in the Old Testament"; "Old Testament Afterlife Themes in Daniel 12") and fully articulated in the New Testament (see "The Afterlife in the New Testament"). The New Testament's teaching on this topic found support in two prominent Old Testament passages, Isaiah 52:13–53:12 and Daniel 7:13–14. The theme of trusting God's promises also made an important contribution.

Isaiah 52:13–53:12 is often cited in the New Testament to describe Jesus's atoning death.[89] In Romans 4:25, however, Paul alludes to this passage in a context where both the death and resurrection of Jesus are in view.[90] Speak-

---

88. Rev. 3:5; 13:8; 17:8; 20:12, 15; 21:27. See also Phil. 4:3.

89. See Acts 8:26–35 (Isa. 53:7–8); 1 Pet. 2:21–25 (Isa. 53:4–6, 9, 12); Matt. 8:17 (Isa. 53:4); Luke 22:37 (Isa. 53:12). Cf. Rom. 10:16; John 12:38 (Isa. 53:1).

90. Because language about death and atonement (as one finds in Isa. 52:13–53:12) is ubiquitous in the New Testament, it can be difficult to tell when an allusion to this passage is in-

ing of righteousness through faith, Paul says that Jesus "was handed over for the sake of our transgressions and raised for the sake of our righteousness" (Rom. 4:25). As background, Isaiah 53:11 states that the servant will "cause righteousness for many" and "bear their iniquities." When Paul says "handed over for the sake of our transgressions," he probably has in mind Isaiah's "bear their iniquities" (Isa. 53:11) or else "pierced for our transgressions" (Isa. 53:5). When Paul says "raised for the sake of our righteousness," he is likely alluding to Isaiah's "cause righteousness for many" and perhaps "raised, lifted up, and highly exalted" (Isa. 52:13). The fact that Paul associates Isaiah's "cause righteousness" (Isa. 53:11) with Jesus's being raised from the dead suggests that he interprets the resurrection of Jesus as a fulfillment of the servant's postmortem vindication in Isaiah 53:10–12. The same interpretation of Isaiah 53 may be reflected in other New Testament passages as well. For example, Acts 3:13 says that God "glorified" (cf. Isa. 52:13 LXX) his "servant" Jesus by raising him from the dead.

Although Daniel 7:9–14 does not explicitly refer to life after death, the New Testament connects it to the afterlife through Jesus's use of the title "Son of Man." Daniel 7 describes a period of harsh persecution against the "saints of the Most High" (vv. 17–25), which is brought to an end by divine judgment against human kingdoms and by the vindication of God's people (vv. 9–14, 26–27). As part of this judgment, one "like a son of man" comes with the clouds of heaven. This figure is presented before the "Ancient of Days" and receives an everlasting kingdom (vv. 13–14).[91] In the New Testament, Jesus employs the designation "Son of Man" to speak of his own future coming in glory.[92] Jesus as the Son of Man is linked to the vindication of the righteous in two ways. First, before his crucifixion Jesus says to his accusers, "You will see the Son of Man seated at the right hand of power, coming on the clouds of heaven" (Matt. 26:64; cf. Luke 22:69). In other words, even though Jesus will be wrongly killed in this life, justice will be fully restored when he returns in power. Second, after encouraging his disciples to save their lives by giving them up (Matt. 16:24–26), Jesus says, "The Son of Man will come in the glory of his Father with his angels, and then he will render to each one according to his deeds" (Matt. 16:27). In other words, when the Son of Man appears, he will reward those who gave up their

---

tended. Possible examples include Matt. 27:12 and Mark 14:61 (Isa. 53:7); Rom. 5:1 (Isa. 53:5); Heb. 9:28 (Isa. 53:12); and Mark 14:48–49 (cf. Isa. 53:9).

91. In Dan. 7:27 the one "like a son of man" may be a personification of God's people. Yet the fact that this figure comes with the clouds of heaven and that he receives not only an everlasting kingdom but also service from all nations suggests that he possesses some kind of divine identity. On the "son of man" in Dan. 7 and the New Testament, see Bock, "Son of Man," 894–900.

92. E.g., Mark 8:38; 13:26; Matt. 24:30; Luke 21:27. In the Gospel of Mark, Jesus predicts his own death by saying that the Son of Man must suffer and die (Mark 8:31; 9:12).

lives for him. In its Old Testament setting, Daniel 7:9–14 depicts God giving justice to his people who suffered in life. According to the New Testament, justice
will be restored when Jesus comes in glory to inaugurate the final judgment.

Justice in the afterlife is an underlying theme throughout Hebrews 11. In
this chapter Old Testament characters are praised because they trusted God
for promises that were not fulfilled during their lifetimes. An essential aspect
of faith according to Hebrews 11 is believing that God rewards those who
seek him (v. 6). If we believe this to be true and yet read that faithful people
in Scripture died without receiving their reward, we might conclude that
God will repay them with blessing in the hereafter. This argument is made in
Hebrews 11:13–16, where it is pointed out that the patriarchs and Sarah died
without receiving the promised land. According to the writer of Hebrews,
these faithful servants of God recognized that they were strangers on this
earth since they were seeking their own homeland—namely, a heavenly one.
But God was preparing for them a heavenly city (cf. Heb. 12:22; 13:14).[93] In
other words, although they did not live long enough to possess the land that
was promised to them, they nevertheless remained faithful to God because
they knew that he would bless them with a heavenly abode in the afterlife.
The book of Genesis does not indicate this expectation explicitly; rather, the
writer of Hebrews deduces this theologically from God's unfolding plan in
Scripture and the characters' faithfulness in the biblical text.

A few specific examples of faith in Hebrews 11 illustrate how afterlife
justice can be inferred theologically from the Old Testament. On the basis
of Genesis 4:10 ("The voice of your brother's blood cries out to me from the
ground"), the author of Hebrews says that Abel spoke despite being dead
(Heb. 11:4). In light of Genesis 5:24 ("Enoch walked about with God, and
he was not, because God took him"), the author concludes that Enoch was
taken up by God and did not see death (Heb. 11:5). As for Abraham, the author explains the remarkable faith Abraham showed in leaving his homeland
(Gen. 12:1–4) by saying that he was looking for a divine city (Heb. 11:8–10).
Furthermore, the author takes Abraham's willingness to offer his son Isaac
(Gen. 22:10), despite having been told that his offspring would come through
Isaac (Gen. 21:12), to mean that Abraham believed that God was able to raise
Isaac from the dead (Heb. 11:19).[94] For Abel and Enoch, the vivid wording of
the biblical text already hints at existence in the hereafter. In light of Jesus's
resurrection, such hints become certainties. In the case of Abraham, the writer

93. Cf. Rev. 3:12; 21:2–22:5.
94. Heb. 11:19 adds, "And he [Abraham] received him [Isaac] from there [the dead] figuratively [*en parabolē*]."

of Hebrews draws insightful theological conclusions from Abraham's extreme faith and God's faithfulness to reward those who trust him.

In conclusion, Old Testament passages contributed to the New Testament's teaching on the afterlife by laying the foundation of key theological themes. Some of these passages no doubt inspired belief in life after death (e.g., Dan. 12), while others were used to explain Jesus's resurrection and eternal life in retrospect (e.g., Ps. 68). The Old Testament prepared the way through its imagery, aspirations, doctrine of God, and sweeping narratives in which plots are not resolved in a single lifetime. The New Testament brings these elements to completion by interpreting them through the lens of Jesus. In fact, when the New Testament cites the Old Testament to talk about the afterlife, it does so most often to demonstrate or interpret Jesus's death, resurrection, or ascension.

Examples of inner-biblical interpretation on this topic occur primarily in the book of Daniel and in the New Testament's use of the Old Testament. The following five insights can be derived from these examples: (1) The New Testament's teachings on final judgment, bodily resurrection, and eternal life are grounded in key texts and themes from the Old Testament. (2) Old Testament passages with implications for the afterlife can be applied to this topic in the New Testament when they are seen as fulfilled in Jesus. (3) Significant experiences, interpreted in light of the whole framework of faith, allow later biblical writers to see new insights in older scriptural traditions. (4) A single key idea in a received scriptural text is enough to make it useful for a later biblical writer's argument. (5) Old Testament images and expressions that were figurative in their original contexts can be interpreted concretely in the New Testament.

Putting the Pieces Together

The Bible offers a variety of perspectives on the afterlife. Much of this variety stems from the difference between the Old Testament's lack of interest in the hereafter on the one hand, and the New Testament's focus on resurrection and eternal life on the other. In many ways, the Old Testament reflects vague ideas about the netherworld, much like its ancient Near Eastern neighbors. In other ways, however, the Old Testament articulates hopes and beliefs that hint at life after death or affirm God's power to restore life to the dead. These hopes and beliefs find confirmation and further development in the New Testament. With rare exceptions, the Old Testament does not counter the New Testament but simply fails to match its level of specificity. Therefore, a coherent theological

picture of the afterlife in Scripture is essentially equivalent to the fully real-
ized perspective of the New Testament. The resurrection of Jesus is both the
basis for Christian confidence in the afterlife and also the interpretive key for
understanding the Old Testament's contribution to this topic.

The death and resurrection of Jesus embody Scripture's core values on
the subject of the afterlife. These values are expressed in Jesus's teaching on
eternal life, final judgment, and recompense in the hereafter. What the New
Testament teaches about the afterlife is the logical outworking of God's love,
power, and justice. These themes appear prominently in the Old Testament,
but their implications for life after death are not fully explored there. The
New Testament takes this further step, informed by a new cultural environment and grounded in Jesus's resurrection.

As is evident from the New Testament, Jesus understood his resurrection
to be the fulfillment of Old Testament teaching, and the apostles agreed with
this. After rising from the dead, Jesus explained to his disciples what the Scriptures said about his suffering and entering into glory (Luke 24:25–27; cf. 1 Pet.
1:10–11). As reported in the book of Acts, Paul spent three days demonstrating
from the Scriptures that the Christ had to suffer and rise from the dead (Acts
17:2–3). Although we do not have transcripts of what Jesus and Paul said on
these occasions, it is reasonable to conclude that the Old Testament passages
that appear in the New Testament to make these points represent a sample
of the passages that Jesus and Paul discussed. In 1 Corinthians 15:3–5 Paul
says that Christ was raised on the third day "according to the Scriptures." It
is worth asking, What Old Testament passage teaches this? I think the most
likely candidate is the book of Jonah, according Jesus's interpretation of the
"sign of Jonah."[95] Another possibility is Hosea 6:2: "He will revive us in two
days, on the third day he will raise us up, and we will live before him" (see
"God's Power over Life and Death in the Old Testament"). Part of the New
Testament's perspective on the afterlife is that Jesus and the apostles stand
in continuity with the Old Testament. For us to adopt this perspective, we
need to be able to find relevant themes in Old Testament texts and interpret
them in relation to Jesus.

Each part of Scripture should be interpreted both in its original context and
within the context of the Bible as a whole. What the New Testament says about
the afterlife can generally be interpreted at a basic level without major difficulties. Of course, wherever New Testament texts offer different perspectives or
emphases, they should be interpreted in light of one another and in harmony

---

95. Matt. 12:38–42; Luke 11:29–32. See "God's Power over Life and Death in the New
Testament."

with Scripture's core values. As for the Old Testament, different types of texts contribute to the Bible's overall teaching in different ways. For example, some passages are skeptical about the afterlife (e.g., Eccles. 3:18–22) or deny that people remember God in death (e.g., Ps. 6:5). Passages like these should be interpreted for the contributions they make to their immediate contexts, but we should not adopt their viewpoints as dogma. Thus, we should enjoy our work as God's gift in view of the fleeting nature of this life (Eccles. 2:24–25; 3:22), and we can petition God to save our lives before we lose the power to bless him in the present world (Ps. 6:4–10). But as Christians, we also believe in the resurrection and eternal life. Other Old Testament passages convey themes that can serve as building blocks for our theological reflection on the afterlife. These passages should first be read in their historical and literary contexts, so we can learn what ideas they communicate and how these ideas contribute to Scripture's teaching. But they can also be interpreted as theological prompts to reflect on a theme (e.g., God's power or justice) that finds its culmination in Jesus and eternal life. If one were looking to preach about Jesus in a sermon on the Old Testament, this would be a valid way to do so.

New Testament writers appropriated Old Testament texts in theologically suggestive ways to demonstrate and explain Jesus's resurrection. This interpretive approach was an essential part of the apostolic message. As we think about how to explain Jesus and the resurrection based on the Old Testament, we should keep a few points in mind. First, we are on surest ground when we base our interpretations on texts that express relevant themes. Second, not every facet of a passage needs to be useful to be employed for theological reflection. Even one core idea is enough, and other facets of the passage need not be pressed. Third, it is the church's experience with Jesus that allows Old Testament texts to yield Christian insights, so Jesus and the New Testament should serve as guardrails for our interpretation. Lastly, sometimes language that was meant metaphorically in the Old Testament can be interpreted concretely in the wake of Jesus's resurrection. We saw this in Acts 2:24–36, which applied the language of Psalm 16:8–11 to Jesus (see "God's Power over Life and Death in the Old Testament"; "God's Power over Life and Death in the New Testament").[96]

---

96. Bishop Diodore of Tarsus (ca. 330–394), a prolific commentator on the Old Testament, believed that certain psalms contain language that was hyperbolic in the text's original context but was fully suitable to a later fulfillment. For example, Ps. 30:3 says, "O LORD, You brought up my life from Sheol, You preserved me alive from going down to the pit" (see "Old Testament Afterlife Themes in the New Testament"). According to Diodore, this language was suitable to its Old Testament context, but at the time, it sounded hyperbolic. In the New Testament era, however, these words are fulfilled in all who will experience the resurrection, to whom the language of the psalm can be applied precisely. See Graves, *Biblical Interpretation*, 137–39.

7

Biblical Interpretation
Then and Now

Principles of Inner-Biblical Interpretation

In the preceding chapters, we have seen many passages where a biblical writer references an earlier biblical tradition to employ it for some fresh purpose. This is the most obvious way in which Scripture interprets Scripture. For each topic discussed in this book, I have given special attention to these examples of inner-biblical interpretation to obtain insights to help interpret Scripture on each topic in question. Although many specific insights on how one biblical text interprets another are found throughout this book, and some insights appear in more than one chapter, I will attempt here to sum up one major insight for each chapter.

Chapter 2. Biblical texts that respond to the formula of transgenerational punishment generally limit its application or emphasize the individual, whereas the responsibility of people to care for one another is consistently affirmed. Thus, biblical traditions can be qualified or clarified in a limiting way, or they can be positively activated for renewed application.

Chapter 3. Both insider and outsider biblical traditions are employed in new settings by later biblical writers. Certain Old Testament texts emphasize earlier traditions that show greater openness to outsiders. Overall the New Testament follows this trajectory. Yet the New Testament also preserves a distinction between inside and outside in keeping with another Old Testament trajectory that focuses on maintaining boundaries.

Chapter 4. Faithfulness to God and concern for human well-being are core principles in biblical texts dealing with marriage, polygamy, and divorce. The teaching of Jesus highlights faithfulness in marriage and envisions a future without marriage. On this topic, biblical writers seem to interpret earlier biblical traditions as upholding core principles, but the specific rules can vary depending on the context.

Chapter 5. Concerning sacrifices, basic concepts such as worship, atonement, and reconciliation remain central throughout Scripture. Some Old Testament writers question the usefulness of sacrificial offerings, focusing instead on inner devotion and ethics. Others promote the ongoing validity of ritual sacrifice. In the New Testament, the latter tradition is affirmed through Jesus's sacrificial death, and the former is affirmed through the figurative application of sacrificial language.

Chapter 6. Whereas the Old Testament says little about the afterlife directly, the New Testament employs Old Testament themes in order to validate and explain its teaching on resurrection and eternal life. In the light of Jesus, New Testament writers see new insights in Old Testament texts and employ Old Testament passages to draw fresh theological conclusions.

Given the specific details of the biblical texts discussed throughout this book, the following general observations can be made about how Scripture interprets Scripture:

1. One biblical text can reapply, adjust, or qualify a previous scriptural tradition when circumstances change or when a new question is being asked.
2. The significance of a scriptural tradition can be interpreted differently by different biblical writers depending on the needs of the context.
3. Biblical writers can affirm more than one side of a complex issue.
4. Sometimes, when a scriptural tradition is redeployed in a new context, only one facet of its original meaning is applied.
5. We typically find fundamental concepts or core values that stand behind the various biblical perspectives on a topic and unite the diverse applications of a scriptural tradition.
6. In the New Testament, the person and work of Jesus can have a transformative influence on how prior scriptural traditions are interpreted.

These observations do not straightforwardly reveal a single interpretive method. But they do suggest general principles that can inform our practice of biblical interpretation. Four principles that I derive from these observations are as follows: (1) Biblical texts make specific statements or take up topics from a particular angle in concrete historical circumstances according to contextual conventions. (2) Although the whole of every text is significant for its function in its context, biblical texts have core ideas that are key to their reapplication in new contexts. (3) The theological unity of the Bible reaches its full measure of coherence at the level of the core ideas that connect all biblical texts together. (4) Our application of the Bible should be informed both by each text's specific content and by its connection to the coherent message of Scripture as a whole.

By seeking to derive principles from explicit cases of inner-biblical interpretation, I have endeavored to take my interpretive cues from Scripture. This does not mean, however, that Scripture gives its own applications apart from the process of interpretation. The argument presented here is not that the Bible simply interprets itself but that biblical writers have much to teach us about how we should interpret the Bible.

Biblical Interpretation as a Process

I will now briefly review the process of biblical interpretation that I introduced in chapter 1. I described this process in the first chapter by explaining four key concepts. On the basis of the preceding analysis of inner-biblical interpretation, I can now describe it in greater detail. I hope that this process is a reasonable application of the observations and principles discussed above.

1. The starting point for interpreting Scripture is faith in Jesus, which entails love of God and neighbor, participation in the church, and the expectation that God has something to teach us from every biblical text.

2. When approaching any biblical text, we should try to understand as much as possible about its contexts: the historical context of the events or composition of the text, the cultural world presupposed by the text, the text's literary form, the location and function of the text within the overall structure of the book, and the text's place in salvation history relative to Jesus. Biblical commentaries are especially helpful for this aspect of interpretation.

3. When studying a specific biblical passage, we should try to recognize and appreciate all the facets of meaning that are present in the text with these various contexts in mind. Our goal should be to understand the text richly, with sensitivity to the various ideas and aims that play out in the text and to be cognizant of how each facet of meaning contributes to what the text communicates in its context. It should be kept in mind that what a biblical text presupposes will not necessarily be the same as what it teaches.

4. The biblical text taken as a whole should be compared with other parts of Scripture that address the same or related themes, speak to issues that are raised by the text, or pertain to questions that are being asked about the text. In doing this, we should be patiently reflective in our own hearts and minds and also ready to listen and learn from others. Examples of one biblical text interpreting an earlier biblical tradition are worthy of special attention. We obviously want to read as widely in Scripture as possible and make use of good resources to help locate and study passages. It is helpful to learn Scripture by memory so that we can remember relevant parallels.

5. The ideas and values communicated in the text and in related biblical passages should be considered in the light of Scripture's core values. These are identified based on Jesus's teachings and example and also based on summative passages found throughout Scripture. The guiding influence of Scripture's core values is yet another way that Scripture helps us interpret Scripture. I offered a brief statement on this in chapter 1 ("We Should Seek a Coherent Picture of What Scripture Teaches"). Other formulations of Scripture's core ideas and values are obviously possible, but Jesus provides a center of gravity that keeps any formulation in balance. Our church and life experiences also shape how we interpret Scripture at this level; this is another reason why we all need to be good listeners to one another.

6. As we study a text at the historical and literary levels (steps 2 and 3), and consider the various facets of meaning in conversation with the whole Christian Bible (steps 4 and 5), we should ask what ideas and values rise to the surface as main teaching points of each passage. We should look for meaning that both emerges from the content of the specific text before us and also fits coherently with what the rest of Scripture teaches. Through the process of interpretation, certain facets of meaning will be activated for application, and others may not be (e.g., Col. 3:22–4:1). Belief that each text communicates a divinely intended message that is useful for application follows necessarily from the doctrine of biblical inspiration (2 Tim. 3:16–17).

7. If we are looking to go deeper into the subject matter addressed by a biblical text, we need to broaden the scope of our study to look in greater detail at other texts that touch on the same subject. In other words, rather than simply looking at parallel passages to gain insight into one text, we should devote serious study to a number of texts. In this way, we will gain a better grasp of Scripture's coherent message.

The best way to begin for anyone who is relatively new to the study of Scripture is to read through the Bible to become broadly familiar with its contents and to listen to good sermons. In today's world it is possible for many Christians to participate in small groups that meet regularly to study the Bible. Many resources are also available to help Christians study Scripture, including study Bibles that address issues of context, exegesis, and theology.[1] For those who will become teachers in the church, advanced training in Scripture and theology is part of seminary education.[2] No one can attain perfect mastery of all Scripture, so we are always growing in our understanding of both individual passages and the Bible as a whole. As with the Christian life in general, learning Scripture requires perpetual striving for a deeper understanding of what lies ahead (cf. Phil. 3:13–14). One does not have to know every verse to grow in faith, hope, and love through Bible study. The key ingredient in Christian biblical interpretation is reading Scripture with the aim of growing in love of God and neighbor.

From the Bible to the Early Church

We have seen numerous examples in the Old Testament of earlier scriptural traditions being redeployed by later biblical writers to address new contexts. This practice of reinterpretation contributed to the diversity of perspectives that can be found on certain topics in the Old Testament, but we also discovered underlying points of conceptual unity that hold the various pieces of Old Testament theology together. This historical process of interpretation and fresh application continued into the New Testament, where Old Testament texts provided the conceptual framework of continuity with the past but also received new significance in light of Jesus and the Greco-Roman world.[3] If we

1. A number of excellent study Bibles are available, some of which focus on specific topics such as biblical languages, ancient contexts, theology, and application. Among the best general study Bibles are the NIV Study Bible (evangelical Protestant), the ESV Study Bible (evangelical Protestant), the New Interpreter's Study Bible (mainline Protestant), and the Roman Catholic Study Bible (Roman Catholic). Anyone reading through one of these study Bibles in its entirety (text, introduction, notes, essays) over a two-year period would gain immense riches in knowledge of Scripture and potential usefulness to the church.

2. Preparation for Christian ministry involves both practical training and academic study. Among the various subjects covered in seminary education, the Bible and theology should have a central place. Academic learning has contributed to the church's mission since its formative years. Most early Christian bishops (who were also preachers) received a solid "secular" education in rhetoric, philosophy, and literary studies. Important catechetical schools of biblical and theological learning in the early church included those in Alexandria, Antioch, and Nisibis. Of the many later schools directly serving the church, two examples worthy of mention are the twelfth-century School of St. Victor in Paris and the sixteenth-century Prophezei of Zurich.

3. The interpretive heritage of the Hebrew Bible was received among Jews in the Greco-Roman world in various ways. The New Testament's appropriation of this heritage is one historical trajectory, which places Jesus at the center of its framework and adopts particular postures toward the broader cultural environment. Another historical trajectory is found in

extend our view, we will see that the Bible's internal trajectory of interpretation continues along recognizable lines into the early church.[4]

In the second century AD, Christian works such as the Epistle of Barnabas (early second century) and writers such as Justin Martyr (d. ca. 165), Melito of Sardis (late second century), and Irenaeus (d. ca. 202) carried on the New Testament's practice of applying biblical texts to new contexts. Scripture was cited to explain and justify Christian teaching and to exercise pastoral care among churches. The kinds of christological and ethical applications that one finds in the New Testament were utilized and expanded by Christian writers of the second and third centuries.[5] Many of the theological commitments evident in these sources are essential to the process of biblical interpretation that I outlined above. These include the continuing relevance of Scripture, the theological harmony of biblical texts, and the symbolic or conceptual application of theological ideas arising from one facet of a biblical text's meaning. However, at least two components of this interpretive process are not explicitly emphasized in these sources—namely, the enduring value of the original context and the usefulness of every biblical text. These two components are brought into clearer focus by Christian interpreters in the third through fifth centuries.

First, beginning especially with Origen of Alexandria (ca. 185–253) and becoming prominent in the fourth century, many Christians adopted methods of classical literary scholarship to better preserve and interpret Scripture.[6] Classical scholar Rudolf Pfeiffer defines "scholarship" as "the art of understanding, explaining, and restoring the literary tradition."[7] By the third century, Christian teachers were applying principles of literary scholarship to sort out differences between biblical manuscripts and expound biblical

---

rabbinic literature, which emphasizes Torah and the Jewish people and adopts different postures toward the Greco-Roman world. On the continuation of the Hebrew Bible's exegetical tradition in rabbinic biblical interpretation, see Fishbane, *Biblical Interpretation in Ancient Israel*, 2–8, 525–43.

4. The best overview of patristic biblical interpretation that gives a sense of historical trajectory is Simonetti, *Biblical Interpretation in the Early Church*. An insightful book that illustrates the theological continuity between the Bible and the church fathers is Daniélou, *From Shadows to Reality*. An accessible discussion of patristic interpretation and biblical inspiration is Graves, *Inspiration and Interpretation of Scripture*. Excellent articles on a range of figures and movements in patristic biblical interpretation can be found in Kannengiesser, *Handbook of Patristic Exegesis*.

5. For an example of this process with regard to the exodus motif, see Graves, "Exodus," 547–60.

6. On Origen and classical scholarship, see Martens, *Origen and Scripture*, 25–106; and Heine, *Origen*.

7. Pfeiffer, *History of Classical Scholarship*, 3. For a recent discussion of this tradition, see Montanari, *History of Ancient Greek Scholarship*.

texts comprehensively (i.e., verse-by-verse). Whereas second-century Christians interacted with Scripture primarily by quoting a limited number of verses in the course of making topical arguments, Origen wrote homilies and commentaries on Scripture that engaged entire biblical books from start to finish.[8] The topical use of Scripture never disappeared, but the comprehensive approach became common in the fourth and fifth centuries. This approach gave Christian preachers and teachers the opportunity to show explicitly their belief that every passage of Scripture is useful for instruction.

Second, Christian interpreters between the third and fifth centuries developed a mode of exegesis that created space for the original contexts of biblical passages to receive explicit attention. A primary vehicle for this was the systematic distinction between a "literal" and a "spiritual" sense.[9] Although this distinction could cause interpretive problems, such as detaching the applied meaning from the text's content, it also provided avenues for sound exegetical work and theological reflection.[10] A commentator who was working through a biblical book and explaining the literal sense could discuss the background or setting of the passage, situate the text in its literary context, explain difficult words, and clarify the flow of thought. In patristic exegesis, exhortations were sometimes made through precept or analogy based on the literal sense. Then, in the spiritual exposition, other passages of Scripture and theological issues were raised that connected the text to the coherent teaching of Scripture as a whole. I do not suggest that patristic commentators always achieved success in expounding Scripture at these levels. But when they did, their attention to the literal sense made the value of the original context clear, not merely implicit as one typically finds in earlier Christian sources.

In short, patristic commentaries and homilies offer numerous examples of biblical interpretation that reflect the same basic values as the process of interpretation described in this book. These may be summarized as the usefulness of every passage, concern for the original contexts, the theological unity of Scripture, readiness to apply one core idea in a text theologically, the importance of interpreting one passage through other passages, and the central place of Jesus in the process of interpretation. I will illustrate these points with a selection from the *Commentary on Matthew* written by Saint

8. As for early Christian commentaries, in addition to Origen's many works, a select commentary on the book of Daniel is preserved from the first part of the third century, ascribed to Hippolytus of Rome.

9. On these senses, see Graves, *Biblical Interpretation in the Early Church*, xxi–xxviii.

10. See Graves, *Inspiration and Interpretation of Scripture*, 53–55.

Jerome (ca. 347–420), who was among the most capable interpreters in the early church.[11] The following are Jerome's comments on Matthew 21:12–13:

> [12]And Jesus entered into the temple of God and drove out all those selling and buying in the temple, and he overturned the tables of the money-changers and the seats of those selling doves, [13]and he said to them: "It is written: 'My house shall be called a house of prayer,' but 'you have made it a den of robbers.'"[12]

> A crowd of believers spread out their garments so that Jesus's colt might proceed with its feet unharmed [Matt. 21:1–11]. Followed by this crowd, Jesus enters the temple. He drives out all who were selling and buying in the temple, overturns the tables of the money-changers, and scatters the seats of those selling doves. Then he speaks to them, citing a testimony from the sacred Scriptures that his Father's house should be a "house of prayer" [Isa. 56:7], not a "den of robbers" [Jer. 7:11] or a "house of business" [John 2:16], as is written in another Gospel.

> First, it should be known that, especially on feast days, the Jewish people would come together from virtually every country to the temple of the Lord [cf. Acts 2:5], which was the most illustrious temple in the whole world,[13] in order to offer countless sacrifices of bulls, rams, and goats in accordance with the commandments of the law. The poor used to offer young doves and turtledoves, so that they would not be without something to sacrifice.[14] Now, it often happened that those who came from far away did not have sacrificial victims. So, the priests thought of a way that they could obtain plunder from the people.[15] They sold all kinds of animals that were needed for sacrifice, so that they might both sell to those who lacked and also receive back what was purchased.

---

11. An introduction to Jerome and his biblical interpretation can be found in Graves, *Jerome*, xxiii–li.

12. For the Latin text of Jerome's commentary, see Hurst and Adriaen, *S. Hieronymi Presbyteri Opera*, 186–88. The English translation is mine.

13. See Josephus, *Antiquities* 7.110–18.

14. Cf. Lev. 5:7; 12:8; 14:22, 30.

15. Jerome would have assumed that sacrificial animals were being sold and bought based on John 2:14–15. Jesus's reference to Jer. 7:11 would have been enough to suggest that those in charge of this commerce were conducting their business dishonestly. Jerome's primary sources for Jewish practices in the time of Jesus were the New Testament itself and the inferences that he drew from it. Some early Jewish sources make general allegations that members of the temple priesthood were acting corruptly, but nothing in these sources corroborates Jerome's account. The Qumran Habakkuk Pesher scroll mentions the figure of the "Wicked Priest" plundering the poor in the sanctuary (1QpHab XII, 7–10; cf. IX, 4–5; IX, 16–X, 1). Charges of corruption against priestly leaders in Jerusalem appear in later sources, such as Josephus (e.g., *Antiquities* 20.213–14) and rabbinic literature (e.g., in Mishnah Keritot 1:7, Rabban Shimon ben Gamliel insists that the price of birds for offerings be lowered; cf. Tosefta Menahot 13:4). See Evans, "Jesus' Action in the Temple," 319–44. These later sources may or may not be relevant for understanding the time of Jesus, but Jerome might have used Josephus or other Jewish sources to fill out his picture of early first-century Jerusalem.

This scam of theirs expanded even further due to the habitual poverty of those who came. Many lacked sufficient financial resources. Not only did they not have proper sacrificial offerings, but they lacked the means to buy even birds or common small gifts. So, the priests appointed "money-changers" who lent money with additional obligation. But since it had been commanded in the law that no one should take interest [Lev. 25:37; Deut. 23:19], and there was no advantage in making a loan that brought no profit and sometimes lost its principal, they devised another scheme to make them "bankers" [*collybistas*] instead of "money-changers."[16] The Latin language does not express the proper meaning of this word. The word *collyba* among them referred to what we call "sweet fruits," that is, common little gifts, such as roasted chickpeas, raisins, and fruits of various kinds.[17] Therefore, because "bankers" who lent money for profit were not allowed to receive interest, they received various gifts that took the place of interest. Their aim was to exact gifts bought with coins, since it was unlawful to exact coins, as if Ezekiel had not warned in advance about this very thing when he said: "You will not receive interest or superabundance!" [Ezek. 22:12]. The Lord, seeing this kind of business, or rather robbery, in his Father's house, was roused to action by the ardor of his spirit in accordance with what is written in the sixty-eighth Psalm: "The zeal of your house has consumed me" [Ps. 69:9].[18] Consequently, he made a whip for himself from cords, and he drove out from the temple a great multitude of men, saying: "It is written: 'My house shall be called a house of prayer, but you have made it a den of robbers'" [Matt. 21:13]. For a man is a robber, and converts the temple of God into a den of robbers, who seeks financial gain from religion. His worship is not so much the worship of God as a pretext for business. This is the sense according to the historical narrative.

Otherwise, according to the mystical sense,[19] Jesus daily enters the temple of his Father and drives out all from his Church, both bishops, priests, and deacons, and also lay people and the whole crowd, and he holds them guilty of a single crime, that is, selling and buying. For it is written: "Freely you have received, freely give" [Matt. 10:8].[20] Moreover, he overturns the tables of the

16. Jerome gives the Greek word *kollybistēs*, "banker," which is found in the original Greek text of Matt. 21:12 in place of the Latin *nummularius*, "money-changer."

17. The Greek word *kollybon* typically refers to a small gold weight, but the plural form of this word (*kollyba*) can be used for small cakes or other desserts. Jerome appeals to this usage to justify his theory that corrupt money-changers or bankers in the temple were accepting gifts as payment for loans to circumvent the prohibition against charging interest.

18. Ps. 68 is the Latin numbering; this psalm is Ps. 69 in English Bibles.

19. For his mystical understanding, Jerome draws on Origen's *Commentary on Matthew* 16.20–23; see Heine, *Commentary of Origen*, 1:261–65. On the reference to "bishops, priests, and deacons," see Origen's *Commentary on Matthew* 16.22 (Heine, *Commentary of Origen*, 1:263).

20. Jerome quotes Matt. 10:8 to make this same point in his homily on Mark 11:15–17 (Matt. 21:12–13), where he also cites the story of Simon Magus (Acts 8:9–24) to illustrate the evil of wanting to buy God's grace; see Ewald, *Homilies of Saint Jerome*, 2:181.

money-changers. Observe that, because of the greed of the priests, the altar of God is designated "tables of money-changers." He also upends the seats of "those selling doves," that is, those who sell the grace of the Holy Spirit and do everything in order to devour the people who are subject to them.[21] Concerning such people it says, "Those who devour my people as if they were eating bread" [Ps. 14:4]. According to the simple understanding, of course, the doves were not on the seats but in cages, unless perhaps the peddlers of the doves were sitting on "seats," but this is completely absurd, since by "seats" the greater honor of teachers is indicated.[22] Yet, this honor is reduced to nothing when it is mixed with greedy profit.

What we have said about the churches, let each person understand also with reference to himself. For the apostle Paul says: "You are the temple of God, and the Holy Spirit dwells in you" [1 Cor. 3:16]. May there be no business in the house of our heart. May there be no commerce of selling and buying. May there be no desire for gifts. Otherwise, an angry and stern Jesus will enter his temple and cleanse it by no other means than with a whip, which he administers in order to make a house of prayer out of a den of robbers and a house of business.

Although many aspects of Jerome's exegesis would benefit from further discussion, I will offer just a few comments on the core values that underlie his approach. First, Jerome exhibits his interest in the immediate literary context by connecting this passage back to the narrative that precedes it (Matt. 21:1–11). Second, he devotes considerable attention to what he understands to be the historical circumstances of the passage as part of his treatment of the "historical narrative" (*historia*). Jerome supposes that corrupt priests were making a profit by selling animals to the people, only to receive them back when they were sacrificed. Furthermore, he imagines that they were making loans at interest to those who were too poor to afford even small sacrifices and were avoiding the biblical prohibition against interest by taking small gifts as interest instead of money. These reconstructions appear to be based on inferences from biblical passages, the specific language of the Greek text,

21. Origen describes "those selling doves" as church leaders who take financial advantage of Christians who are innocent like doves (Heine, *Commentary of Origen*, 1:263; cf. Matt. 10:16). Jerome agrees with Hilary of Poitiers in seeing the doves as symbolic of the Holy Spirit (cf. Matt. 3:16; Mark 1:10; Luke 3:22; John 1:32); see Williams, *St. Hilary of Poitiers*, 221.

22. Jerome's comment on the "simple understanding" addresses two issues. First, he clarifies the language of the Latin text, to make the obvious point that it is not the doves but those who sell doves who could sit on "seats." Second, he points out that in normal ecclesiastical Latin usage, to sit on a "seat" (*cathedra*) is an honor associated with teaching authority, both in connection with the bishop's "seat" and with reference to Matt. 23:2. Because peddlers of doves would not possess such honor according to the simple understanding, Jerome thinks that the text is alluding to authoritative teachers whose honor is reduced by their greed (cf. Heine, *Commentary of Origen*, 1:264).

and probably Jewish historical sources such as Josephus. Third, he shows his belief in the usefulness of the text by deriving lessons from the passage, not only at the "mystical" level but even at the historical level (e.g., we should not seek financial gain from religion).

Fourth, Jerome affirms the theological unity of Scripture and the importance of intertextual biblical connections through the various parallel passages he cites in his mystical interpretation. The notion of biblical usefulness also comes into play. According to Jerome, we should interpret the concrete details of Matthew 21:12–13 not merely as literary embellishments but as avenues for Christian instruction. Jesus opposes not simply buying and selling, or even illicit business practices in general, but the conducting of such business in God's temple. Jerome's application of this detail is grounded in 1 Corinthians 3:16, which states that Christians are God's temple (cf. 2 Cor. 6:16). Jerome understands this application at two levels, both for the church and for the individual Christian. Just as leaders in the temple were wrong to make use of their religious authority for personal gain, leaders in the church are wrong to do the same. He supports this by the quotation of Matthew 10:8, which comes from Jesus's commission to the Twelve to preach the kingdom of heaven. And he confirms God's disapproval of such wicked church leaders by quoting Psalm 14:4. Moreover, just as those in the temple were wrong to put financial gain ahead of prayer, individual Christians are wrong to let financial concerns take precedence in their hearts over prayer and the Holy Spirit. If church leaders or individual Christians allow these sins to take root, they can expect Jesus to rebuke them as he did the sinful people mentioned in Matthew 21:12–13. As a fifth and final point, these applications show Jerome's readiness to apply a core idea in the text theologically, and they naturally reflect his view that Jesus is central to the process of interpretation.[23] It should be observed that Jerome's mystical interpretations are not only grounded in parallel passages of Scripture but also flow logically from his "historical" lesson (e.g., we should not seek financial gain from religion). Of course, I am not suggesting that every aspect of Jerome's exposition is worth emulating. But this example shows that Jerome approaches biblical interpretation in a manner analogous to the process of interpretation that I have described in this book.

---

23. Jerome's commitment to interpreting Scripture through the lens of Jesus is more strikingly evident in his Old Testament commentaries. A good example can be found in his *Commentary on Ecclesiastes* 3:18–21. For this passage Jerome describes the sense of the text in context, explains his view that all the dead went to Hades prior to the coming of Christ, argues that the literal sense still allows for the survival of the soul after the death of the body, and then gives a Christian spiritual interpretation that employs the theme of reversal between appearances on earth and rewards in heaven; see Goodrich and Miller, *St. Jerome*, 62–64.

To sum up this section, I am suggesting that (1) the practice of interpretation seen within the Bible itself continued on into the early church, and (2) the basic approach that one sees in the best of classical patristic exegesis is the model for the process of interpretation that I am proposing. I am not arguing that my approach is exactly what biblical writers or early Christians did, because the interpretations they gave and the manner in which they gave them were specific to their contexts. The point I intend to make is that my approach to biblical interpretation is not one that I have newly discovered. On the contrary, I am endeavoring to interpret Scripture based on lessons learned from Scripture itself in harmony with interpretive concepts that played an important role in the history of biblical interpretation. If my descriptions of inner-biblical interpretation and the way I formulate the process of interpretation are useful for others, I will be pleased, but I hope that most of the interpretive moves that I make throughout the book are already familiar to Christian readers.

Biblical Interpretation: Past, Present, and Future

Although the Bible is a collection of ancient texts, as sacred Scripture it remains always relevant. This perpetual timeliness is the result of divine inspiration, and it is put into effect through interpretation. If we engage Scripture with reverence and diligence, we can learn what is essential for honoring God, doing right by our neighbors, and experiencing God's blessing. The fact that we are required to participate actively in interpreting Scripture seems to be by design, partly because it involves our responding to Jesus's call to follow him and partly because it binds us together as Christians, since biblical interpretation involves traditions, resources, and insights that are beyond the possession of any single individual. As we have seen, the enduring relevance of biblical teaching is made clear to us when we pay attention to how Scripture interprets Scripture.

Because biblical books come from the past, our starting point for interpretation needs to be the ancient contexts in which these books were written. We should pay attention to what each passage said in its context and how biblical writers interacted with prior biblical traditions. Giving proper consideration to the original contexts of Scripture helps us to understand the various viewpoints we sometimes encounter on specific topics so that we learn from the full spectrum of wisdom that the Bible offers. Recognizing the concrete circumstances behind a biblical text invites us to think about how we can apply the text's teaching concretely today. We will often find models and principles in our historical study that suggest possible contemporary applications. If we take it seriously, the Bible's past is a help, not a hindrance, to present-day biblical interpretation.

As we turn to the present, our need to apply biblical teaching creates new obligations and opportunities. It is essential that we address today's questions, listen to today's voices, and make faithful use of today's resources. Our belief in the divine inspiration and usefulness of all Scripture leads us to seek a coherent picture of biblical teaching on contemporary issues. A cohesive but not blandly uniform understanding of what Scripture teaches enables us to see each individual passage's unique contribution within the framework of the Bible as whole. The search for theological coherence is not merely an intellectual exercise; on the contrary, it is a key step in making biblical teaching comprehensible so that we can apply it in real life. It is through practical application that Scripture helps us to be transformed into what God intends us to be.

The Bible is relevant today, not because it portrays a futuristic utopian society that we can imitate but because through its diverse ancient literary forms it preserves and commends a sacred deposit of enduring truths about God and humanity. Our goal in interpreting Scripture should not be to reconstruct the ancient cultures that are presupposed in Scripture. Biblical writers did not use earlier biblical traditions this way, and in any case the Bible as a whole reflects more than one ancient culture. Instead, we should endeavor to interpret and apply Scripture to help bring about a world that is better than what the Bible presupposes. This happens primarily by progress in holiness among Christians, the dissemination of the good news of Jesus, and the positive influence of the church on society. It should not be imagined that God needs to improve. It is we who must increase in love of God and neighbor. We can do this by applying the teaching of Scripture to our present world in keeping with the example we learned from how Scripture interprets Scripture.

Bibliography

Abernethy, Andrew T. *The Book of Isaiah and God's Kingdom: A Thematic-Theological Approach*. New Studies in Biblical Theology 40. Downers Grove, IL: InterVarsity, 2016.

Alexander, Desmond. "The Old Testament View of Life after Death." *Themelios* 11 (1986): 41–46.

Anderson, Gary A. "Sacrifice and Sacrificial Offerings: Old Testament." In *The Anchor Bible Dictionary*, edited by David Noel Freedman, 5:870–86. New York: Doubleday, 1992.

Augustine. *On Christian Teaching*. Translated by R. P. H. Green. Oxford: Oxford University Press, 1997.

Averbeck, Richard E. "The Cult in Deuteronomy and Its Relationship to the Book of the Covenant and the Holiness Code." In *Sepher Torath Mosheh: Studies in the Composition and Interpretation of Deuteronomy*, edited by Daniel I. Block and Richard L. Schultz, 241–56. Peabody, MA: Hendrickson, 2017.

———. "Reading the Ritual Law in Leviticus Theologically." In *Interpreting the Old Testament Theologically: Essays in Honor of Willem A. VanGemeren*, edited by Andrew T. Abernethy, 135–49. Grand Rapids: Zondervan, 2018.

———. "Sacrifices and Offerings." In *Dictionary of the Old Testament: Pentateuch*, edited by T. Desmond Alexander and David W. Baker, 706–33. Downers Grove, IL: InterVarsity, 2003.

Babbitt, F. C., trans. *Plutarch: Moralia, Volume 2*. Loeb Classical Library 222. Cambridge, MA: Harvard University Press, 1928.

Beale, G. K. *Handbook on the New Testament Use of the Old Testament: Exegesis and Interpretation*. Grand Rapids: Baker Academic, 2012.

Beaton, R. "Song of Songs 3: History of Interpretation." In *Dictionary of the Old Testament Wisdom, Poetry, & Writings*, edited by Tremper Longman III and Peter Enns, 760–69. Downers Grove, IL: IVP Academic, 2008.

Becker, A., J. Renger, J. Quack, V. Haas, T. Podella, J. N. Bremmer, C. R. Phillips, and P. Wick. "Sacrifice." In *Brill's New Pauly: Encyclopaedia of the Ancient World*, vol. 12, edited by Hubert Cancik and Helmuth Schneider, 832–56. Leiden: Brill, 2008.

Beckwith, Roger T., and Martin J. Selman, eds. *Sacrifice in the Bible*. Grand Rapids: Baker, 1995.

Berman, Joshua. *Inconsistency in the Torah: Ancient Literary Convention and the Limits of Source Criticism*. Oxford: Oxford University Press, 2017.

Bock, D. L. "Son of Man." In *Dictionary of Jesus and the Gospels*, 2nd ed., edited by Joel B. Green, Jeannine K. Brown, and Nicholas Perrin, 894–900. Downers Grove, IL: InterVarsity, 2013.

Boring, M. Eugene, Klaus Berger, and Carsten Colpe, eds. *Hellenistic Commentary on the New Testament*. Nashville: Abingdon, 1995.

Borowski, Oded. *Daily Life in Biblical Times*. Atlanta: Society of Biblical Literature, 2003.

Bottéro, Jean. *Mesopotamia: Writing, Reasoning, and the Gods*. Translated by Zainab Bahrani and Marc Van De Mieroop. Chicago: University of Chicago Press, 1992.

Bruce, Barbara J., trans. *Origen: Homilies on Joshua*. Fathers of the Church 105. Washington, DC: Catholic University of America Press, 2002.

Cataldo, Jeremiah W. *A Theocratic Yehud? Issues of Government in a Persian Period*. New York: T&T Clark, 2009.

Chapman, Stephen B., and Marvin A. Sweeney, eds. *The Cambridge Companion to the Hebrew Bible/Old Testament*. Cambridge: Cambridge University Press, 2016.

Charlesworth, James H., ed. *The Old Testament Pseudepigrapha*. 2 vols. New York: Doubleday, 1983.

Christmas Carols; or Sacred Song Suited to the Festival of Our Lord's Nativity; with Appropriate Music, and an Introductory Account of the Christmas Carol. London: John William Parker, 1833.

Dalley, Stephanie. "The Descent of Ishtar to the Underworld." In *The Context of Scripture*, edited by William W. Hallo and K. Lawson Younger Jr., 1:381–84. Leiden: Brill, 2003.

———. *Myths from Mesopotamia: Creation, the Flood, Gilgamesh, and Others*. Oxford World's Classics. Oxford: Oxford University Press, 1989.

———. "Nergal and Ereshkigal." In *The Context of Scripture*, edited by William W. Hallo and K. Lawson Younger Jr., 1:384–89. Leiden: Brill, 2003.

Danby, Herbert, trans. *The Mishnah*. Oxford: Oxford University Press, 1933.

Daniélou, Jean. *From Shadows to Reality: Studies in the Biblical Typology of the Fathers*. Translated by Wulstan Hibberd. London: Burns & Oates, 1960.

Danylak, Barry. *Redeeming Singleness: How the Storyline of Scripture Affirms the Single Life*. Wheaton: Crossway, 2010.

Darnell, John C., and Colleen M. Darnell. *The Ancient Egyptian Netherworld Books*. Atlanta: SBL Press, 2018.

Day, John. "The Development of Belief in Life after Death in Ancient Israel." In *After the Exile: Essays in Honour of Rex Mason*, edited by John Barton and David J. Reimer, 231–57. Macon, GA: Mercer University Press, 1996.

Dixon, Suzanne. "Sex and the Married Woman in Ancient Rome." In *Early Christian Families in Context*, edited by David L. Balch and Carolyn Osiek, 111–29. Grand Rapids: Eerdmans, 2003.

Elledge, C. D. *Resurrection of the Dead in Early Judaism 200 BCE–CE 200*. Oxford: Oxford University Press, 2017.

Evans, Craig A. "Jesus' Action in the Temple and Evidence of Corruption in the First-Century Temple." In *Jesus and His Contemporaries: Comparative Studies*, 319–44. Leiden: Brill, 2001.

Ewald, Marie L., trans. *The Homilies of Saint Jerome*. 2 vols. Fathers of the Church 57. Washington, DC: Catholic University of America Press, 1965.

Faulkner, Raymond O., Ogden Goelet Jr., J. Daniel Gunther, Carol A. R. Andrews, Eva Von Dassow, and James Wasserman, eds. *The Egyptian Book of the Dead: The Book of Going Forth by Day*. Rev. ed. San Francisco: Chronicle Books, 2015.

Feldman, Louis H. *Flavius Josephus: Judean Antiquities 1–4, Translation and Commentary*. Leiden: Brill, 2004.

Ferguson, Everett. *The Rule of Faith: A Guide*. Eugene, OR: Cascade, 2015.

Fishbane, Michael. *Biblical Interpretation in Ancient Israel*. Oxford: Clarendon, 1985.

Foster, Benjamin R. *Before the Muses: An Anthology of Akkadian Literature*. 3rd ed. Bethesda, MD: CDL, 2005.

France, R. T. *Women in the Church's Ministry: A Test Case for Biblical Interpretation*. Carlisle, UK: Paternoster, 1995.

Fried, Lisbeth S. *The Priest and the Great King: Temple-Palace Relations in the Persian Empire*. Winona Lake, IN: Eisenbrauns, 2004.

Gadotti, Alhena. *"Gilgamesh, Enkidu, and the Netherworld" and the Sumerian Gilgamesh Cycle*. Berlin: de Gruyter, 2014.

Goldingay, John. *Theological Diversity and the Authority of the Old Testament*. Grand Rapids: Eerdmans, 1987.

Goodrich, Richard J., and David J. D. Miller, trans. *St. Jerome: Commentary on Ecclesiastes*. Ancient Christian Writers 66. New York: Newman, 2012.

Gorman, Michael J. *Elements of Biblical Exegesis: A Basic Guide for Students and Ministers*. 3rd ed. Grand Rapids: Baker Academic, 2020.

Graves, Michael, ed. *Biblical Interpretation in the Early Church*. Minneapolis: Fortress, 2017.

———. "Exodus." In *The Oxford Handbook of Early Christian Biblical Interpretation*, edited by Paul M. Blowers and Peter W. Martens, 547–60. Oxford: Oxford University Press, 2019.

———. *The Inspiration and Interpretation of Scripture*. Grand Rapids: Eerdmans, 2014.

———, trans. *Jerome: Commentary on Jeremiah*. Ancient Christian Texts. Downers Grove, IL: IVP Academic, 2011.

Haas, Volkert. "Death and the Afterlife in Hittite Thought." In *Civilizations of the Ancient Near East*, edited by Jack M. Sasson, 3:2021–30. New York: Scribner's Sons, 1995.

Hadot, Pierre. *Philosophy as a Way of Life*. Edited by Arnold I. Davidson. Translated by Michael Chase. Oxford: Blackwell, 1995.

Hallo, William W., and K. Lawson Younger Jr., eds. *The Context of Scripture*. 4 vols. Leiden: Brill, 2003–17.

Hammer, Reuven, trans. *Sifre: A Tannaitic Commentary on the Book of Deuteronomy*. New Haven: Yale University Press, 1986.

Hays, Richard B. *Echoes of Scripture in the Gospels*. Waco: Baylor University Press, 2016.

Heine, Ronald E., trans. *The Commentary of Origen on the Gospel of St. Matthew*. 2 vols. Oxford Early Christian Texts. Oxford: Oxford University Press, 2018.

———. *Origen: Scholarship in the Service of the Church*. Oxford: Oxford University Press, 2010.

Hess, Richard S. "War in the Hebrew Bible: An Overview." In *War in the Bible and Terrorism in the Twenty-First Century*, edited by Richard S. Hess and Elmer A. Martens, 19–32. Winona Lake, IN: Eisenbrauns, 2008.

Hill, Robert C., trans. *Theodore of Mopsuestia: Commentary on Psalms 1–81*. Writings from the Greco-Roman World. Atlanta: Society of Biblical Literature, 2006.

———. *Theodoret of Cyrus: Commentary on the Song of Songs*. Brisbane: Centre for Early Christian Studies, 2001.

Hillman, Eugene. *Polygamy Reconsidered: African Plural Marriages and the Christian Churches*. Maryknoll, NY: Orbis Books, 1975.

Hitchcock, Christina S. *The Significance of Singleness: A Theological Vision for the Future of the Church*. Grand Rapids: Baker Academic, 2018.

Hoffmeier, James K. "The (Israel) Stela of Merneptah." In *The Context of Scripture*, edited by William W. Hallo and K. Lawson Younger Jr., 2:40–41. Leiden: Brill, 2003.

Holmstedt, Robert D. *Ruth: A Handbook on the Hebrew Text*. Baylor Handbooks on the Hebrew Bible. Waco: Baylor University Press, 2010.

Hurst, D., and M. Adriaen, eds. *S. Hieronymi Presbyteri Opera, Commentariorum in Matheum Libri IV*. Corpus Christianorum Series Latina 77. Turnhout, Belgium: Brepols, 1969.

Instone-Brewer, David. *Divorce and Remarriage in the Bible: The Social and Literary Context*. Grand Rapids: Eerdmans, 2002.

Janzen, David. *The Social Meanings of Sacrifice in the Hebrew Bible*. Berlin: de Gruyter, 2004.

Johnston, Philip S. *Shades of Sheol: Death and Afterlife in the Old Testament*. Downers Grove, IL: IVP Academic, 2002.

Kaminsky, Joel S. *Corporate Responsibility in the Hebrew Bible*. Sheffield: Sheffield Academic, 1995.

Kannengiesser, Charles, ed. *Handbook of Patristic Exegesis: The Bible in Ancient Christianity*. 2 vols. Leiden: Brill, 2004.

Kaplan, Jonathan. *My Perfect One: Typology and Early Rabbinic Interpretation of the Song of Songs*. Oxford: Oxford University Press, 2015.

Katz, Dina. *The Image of the Netherworld in the Sumerian Sources*. Bethesda, MD: CDL, 2003.

Keener, Craig. *And Marries Another: Divorce and Remarriage in the Teaching of the New Testament*. Peabody, MA: Hendrickson, 1991.

Kelly, J. N. D. *Early Christian Creeds*. 3rd ed. New York: Longman, 1972.

King, Philip J., and Lawrence E. Stager. *Life in Biblical Israel*. Louisville: Westminster John Knox, 2001.

Klawans, Jonathan. *Purity, Sacrifice, and the Temple: Symbolism and Supersessionism in the Study of Ancient Judaism*. Oxford: Oxford University Press, 2006.

Knight, George W., III. *The Pastoral Epistles: A Commentary on the Greek Text*. New International Greek Testament Commentary. Grand Rapids: Eerdmans, 1992.

Köstenberger, Andreas J., and Margaret E. Köstenberger. *God's Design for Man and Woman: A Biblical-Theological Survey*. Wheaton: Crossway, 2014.

Kraemer, Ross S. "Typical and Atypical Jewish Family Dynamics: The Cases of Babatha and Berenice." In *Early Christian Families in Context*, edited by David L. Balch and Carolyn Osiek, 114–39. Grand Rapids: Eerdmans, 2003.

Lee-Barnewall, Michelle. *Neither Complementarian nor Egalitarian: A Kingdom Corrective to the Evangelical Gender Debate*. Grand Rapids: Baker Academic, 2016.

Lesko, Leonard H. "Death and the Afterlife in Ancient Egyptian Thought." In *Civilizations of the Ancient Near East*, edited by Jack M. Sasson, 3:1763–74. New York: Scribner's Sons, 1995.

Levinson, Bernard. *Legal Revision and Religious Renewal in Ancient Israel*. Cambridge: Cambridge University Press, 2008.

Lewis, Theodore J. *Cults of the Dead in Ancient Israel and Ugarit*. Atlanta: Scholars Press, 1989.

———. "The Rapiuma." In *Ugaritic Narrative Poetry*, edited by Simon B. Parker 196–205. Atlanta: Scholars Press, 1997.

Lichtheim, Miriam. "Instructions: Merikare." In *The Context of Scripture*, edited by William W. Hallo and K. Lawson Younger Jr., 1:61–66. Leiden: Brill, 2003.

Loader, William. *The New Testament on Sexuality*. Grand Rapids: Eerdmans, 2012.

Lucas, Ernest. *Daniel*. Apollos Old Testament Commentaries. Downers Grove, IL: InterVarsity, 2002.

MacDonald, Margaret Y. "Marriage, NT." In *The New Interpreter's Dictionary of the Bible*, edited by Katharine Doob Sakenfeld, 3:812–18. Nashville: Abington, 2008.

Malherbe, Abraham J., and Everett Ferguson, trans. *Gregory of Nyssa: The Life of Moses*. Classics of Western Spirituality. New York: Paulist Press, 1978.

Marshall, I. Howard, with Philip H. Towner. *A Critical and Exegetical Commentary on the Pastoral Epistles*. International Critical Commentary. London: T&T Clark, 1999.

Martens, Peter W. *Origen and Scripture: The Contours of the Exegetical Life*. Oxford: Oxford University Press, 2012.

Martínez, Florentino García, and Eibert J. C. Tigchelaar, eds. *The Dead Sea Scrolls Study Edition*. 2 vols. Leiden: Brill, 1997.

Matter, E. Ann. *The Voice of My Beloved: The Song of Songs in Western Medieval Christianity*. Philadelphia: University of Pennsylvania Press, 1990.

Matthews, Victor H., and Don C. Benjamin. *Old Testament Parallels: Laws and Stories from the Ancient Near East*. 4th ed. Mahwah, NJ: Paulist Press, 2017.

Mattison, Kevin. *Rewriting and Revision as Amendment in the Laws of Deuteronomy*. Tübingen: Mohr Siebeck, 2018.

McConville, J. G. *Deuteronomy*. Apollos Old Testament Commentary. Downers Grove, IL: InterVarsity, 2002.

Montanari, Franco, ed. *History of Ancient Greek Scholarship: From the Beginnings to the End of the Byzantine Age*. Leiden: Brill, 2020.

Moyise, Steve. *Paul and Scripture: Studying the New Testament Use of the Old Testament*. Grand Rapids: Baker Academic, 2010.

Norris, Richard A., trans. and ed. *The Song of Songs: Interpreted by Early Christian and Medieval Commentators*. The Church's Bible. Grand Rapids: Eerdmans, 2003.

Ntagali, Stanley, and Eileen Hodgetts. *More Than One Wife: Polygamy and Grace*. Kampala, Uganda: Orombi, 2011.

Oldfather, W. A., trans. *Epictetus: The Discourses as Reported by Arrian, the Manual, and Fragments*. Loeb Classical Library 218. Cambridge, MA: Harvard University Press, 1928.

Ollenburger, Ben C. "If Mortals Die, Will They Live Again? The Old Testament and Resurrection." *Ex Auditu* 9 (1993): 29–44.

Parker, Simon B., trans. "Aqhat." In *Ugaritic Narrative Poetry*, edited by Simon B. Parker, 49–80. Atlanta: Scholars Press, 1997.

Petterson, Anthony R. *Haggai, Zechariah & Malachi*. Apollos Old Testament Commentaries. Downers Grove, IL: InterVarsity, 2015.

Pfeiffer, Rudolf. *History of Classical Scholarship: From the Beginnings to the End of the Hellenistic Age*. Oxford: Clarendon, 1968.

Pope, Marvin H. *Song of Songs: A New Translation with Introduction and Commentary*. Anchor Bible. New York: Doubleday, 1977.

Porten, Bezalel. "Egyptian Aramaic." In *The Context of Scripture*, edited by William W. Hallo and K. Lawson Younger Jr., 3:141–98. Leiden: Brill, 2003.

Pritchard, James B., ed. *Ancient Near Eastern Texts Relating to the Old Testament*. Princeton: Princeton University Press, 1969.

Rainey, A. F. "The Order of Sacrifices in Old Testament Ritual Texts." *Biblica* 51 (1970): 485–98.

Renger, J. "Sacrifice II A: Mesopotamia." In *Brill's New Pauly: Encyclopaedia of the Ancient World*, vol. 12, edited by Hubert Cancik and Helmuth Schneider, 838–39. Leiden: Brill, 2008.

Roberts, Barbara. *Not under Bondage: Biblical Divorce for Abuse, Adultery and Desertion*. Ballarat, Australia: Maschil, 2008.

Roth, Martha. "The Laws of Hammurabi." In *The Context of Scripture*, edited by William W. Hallo and K. Lawson Younger Jr., 2:335–53. Leiden: Brill, 2003.

———. "The Middle Assyrian Laws." In *The Context of Scripture*, edited by William W. Hallo and K. Lawson Younger Jr., 2:353–61. Leiden: Brill, 2003.

Sanders, John, ed. *What About Those Who Have Never Heard? Three Views on the Destiny of the Unevangelized*. Downers Grove, IL: InterVarsity, 1995.

Sasson, Jack M. *Jonah: A New Translation with Introduction, Commentary, and Interpretations*. Anchor Yale Bible. New Haven: Yale University Press, 1990.

Schipper, Jeremy. *Ruth: A New Translation with Introduction and Commentary*. Anchor Yale Bible. New Haven: Yale University Press, 2016.

Scurlock, Jo Ann. "Death and the Afterlife in Ancient Mesopotamian Thought." In *Civilizations of the Ancient Near East*, edited by Jack M. Sasson, 3:1883–93. New York: Scribner's Sons, 1995.

Sigvartsen, Jan A. *Afterlife and Resurrection Beliefs in the Apocrypha and Apocalyptic Literature*. London: T&T Clark, 2019.

———. *Afterlife and Resurrection Beliefs in the Pseudepigrapha*. London: T&T Clark, 2019.

Simon, Maurice, trans. *Midrash Rabbah: Song of Songs*. London: Soncino, 1983.

Simonetti, Manlio. *Biblical Interpretation in the Early Church*. Translated by John A. Hughes. Edinburgh: T&T Clark, 1994.

Smith, Mark S., trans. "The Baal Cycle." In *Ugaritic Narrative Poetry*, edited by Simon B. Parker, 81–180. Atlanta: Scholars Press, 1997.

Sprinkle, Joe M. *Biblical Law and Its Relevance: A Christian Understanding and Ethical Application for Today of the Mosaic Regulations*. Lanham, MD: University Press of America, 2006.

Spronk, Klaas. *Beatific Afterlife in Ancient Israel and in the Ancient Near East*. Kevelaer, Germany: Butzon & Bercker, 1986.

Stackhouse, John G., Jr. *Partners in Christ: A Conservative Case for Egalitarianism.* Downers Grove, IL: IVP Academic, 2015.

Strauss, Mark L. *Remarriage after Divorce in Today's Church: 3 Views.* Grand Rapids: Zondervan, 2006.

Tigay, Jeffrey H. *Deuteronomy.* JPS Torah Commentary. Philadelphia: Jewish Publication Society, 1996.

Tromp, Nicholas J. *Primitive Conceptions of Death and the Nether World in the Old Testament.* Rome: Pontifical Biblical Institute, 1969.

Tucker, W. Dennis, and Jamie A. Grant. *Psalms.* 2 vols. NIV Application Commentary. Grand Rapids: Zondervan, 2018.

van Bavel, T. J. "The Influence of Cicero's Ideal of Friendship on Augustine." In *Augustiniana Traiectina*, edited by J. den Boeft and J. van Oort, 59–72. Paris: Études Augustiniennes, 1987.

Webb, William J. *Slaves, Women, and Homosexuals: Exploring the Hermeneutics of Cultural Analysis.* Downers Grove, IL: InterVarsity, 2001.

Weiss, Dov. "Sins of the Parents in Rabbinic and Early Christian Literature." *Journal of Religion* 97 (2017): 1–25.

Wenham, Gordon J. *Jesus, Divorce, and Remarriage in Their Historical Setting.* Bellingham, WA: Lexham, 2019.

Westbrook, Raymond. "Biblical and Cuneiform Law Codes." *Revue Biblique* 92 (1985): 247–64.

———. *Law from the Tigris to the Tiber: The Writings of Raymond Westbrook.* Vol. 2, *Cuneiform and Biblical Sources.* Edited by Bruce Wells and F. Rachel Magdalene. Winona Lake, IN: Eisenbrauns, 2009.

Williams, D. H., trans. *St. Hilary of Poitiers: Commentary on Matthew.* Fathers of the Church 125. Washington, DC: Catholic University of America Press, 2012.

Xella, Paolo. "Death and the Afterlife in Canaanite and Hebrew Thought." In *Civilizations of the Ancient Near East*, edited by Jack M. Sasson, 3:2059–70. New York: Scribner's Sons, 1995.

Yarhouse, Mark, and Olya Zaporozhets. *Costly Obedience: What We Can Learn from the Celibate Gay Christian Community.* Grand Rapids: Zondervan, 2019.

Younger, K. Lawson, Jr. "The Figurative Aspect and the Contextual Method in the Evaluation of the Solomonic Empire (1 Kings 1–11)." In *The Bible in Three Dimensions*, edited by David J. A. Clines, Stephen E. Fowl, and Stanley E. Porter, 157–75. Sheffield: Sheffield Academic, 1990.

———. *Judges and Ruth.* NIV Application Commentary. Grand Rapids: Zondervan, 2002.

Zurlo, Luanne. *Single for a Greater Purpose: A Hidden Joy in the Catholic Church.* Manchester, NH: Sophia Institute Press, 2019.

Scripture and Ancient Writings Index

Subject Index